The NIGHTMARE
ENCYCLOPEDIA

Your Darkest
Dreams
Interpreted

By

Jeff Belanger

and

Kirsten Dalley

NEW PAGE BOOKS
A division of The Career Press, Inc.
Franklin Lakes, NJ

THE NIGHTMARE ENCYCLOPEDIA
TYPESET BY EILEEN DOW MUNSON
Cover design by Cheryl Cohan Finbow
Printed in the U.S.A. by Book-mart Press
Cover image *The Nightmare*, 1781
Henry Fuseli
Founders Society Purchase with funds from Mr. and Mrs. Bert L. Smokler and Mr. and Mrs. Lawrence A. Fleischman
Photograph © 1886 The Detroit Institute of Arts
Other interior art from Clipart.com and Library of Congress

To order this title, please call toll-free 1-800-CAREER-1 (NJ and Canada: 201-848-0310) to order using VISA or MasterCard, or for further information on books from Career Press.

The Career Press, Inc., 3 Tice Road, PO Box 687,
Franklin Lakes, NJ 07417
www.careerpress.com
www.newpagebooks.com

Library of Congress Cataloging-in-Publication Data

Belanger, Jeff.
   The nightmare encyclopedia : your darkest dreams interpreted / by Jeff Belanger and Kirsten Dalley
      p. cm.
   Includes bibliography and index.
   ISBN 1-56414-762-2 (paper)
      1. Nightmares. 2. Dream interpretation. I. Dalley, Kirsten. II. Title.

BF1099.N53B45 2005
154.6'32--dc22

2005054048

Contents

Introduction

Sleep is a sweet and necessary reward for the hard-fought battles of the day. In sleep, we dream. No one knows exactly why we dream, but science can attest that during the deepest stages of sleep (rapid eye movement, or *REM*, sleep), our brains remain incredibly active. Dreams are the language of our souls. The sights, sounds, and sensations we experience in our dreams speak directly to us, and for us, while we're unconscious. While it is mysterious, and sometimes even frightening, this intensely personal, private, and intimate dream world ultimately provides a way for us to make sense of our conscious, waking lives. Unfortunately, when we awake we often remember only a fraction of what we dream, and sometimes we don't remember any of our dreams at all. But everyone dreams, and those who remember their dreams know that they're not always pleasant.

Sometimes our dreams take us to a place that we'd rather not go, and offer us episodes that rock our very core, increase our heart rates, open our pores to sweat, and sometimes shake us—and our bedmates—awake in a fit of terror. Nightmares are those dreams that venture into the darkest, murkiest corners of the psyche and the unconscious human experience. Nightmares keep children and adults alike awake at night: as tired as we may be, all of us are familiar with the fear of the monsters and sinister scenes waiting beyond the veil of sleep. Recurring nightmares can torment us for weeks, months, or even years, to the point that we're affected psychologically. Nightly nightmares may even cause sleep deprivation, robbing us of a precious necessity. People who have been unfortunate enough to experience a traumatic event often suffer from recurring nightmares and waking flashbacks that replay the terrifying event or events in a predictable, but no less terrifying, tableau.

On the flip side, nightmares can also bring inspiration. A nightmare about getting into a horrible automobile accident may prompt us to drive more carefully, or a nightmare involving lung cancer may motivate us to quit smoking for good. On a larger scale, nightmares have inspired and informed virtually every conceivable artistic and creative medium, as the artist has attempted to comprehend, integrate, and even exploit the deep sense of terror and dislocation he has experienced. Who can forget Freddy Krueger, the razor-fingered monster from the *Nightmare on Elm Street* movies, who hunts and kills his prey within their worst dreams? And what of Mary Shelley's *Frankenstein*, said to have come to the author in a nightmare? And let's not forget Ebenezer Scrooge's life-changing nightmare in Charles Dickens's classic, *A Christmas Carol*.

Nightmares seem to express and evoke our worst fears, primary among these our fear of death—the ultimate unknown. William Shakespeare links the ideas of sleep and death in *Hamlet*. During Hamlet's "To be, or not to be" soliloquy, he muses:

> To die, to sleep;
> To sleep: perchance to dream: ay, there's the rub;
> For in that sleep of death what dreams may come
> When we have shuffled off this mortal coil.

What dreams indeed may come in the unending "sleep" of death? A nightmare from which we cannot wake would be a hell worse than any priest, artist, or author could ever conceive of. Nightmares are our own creation, and our subconscious minds seem to know what scares us the most, more than our conscious minds do, and certainly more than any movie, book, or work of art.

References to nightmares are found in all cultures and throughout the whole of history. They are in holy books such as the Bible, Koran, and Talmud, as well as in "profane" literature, music, and popular culture. Dreams and nightmares have influenced political leaders and altered the course of world history. Even the blind have nightmares, though the dreams of people who have been blind from birth are auditory and not visual.

Theories of dreams and dreaming are perhaps as diverse and varied as the dreams themselves: Sigmund Freud speculated that dreams are simply wish fulfillment; Carl Jung believed that all dreams, nightmares included, are objective facts about our perceptions of ourselves and the world around us. Some people believe that our souls, or essences, can leave our bodies during dreams and travel to an astral realm. Others feel we are prone to supernatural attacks and spirit visitations from demonic entities during the sleep state, which are then experienced as nightmares. However, most modern dream analysts contend that we are problem-solving in our dreams, and perhaps no one is better suited to interpret the meaning of a dream (and the problem or crisis it represents) than the dreamer.

It is important to remember that, in dream interpretation, context is everything. It just isn't possible to definitively say that one dream image means the same thing for all people. For example, take water: If the dreamer is a deep-sea fisherman, he will have a different and probably more nuanced relationship with water than, say, an investment banker or farmer. In dream interpretation, it is very important to take into account such variables as the dreamer's physical and psychological health, diet, socioeconomic status, ethnicity, religion, gender, and age, as well as the influence of surrounding culture. But perhaps the most important overriding factor to keep in mind in dream interpretation is the dreamer's emotional state before, during, and after the dream. The emotion will guide and inform the symbolism and imagery in the dream, as well as the dreamer's response to it. As the psychiatrist Ernest Hartmann puts it, the dream or nightmare "contextualizes," or provides a symbolic context for, the dreamer's dominant emotional state. Remember this when you read the various symbols and possible meanings and explanations provided herein. These interpretations are to be taken as a general guide only—use them as a springboard to inspire your own creative response and interpretation. Sometimes, however, you may need help that goes beyond the scope of this book when grappling with your dreams. Certainly, if dreams or nightmares are recurring and/or becoming very distressing or intrusive, there is no substitute for discussing this with others, preferably with a trained therapist or analyst.

Though there are no absolutes, there are more or less universal patterns, stories, and archetypes that can provide some direction in discerning the meaning of dreams. To this end we explore the history, folklore, and myth narratives of many cultures that often shape nightmare imagery; the people who study and comment on dreams and nightmares; the artists and pop culture figures who incorporate these dark, nocturnal images into their work; and finally the nightmare images and symbols themselves. The meanings of the dream images presented in this book are from the authors' research and from personal interviews with dreamers. Again, they are guides intended to lead you into deeper study and understanding of your own dreams and nightmares, and hopefully into a larger, more complete comprehension of yourself, your world, and your place in it.

Throughout the book you will also find several nightmare spotlights from various nightmare sufferers whom the authors had the opportunity to interview. Included in these profiles are interpretations based on the symbols from this book. By seeing the interpretation process at work in the spotlighted dreams, you will, hopefully, better understand the possible applications in your own life.

To understand your dreams and nightmares is to better understand yourself, especially that part of you that would prefer to remain hidden and uncharted. If the modern theorists are correct, a nightmare may only be your subconscious mind's way of getting your conscious mind's attention. Maybe a nightmare really *is* only an ephemeral and harmless representation of all the thoughts, fears, and impulses residing in your psyche that are unpleasant or somehow unacceptable. Or maybe the old stories are right: maybe there really *are* monsters or demons lurking in the deep recesses of your sleeping mind. If you take the time to read this book, keep a dream journal, and study the images from your own nightmares, you just may find out.

Deciphering the Nightmare:

When Nightmares Aren't Just Female Horses of the Night

By Evelyn Dorothy Oliver

When examining other dream dictionaries, many interpretations have outraged my logic or violated my sense of propriety. Dream dictionaries often predict tragic and frightening outcomes to many otherwise innocuous dreams. One example of this type of interpretation is:

> Losing a wedding ring means the death of a lover or the loss of one's family members, their job, or the end of their marriage.

If taken seriously, predictions such as these could make a person feel hopeless and helpless. Many of them can be psychologically damaging to the reader.

When you read nightmare symbol interpretations, always keep in mind that they are intended to be suggestive rather than definitive: they exemplify how one might go about exploring the range of possible valences of a dream symbol rather than claiming to offer the final word on its meaning. As with all such symbols, the feeling, tone, and other settings of the dream indicate whether any of the proffered interpretations are appropriate. When the interpretations are clearly inapplicable, the reader should not feel bound to accept them. Also, if you suffer intense and recurring nightmares, your best guidance is to embark upon their exploration with the assistance of a competent, licensed healthcare professional because nightmares are no laughing matter.

In my 34 years as a therapist for both business and personal issues, my diagnostic insights and solutions often originate from the intuitive, "spiritual" aspect of my being, rather than from linear thinking alone. Being aware of the unique meanings that dream images can hold for each individual, it is difficult to compose interpretations from which readers can obtain anything like an adequate understanding of their nightmares. In lieu of the therapeutic context of personal contact between therapist and client, I have created a structure that will help contextualize one's nightmares. The following format outlines categories in which readers can find themselves and assist in their understanding of what a nightmare might indicate for them.

When you read some of the following questions, you will realize you don't have to be a trained therapist or scientist to gain some perspective on your nightmares. A good starting point is to locate yourself in one or more of the following categories:

Category I

Q: Have you been a victim of crime or the perpetrator of a crime?

A: _____

_____

_____

Q: Are you living in a country where daily life used to be simple, safe, and peaceful, but has recently become threatened?

A: _____

_____

_____

Q: Were you personally affected by 9/11, the tsunami tragedy, or similar events in which friends or loved ones were killed?

A: _____

_____

_____

Q: Are you or a member of your family in the military or on leave, or have recently served in the military or been discharged as a casualty of war?

A: _____

_____

_____

Q: Have you personally been a victim of an assault, sexual abuse, or crime? Has a family member? Is there a history of rape?

A: _____

_____

_____

_____

Q: Have you caused bodily harm to another person or animal, or fantasized about committing violence against yourself or others?

A: _____

_____

_____

_____

Category II

Q: What are you dealing with in your emotional life? Divorce; remarriage; layoffs; firings; job relocation; sale or purchase of a home; adoption, sterilization, or fertilization; death of a child; death of one or more friends via accident, murder, suicide, drug overdose, or medical mishap?

A: _____

_____

_____

_____

Q: Are you dealing with health issues—your own or someone else's? Medicine, food, eating, defecating, vomiting, urination, bleeding, surgery, doctors, nurses, and so on?

A: _____

_____

_____

_____

Q: Are you dealing with authority figures? Going back to school as an adult, graduation, dropping out, teachers, students, test-taking, homework, or tardiness? Also, lawyers, police officers, prison, drunk and disorderly charges, convictions, and so on?

A: _____

_____

_____

_____

Q. Are you overextended at your workplace? Unfair compensation or acknowledgment, or stressful work conditions (for example, someone else always gets the credit, can't keep up with the pace, can't remember things)?

A: _____

_____

_____

_____

Category III

Q: What are you indulging in? Food and alcohol intake before going to bed?

A: _____

_____

_____

_____

Q: Are you indulging in movies and TV horror shows?

A: _____

_____

_____

_____

Q: Are you exercising too much, or do you feel guilty when you neglect to exercise?

A: _____

_____

_____

Q: What did you eat, drink, or take prior to sleep?

A: _____

_____

_____

_____

Q: Are sports on the brain too much, too often?

A: _____

_____

_____

_____

Q: Is your sex life too excessive? Too many partners? Or are there no partners, no libido?

A: _____

_____

_____

_____

While there are more categories of human experiences, I have attempted to highlight some of the more common ones. Any of these stressful conditions can enter into and shape our nightmares. And these general conditions need to be considered as the larger context for interpreting specific nightmare symbols.

Abandonment

For children, one of their deepest fears is to be abandoned by their parents or guardian. To be left behind or forgotten would mean they are unwanted and unloved—a sad and lonely feeling. Although this dream is most common in children, the nightmare of being stranded or forgotten also occurs in adults. To dream of being abandoned speaks to the interpersonal relationships in the dreamer's life. Possibly a friendship or love affair has ended, and the dreamer is coping with being alone, or perhaps there was in fact an instance of abandonment as a child that is being replayed or re-narrated through the dream.

Aging

Aging is a natural process for every living thing, yet we see it as unnatural—something to avoid and suppress at all costs. We fear the signs of aging: wrinkles portend the loss of youthful beauty, the body grows more frail and weak, and even the mind loses its vigor and elasticity. To have a nightmare

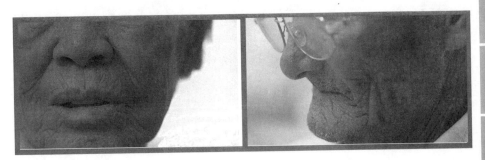

about aging could be a sign of narcissism, or merely of feeling vulnerable to the inevitable loss of virility. In the more extreme version of this nightmare, one might witness oneself or another person age in an unnaturally rapid way, so that years are converted to seconds. This more horrific vision could represent a fear of growing out of one's comfort zone in either a work or relationship situation.

Aguaruna (Also known as the *Aguajun* or *Ahuajun*)

The Aguaruna are an indigenous people found in the northern region of Peru. Numbering approximately 45,000, today they are found mainly along the Cenepa and Maranon Rivers. Although general interest in dreams and nightmares among this people has been declining somewhat in recent years, dreams still play an important role in the people's individual and corporate responses to contemporary problems and day-to-day decision-making.

According to the Aguaruna, dreams are generally regarded as the journeys of the itinerant soul during sleep, this soul's encounters with other souls, and the means of discovering the hidden and possibly harmful intentions of others. As such, dreams are largely construed as prophetic in function and are thought to reveal events that are yet to transpire or become fully manifest. Therefore, dreams or omens are heavily relied upon to plan the course of the day. However, the exposure of the Aguaruna to the Christian construct of the soul has complicated their understanding of the dream experience, and some of the Aguaruna now argue that "soul loss" of any kind (dreaming included) is a cause of illness.

In any case, dreaming is considered an intimate and personal experience, fully known and understood only by the dreamer. Dreams that are intentionally sought are seen as more significant than those that occur spontaneously in that they require effort on the part of the dreamer and offer greater potential rewards for the dreamer's personal and political agency. The types of Aguaruna dreams include:

○ The *kuntuknar*: Dreams about human beings that symbolize events in the natural world, such as a successful hunt. These dreams always hold positive connotations for the tribe and are interpreted metaphorically.

○ The *mesekramprar*: Dreams about the natural world that symbolize future problems, such as raids from other tribes, diseases, and accidents, all of which are believed to be caused by a shaman from another tribe. These too are taken metaphorically.

○ The *penke karamprar*: The "true dreams," in which the dreamer's soul visits the soul of a deceased neighbor or relative. These dreams can be construed as good or bad. The bad dream, or *emesak*, is one in which the dreamer sees the souls of opponents he has killed in battle. This dream is always taken literally.

Dreams concerning success in hunting and warfare are considered by the Aguaruna to be the most powerful and influential, and are thought to exercise the same control over the waking world as magical songs or spells. For example, the nightly dreams of a husband or wife will set the tribe's hunting patterns, and predicts and/or determines what may be caught the next day. The establishment of contact between a man and an ancient warrior soul is a particularly honored warfare dream experience. This type of dream usually consists of an initial vision of a terrifying entity that the dreamer must confront, followed by the apparition of the ancient warrior who acknowledges the dreamer and confirms his future triumph over an attack and his ultimate victory in battle. In this way, dreams are often used as vehicles for the expression of authority by leaders and people in positions of power, and as a means to retain that power and authority.

For the Aguaruna, dreams, nightmares, and omens are ultimately seen as an arena for exercising influence and control over the natural world, largely because they provide a conduit between people and powerful supernatural beings.

Airplanes

Riding in an airplane puts one in a uniquely vulnerable position, a feeling that can cause severe phobias—and nightmares—in many. Riding on a commercial airliner is the great equalizer—aside from the pilot, no one has any real control over the outcome of the flight. Traveling at altitudes too high to even breathe in and at speeds that would literally tear one apart creates a feeling of powerlessness. Unfortunate images of airline disasters in the media help feed this fear and supply ample imagery for the dreamer's imagination. If there are problems with the plane in your dream, your fight-or-flight response goes into overdrive: Are you a very long minute or two of freefall away from doom, or will the plane recover? Is there any possible way to escape? A normal dream about flying may represent freedom of thought or expression, but to experience the plane—and your life—in peril means you may be feeling a significant lack of control over life events, or perhaps a feeling of vulnerability while at the top of your professional game.

Alarms

When you hear an alarm in your waking state, it usually indicates a necessity for immediate action. If you hear an alarm in your nightmare, the meaning should be

taken just as literally. It's time to pay attention and focus—take note of where you are in your dream when an alarm goes off: Are you at work? In school? At home? If you're at the office, the alarm might be your subconscious mind getting your attention to focus on a time-sensitive issue at work. No matter where this occurs, however, there may be an important issue that you have neglected at your peril.

Alcohol

While the average adult sleeps seven to eight hours per night, there is abundant evidence to suggest that a lack of sleep—or, more specifically, rapid eye movement (REM) sleep—can have serious consequences. Even the occasional use of alcohol can have a significant impact on sleep and dreaming, and frequent or excessive drinking disrupts the natural patterns of sleep over the long term. For alcoholics, the sedating effects are required for rest, and as dependence on the alcohol grows, progressively more must be consumed in order to fall asleep. People with the problem of increasing dependency often wake in the middle of the night when the sedating effects of the alcohol wear off.

A person under the influence of alcohol may experience a decrease in the length of REM sleep, while the fourth stage of sleep, which is the deepest sleep, increases in length. This creates the false impression that sleep has been deeper and sounder; however, the reality is that the sleeper is depriving him- or herself of the very stage of sleep that is necessary for overall health. While this improves slightly after the symptoms of withdrawal, even chronic alcoholics who have abstained for a protracted period of time have been shown to exhibit abnormal sleep patterns. It has been speculated that the disruption of sleep patterns by alcoholism, particularly the reduction of REM sleep, can result in irreversible brain damage.

Alcohol consumption actually tends to *lessen* the occurrence of dreaming and nightmares. However, individuals with post-traumatic stress disorder who are alcohol-dependant (a common means of "numbing" the pain and severe anxiety associated with this disorder) can experience a significant *increase* in their recurring nightmares during withdrawal.

(See also *Recurring Nightmares*, *Rapid Eye Movement (REM) Sleep*, and *Post-Traumatic Stress Disorder*)

Alice in Wonderland

In 1865, British mathematician and author Reverend Charles Lutwidge Dodgson published the children's fable *Alice's Adventures Underground* under the pseudonym Lewis Carroll. (It was later renamed *Alice in Wonderland*, which is the title most of us recognize.) The book tells the story of a girl named Alice who, in her dream or nightmare (it's difficult to tell which), falls down a rabbit hole into a genial yet nightmarish underworld of paradox, the absurd, and the improbable.

In the dream, Alice meets memorable characters such as the March Hare, Mad Hatter, Cheshire Cat, and an anthropomorphized deck of cards. As in most nightmares, the dream is often bizarre, as Alice finds herself to be alternately too large and too small. In the chapter "The Pool of Tears," Alice discovers with horror that she's rapidly shrinking into nothingness:

> "I must be growing small again." She got up and went to the table to measure herself by it, and found that, as nearly as she could guess, she was now about two feet high, and was going on shrinking rapidly: she soon found out that the cause of this was the fan she was holding, and she dropped it hastily, just in time to avoid shrinking away altogether.
>
> "That was a narrow escape!" said Alice, a good deal frightened at the sudden change, but very glad to find herself still in existence.
>
> (*Alice's Adventures in Wonderland & Through the Looking-Glass*, New American Library, 2000)

Unidentified Flying Nightmare

Brooke Harris is a 27-year-old housewife and mother of three living in Jacksonville, Alabama. She's been having a recurring alien nightmare.

The Nightmare:

> *I've been having dreams about UFOs now for about eight months. They always take place at night in the house I lived in about three years ago.*
>
> *My family and I are sitting in the living room watching TV, and then we all hear a strange humming sound coming from outside. A few of us get up to look out the window and that's when we see a big, bright, colorful UFO slowly circling my house.*

We lived in a secluded area with only one street lamp, but the UFO has everything lit up. We get really scared and run to the basement to hide. There is a big, glass double door in there and we see that the UFO has landed in the field next to the house. We all try to find a good place to hide while I cry and scream for it all to be a dream. I'm convinced it's all real. I turn a corner and see a short, thin, gray alien looking at me. I turn to run up the stairs, but I can't move. I stand there and scream, hearing my family do the same. Then I wake up shaking and crying. It usually stays with me for the rest of the day. No other nightmare compares to this one.

Brooke said she's been having this nightmare once every other month or so.

The Analysis:

The UFO and alien represent an unknown factor that may be gnawing at Brooke. The imagery suggests she senses some changes coming up in her life, and she's having difficulty seeing beyond them. The unknown is what causes the fear.

■　　■　　■

Dodgson's fantasy is a perfect example of "dream art," in which dreams or nightmares have directly influenced or inspired the theme and aesthetics of the work.

(See also *Art*)

Aliens

When E.T. attacks, you should be wondering why. Extraterrestrials coming down from space *en masse* within your dreams is a reason to run, but this image is a good indication that you probably don't understand exactly what you're running from. Aliens represent the unknown, so to dream of aliens may mean that a big change is coming and you're unsure what that alteration will bring. Recurring nightmares of aliens indicate the necessity for evaluating the changes taking
place in your life. By "unpacking" your feelings and responses to these changes, the unknown becomes known and hence will no longer be something to fear.

Alley

An alley usually connotes a sinister or overtly violent confrontation. Dreaming of alleys in a threatening context may indicate a shortcut being taken in your personal or business life, which later may have unfortunate results. The seedy setting of an alley may also indicate your discomfort concerning friendships or alliances with questionable or unscrupulous people.

Ambush

An ambush is a surprise attack, so this nightmare may represent vulnerability to some symbolic or actual unpleasant surprise. Experiencing an ambush in your dreams may signify a sudden loss or emotional upheaval. People who have been ambushed or attacked in waking life (such as in a war or a domestic violence situation) may have traumatic nightmares in which the precipitating event is replayed over and over again.

Amputation

This nightmare often represents the abandonment or neglect of talents and powers represented by the amputated limb. Or it may simply indicate a general loss of perceived agency or control over life's events. The loss of a hand might mean you are unable to handle a situation, while a severed leg may indicate a need to get a "leg up" on a project, or that your ideas don't have a leg to stand on. The loss of an arm may signify that your efforts to attain a goal may be in vain.

Analyze This

The 1999 movie *Analyze This*, starring Robert De Niro, is in some ways a caricature of our excessive faith in dream interpretation and of Freudian dream analysis itself, reflecting our fascination with the prospect of quick cures through dream therapy.

The movie starts with psychiatrist Ben Sobel (Billy Crystal) backing into gangster Paul Vitti's (Robert De Niro's) car. Vitti subsequently dispatches henchmen to bring Sobel to him so he can listen to Vitti's dreams. He has a persistent nightmare in which he sees himself drinking black milk. He also suffers from sudden anxiety attacks, which prevent him from fulfilling his role as a Mafia don. Sobel analyzes Vitti's dream as a representation of repressed guilt over his father's death, and interprets the symbol of the black milk as the negative nurturing he received in childhood. Eventually, through successful dream analysis and therapy, the don recovers from his panic disorder.

Analyze This is based on an earlier movie, the *Dark Past*, in which an escaped convict barges into a house during a dinner party. The convict has a persistent nightmare problem that a psychologist at the party analyzes. This convict is so overwhelmed by the process that he cannot pick up his gun when the police arrive, and he gets killed at the end of the film.

(See also *Freud, Sigmund*)

Angel of Death

The angel of death is a familiar personification of death in traditional, mythical, and especially religious iconography. In the Bible, death is represented in the form of an angel sent by God, with such names as the "angel of the Lord," the "destroying angel," the "destroyer," or in the plural as "destroying angels." Proverbs 16:14 is the first passage in the Bible to explicitly use the term "angels of death."

(See also *Bible* and *Grim Reaper*)

Anger and Aggression

Violence or aggression in a dream or nightmare is a direct result of anger and frustration in our waking lives. These two emotions, combined with anxiety, are twice as likely to occur in a nightmare as are more pleasant feelings.

There have been numerous studies on the different factors influencing the frequency of anger and aggression in dreams and nightmares—factors such as age, gender, birth order, social class, and geographical location. The most compelling of these factors seems to be gender. In general, females of all ages remember their dreams more often than their male counterparts, and their dreams are longer, more detailed, and contain more friendly interactions. In contrast, males report slightly more aggressive encounters, even though they remember a significantly lower number of their dreams than do women. Renowned psychiatrist and author, Ernest Hartmann suggests that, because of socialization and commonly accepted gender stereotypes, women are more likely to admit to having nightmares than men. Having nightmares is not an especially "manly" affliction: they are associated with fear (and hence weakness), and are therefore construed as feminizing—an image that doesn't dovetail with the modern model of solitary male strength and machismo.

For children, the statistics concerning the role of gender in aggression appearing in dreams are less conclusive than those regarding age. Most studies indicate that, for boys and girls between the ages of 2 and 12, the level of aggressiveness in dreams is commensurate; however, at the age of 12 (around the time

of puberty), these levels begin to drop for girls. In males, these levels do not drop until their 30s at the earliest, and they have been known to remain high until men are in their 70s or 80s.

Nightmares in children usually involve strange people, monsters, and wild animals. It is generally believed that children's nightmares are early anxiety dreams stemming from inchoate fears of a largely unfamiliar waking world.

Work status is another factor that affects the incidence of aggression in dreams. A study was done on a group of working mothers with preschool children and stay-at-home mothers with children of the same age. The working mothers reported more male characters in their dreams, fewer indoor environments, and experienced more unpleasant feelings, such as failure, anger, and aggression than the stay-at-home mothers. Conversely, the stay-at-home mothers had more friendly encounters, but contended with more misfortune and hostility while dreaming. It was also discovered that mothers with dual roles—mother and provider—experienced more work-related dreams than their male counterparts.

Birth order also plays a role in aggression in dreams. Although men typically experience more aggressive dreams than women, this is not always true if the male is the firstborn. In this case, the male typically sees himself in a more positive manner than his younger male siblings, with the possible result being more positive encounters in his dreams. Conversely, firstborn females tend to have more aggressive characters in their dreams and are more likely to be aggressive than other females of the same age group who are not firstborn.

Perhaps not surprisingly, geography also seems to be an important factor that affects the incidence of aggression in our dreams. In an East Coast survey, 40 percent of the total study group reported being the initiator of a violent act in their dreams. The same study was done on the West Coast and in the Midwest. On the West Coast, that figure dropped to 22 percent, and to 10 percent in the Midwest. Whether this was a result of crowding or some other factor is unclear.

Finally, socioeconomic status also plays a role. Members of lower social classes reported more violently aggressive dreams and/or nightmares than those in the middle or upper classes. They also experienced more dreams of anger and misfortune. The most noteworthy finding in this area was that lower-class high school girls experienced more angry and aggressive dreams than their male or female counterparts.

Animals

People have been dreaming about animals for ages. It has been speculated that some of the ancient cave paintings of animals may be the dream images of cave dwellers whose lives were mostly spent hunting and taming animals. In ancient Egypt, human-figured deities with animal heads also suggest dreamlike images.

Modern studies have shown that children have more animal dreams than adults. A well-known study by Robert L. van de Castle found a significantly larger number of animal dreams in children than in adults. Dreams of a group of 741 children (383 girls and 358 boys), ages 4 to 16, were examined for the presence of animal figures. Animal figures were present in 39.4 percent of dreams from the 4- and 5-year-old children, with the percentage steadily dropping for each subsequent age grouping (6- and 7-year-olds: 35.5 percent; 8- and 9-year-olds: 33.6

percent; 10- and 11-year-olds: 29.8 percent; 12- and 13-year-olds: 21.9 percent; and 14- through 16-year-olds: 13.7 percent). Boys had higher animal figures percentages at ages 4 through 6 (44 percent versus 34 percent for girls), while girls had higher figures at ages 9 through 11 (36 percent versus 26 percent for boys). Overall, animal figures appeared in 29 percent of the combined girls' dreams and 29.6 percent of the combined boys' dreams. The animal figures that occurred most frequently were dogs (30 times), horses (28 times), cats (15 times), snakes (15 times), bears (14 times), lions (13 times), and mythical creatures or monsters (for example, dragons or the Wolf Man) (13 times).

If the rate of occurrence for all animal figures is considered, it is clear that young children dream more frequently of large and/or threatening wild animals, while young adults up to college age dream more often of pets and domesticated animals. Bears, lions, tigers, gorillas, elephants, bulls, dinosaurs, dragons, and monsters accounted for 27 percent of the animal figures in children's dreams but only 7 percent of the animal figures in adult dreams. This collection of wild animals appeared more frequently in boys' dreams (44 times) than in girls' dreams (27 times). Several theorists have suggested that these large, threatening animals in the dreams of children may represent unsympathetic or hostile parental figures. In addition, an interesting gender difference was found with regard to the types of animals reported. Women and girls cited significantly more mammals, while men and boys cited significantly more non-mammals. This difference in type may reflect an unconscious female identification with other forms of life that nurse their young.

There is also lively debate as to whether animals themselves dream. At least some form of sleep seems to be widespread in the animal kingdom. Mammals, birds, reptiles, and even insects show some forms of behavioral sleep, while the brain waves that occur during REM and non-REM sleeps are found in mammals, birds, and reptiles—but not in amphibians and fish.

It has been suggested that when animals dream, they are focused on the sorts of things they usually do in their waking state. For example, animals that are smell-oriented, such as dogs, seem to have dreams with a significant olfactory component. Similarly, monkeys that were taught to respond to visual stimuli by pressing a button later made similar hand motions when they were sleeping, sug-

gesting that they were reenacting the motion in a dream. Finally, in an experiment on cats, portions of the brain stem responsible for muscle inhibition during REM sleep were damaged. Instead of lying quietly with their eyes moving, as is typical during REM sleep, the cats actually got up and chased imaginary creatures—as if they were acting out their dreams without waking up. What is not known is whether or not animals dream about us, their human counterparts in the animal kingdom.

Ankou

The personification of Death as a living, sentient entity is a concept that has existed in virtually all societies. Ankou is the collector of souls from the world of Celtic fairy lore. He is represented as a dark, robed character pushing a black cart or driving a black horse-drawn carriage, his arrival usually heralded by a cold gust of wind. The cart is pulled along either by two horses—one old, thin, and sickly; the other youthful and strong—or by four black horses of unspecified age. Ankou wears a dark hat or covering over his face. (According to the lore, no one can ever see his face and live to tell about it.) In some tales, he has two companions: skeletons that follow behind his cart, into which they toss the dead souls. The folklore of how Ankou acquired this horrible occupation recounts that he was once a prince who loved to hunt and engage in games of fortune, luck, and chance. While on one of his hunts, Ankou comes upon Death riding a black horse. Death challenges Ankou to a hunting contest in which the victor can determine the loser's fate. When Death inevitably wins, he sentences Ankou to an eternity of hunting the souls of men.

Although the specter of Ankou is largely forgotten in Cornwall, Wales, and Ireland, he remains part of the living folklore—and presumably the nightmares as well—of the people of French Brittany.

(See also *Grim Reaper* and *Angel of Death*)

Ants

Is something bugging you? If ants are crawling on your body in a nightmare and you feel them biting or stinging, perhaps you are experiencing the sum total of your current life situations as a real threat, or perhaps you are besieged by many little problems that are out of your control. If you are plagued by recurring nightmares about ants (or any other creeping thing), take preventative steps and "re-narrate" the dream by deciding to call an exterminator into your next nightmare.

(See also *Lucid Dreaming*)

Anubis

Anubis is the Greek name for the ancient god of the underworld in Egyptian mythology. Prayers to Anubis have been found carved on the surface of the most ancient tombs in Egypt. His name can be translated as something such as *putrefaction*. (Interestingly, Anubis is also identified as the father of Kebechet, the goddess of the purification of bodily organs.)

Ancient texts indicate that Anubis silently walks through the shadows of life and death like a jackal, lurking in the dark places, watchful by day as well as by night. In art, he is represented as a combination of human and jackal-like characteristics—usually as a man with the head of a jackal, alert ears, and often wielding a whip. On very rare occasions, Anubis is depicted as fully human, or, slightly more frequently, as fully jackal. However, like most personifications of death, Anubis is always black in color.

He was given titles such as "He who is set upon his mountain," in reference to his sitting atop desert cliffs to guard the necropolises (graveyards or abodes of the dead); and "Lord of the Westerners," in reference to Egyptian belief that the entrance to the underworld was toward the west. As king of the underworld, it was thought that he weighed the hearts of the dead against the feather of Ma'at (the concept of truth), earning him the title "He who counts the hearts." It is commonly known that the ancient Egyptians took great care to preserve their dead with sweet-smelling herbs and oils, in part because they believed that Anubis would check each person with his keen canine nose—they would be granted entrance into the Kingdom of the Dead only if they smelled pure.

As the myth narrative evolved, Anubis eventually became the gatekeeper of the underworld, the "Guardian of the Veil" (or "of death"). He was said to protect souls as they journeyed there, and thus he became the patron of lost souls and orphans, and the god of dying and funeral arrangements—a significant (and much more sympathetic) title in ancient Egyptian culture.

Apnea

Apnea is a sleep disorder in which the sleeper's breathing is disrupted and even stopped, causing the sleeper to wake. As this can happen repeatedly throughout a given night, the sleeper cannot experience the continuous, uninterrupted REM stage of sleep so necessary for health and well-being. Unexplained fatigue during waking hours and the feeling that one has never slept soundly is usually the result. Sleep apnea can sometimes be accompanied by nightmares in which the dreamer experiences the sensation of drowning or being choked. This disorder can be treated with medications and with devices that force the sleeper to stay on his or her side.

Apocalypse

This word comes from the Greek *apokalupsis*, meaning "revelation" (literally, "a lifting of the veil," or "disclosure"). Apocalyptic literature reveals mysteries and portents beyond the normal scope of human knowledge, usually through the first-person narrative description of a dream or nightmare predicting future events. Many religious texts are filled with vivid descriptions and predictions regarding the end of the world. In the King James Bible, Revelations 16:16-21 reads:

> [16] And he gathered them together into a place called in the Hebrew tongue Armageddon. [17] And the seventh angel poured out his vial into the air; and there came a great voice out of the temple of heaven, from the throne, saying, It is done. [18] And there were voices, and thunders, and lightnings; and there was a great earthquake, such as was not since men were upon the earth, so mighty an earthquake, and so great. [19] And the great city was divided into three parts, and the cities of the nations fell: and great Babylon came in remembrance before God, to give unto her the cup of the wine of the fierceness of his wrath. [20] And every island fled away, and the mountains were not found. [21] And there fell upon men a great hail out of heaven, every stone about the weight of a talent: and men blasphemed God because of the plague of the hail; for the plague thereof was exceeding great.

At times, religion can fill our minds with disturbing doomsday images, and these same images may "play" again in our dreams. An end-of-the-world nightmare may bode a major change in the dreamer's life—some part of the dreamer's world may be ending. Apocalyptic imagery could also be a response to the death of someone close to the dreamer, a bankruptcy, a divorce, or some other major, life-changing event.

Aquinas, Thomas

Thomas Aquinas was born into nobility in Rocca Secca in the kingdom of Naples, Italy, most likely in early 1225 C.E. The son of a count and countess, he was related to the Hohenstaufen dynasty of the Holy Roman emperors. His mother sought out a local religious hermit before his birth in order to divine the child's future, and the hermit related that he would be a great man, devoted to the church, and that the impact of his words would endure throughout all of time.

At 5 years of age, he was sent for his early education to the Monte Cassino monastery, of which his uncle was abbot. Later, after studying at the University of Naples, Thomas joined the Dominican Order, which represented a revolutionary challenge to the established clerical systems of early medieval Europe. This also meant that he had effectively embraced the lifestyle of a pauper. This garnered the disapproval of his noble family, and he was subsequently seized by his brothers and brought back to his parents at the castle of San Giovanni. Here he was quite literally held captive for almost two years in order to redirect his ambitions and vocation.

According to some of his earliest biographers, angels appeared to him once in a nightmarish dream in which they wrapped him up in a cord of fire—an experience so horribly painful that he woke with a scream. According to many accounts, the cord was a girdle of eternal chastity, and he never again suffered from the "desires of the flesh," preferring instead to live the remainder of his life in celibacy. The duration of his imprisonment he then spent in study, just as he would have if he had actually been in Paris. Eventually, his mother granted him his freedom, and Thomas was able to return to the Dominicans. They were relieved to discover that he was as educated in theology and the Scriptures as he would have been if not for his captivity, if not more so.

At some point during 1244–1245, he became a student of Albertus Magnus, a renowned professor of the order, and they traveled to Cologne together, where Magnus was to teach at the university. (Magnus initially thought that Thomas was slow, due in part to the boy's enduring modesty and quiet humility. However, Magnus changed his opinion after reading Thomas's brilliant defense of a particularly difficult thesis.) In 1250, Thomas Aquinas finally achieved his place among the priesthood.

After spending a year in Cologne, Thomas traveled to Paris to attend the university and earn his doctorate of theology. It was at this university that Thomas wrote *The Majesty of Christ*, said to be prompted by a dream in which a heavenly visitor instructed him. He finally received his doctorate in 1256, and a full nine years passed before the Pope chose to honor Thomas Aquinas with the position of Archbishop of Naples. (If he had received the position earlier, he probably would never have had the chance to write his chief work, the *Summa Theologica*.) He died at Fossa Nova on March 7, 1274, and on July 18, 1323, he was finally canonized by Pope John XXII.

Although he lived for less than 50 years, St. Thomas Aquinas signed his name

to more than 66 religious masterpieces, each exemplifying remarkable insight and piety. The *Summa Theologica* was a more mature, well-developed, and structured version of his earlier work, and ultimately survived as his *magnum opus*. St. Thomas claimed that certain passages of this work were a direct result of advice from the apostles Peter and Paul, which he received while dreaming. Regardless of the mystical and distinctly non-Aristotelian dreams that plagued him throughout his life, St. Thomas attempted to downplay and discourage the importance most common people invested in their dreams. He asserted that divination through dreams was lawful as long as one was certain that the dream found its origin in divine design, and that the dreaming state lacked artificial influences such as alcohol. Not surprisingly, he also conceded a demonic influence in the common occurrence of prophetic dreams and nightmares.

Archetypes

While the notion of the archetype is at least as old as Plato, it is most familiar to the modern world through the work of the prominent Swiss psychotherapist Carl Jung. In contrast to his mentor Sigmund Freud, Jung divided the unconscious mind into two subdivisions: the personal unconscious and the collective unconscious. Jung posited that while the personal unconscious is shaped by our personal experiences, the collective unconscious represents our inheritance from the collective experience of humankind, amassed and stored over the centuries. This inheritance, or storehouse, of humanity's experiences arises at least partially through the evolutionary process, and resides in the objective psyche in the form of archetypes. Archetypes find their expression in myth, folklore, religion, popular stories, and, of course, dreams.

The archetypes function as paradigms in that they unconsciously predispose us to organize, or "filter," our personal experiences in certain ways. We are, for instance, inclined to perceive an older male figure in our early environment as a father because of the father archetype. If our biological father is absent during our early years, someone else (for example, an older brother or an uncle) is assimilated into and filtered by this archetype, providing concrete images for our father *complex* (a group of memories and interpretations closely associated with and shaped by the archetype).

Some of Jung's archetypes and their meanings are:

○ *Anima/Animus*: Jung noticed that both genders had underlying attributes and potentials of the opposite sex. *Anima* represents the feminine side of a man's personal unconscious, and *animus* represents the masculine side of a woman's personal unconscious. (Jung was unclear if the anima/animus archetype was totally unconscious or not, instead preferring to call it "a little bit conscious *and* unconscious.") The anima is usually an aggregate of a man's mother combined with aspects of sisters, aunts, and teachers, while the woman's animus is usually an aggregate of corresponding male figures. The concept of anima/animus is considered one of Jung's most important contributions to psychology.

○ *Syzygy*: This archetype denotes a pairing of contrasexual opposites, which symbolizes the communication of the conscious and unconscious minds. This archetype also represents the coming together of opposites for a perfect whole, the internal union of the male and female parts of the self, and the union of souls in relationships. The Japanese concept of yin/yang could be considered a permutation of the syzygy archetype.

○ *Child*: More commonly known as the "inner child" today, this archetype represents the innocent hope inside all of us, and the part of us that can still see the wonder in things. A child who speaks wisely beyond his/her years can also represent the child archetype.

○ *Father*: Although almost every culture in history can arguably be described as patriarchal, Jung felt the archetype of father wasn't nearly as important as mother. The hero and wise old man archetypes both incorporate the most positive or active elements of the "father," which may explain why Jung gave so little focus to this archetype.

○ *Hero*: The hero is one of the dominant and repeating themes Jung noticed throughout the history of folklore and mythology. Jung found a common thread throughout all heroic legends: significant lineage (such as the child of a god or royalty) with a descent into a place such as hell, where the hero must suffer through and ultimately overcome great battles or hardships in order to be reborn as someone greater. There is hero in all of us—whether it involves overcoming our own shadows or demons, or rising above the odds to save a life from a burning building—the hero is the archetype we understand during moments of suffering and triumph.

○ *Mother*: Jung felt that the mother archetype was particularly powerful in that it must be able to balance the predominance of male influence found in most, if not all, cultures. Jung valued the feminine in all forms, but felt the role of mother to be the most significant and influential of these forms.

○ *Persona*: The persona is the mask or appearance—almost a caricature—that one presents to the world. It is the image one offers to the public. It may appear in dreams under various guises: the pious churchgoer, the sharp and polished professional, the studious intellectual, the wild child, the stylish clotheshorse, and the quiet-but-tough blue-collar worker are just some of the personas people adopt in an effort to shape a public (and private) identity. Problems may arise when there is too much of a disconnect between the persona and the core personality.

○ *Self*: This represents the perfect, whole personality. Jung believed that it could not be brought to completion until death; representations such as Jesus and Buddah are good examples of this concept. The self archetype constitutes our authentic, conscious self-image or self-concept. In dreams, this self can be represented in a variety of ways, often in the form of a circle, or *mandala* (a circular diagram used as a meditative aid in Hinduism and Buddhism), or often in images of the *quaternity* (according to Jung, the number of wholeness and, hence, a symbol of the self).

○ *Shadow*: A part of the unconscious mind that is mysterious and often disagreeable to the conscious mind, but which is also relatively close to the conscious mind. The shadow represents the darker side of the self—the immoral thoughts and impulses and shameful actions that are suppressed. Jung felt that people need to acknowledge and address the inner shadow no matter how embarrassing in order to achieve integration and psychological health. The shadow self makes its presence felt most commonly in disturbing dreams and nightmares.

○ *Trickster*: A divine entity or human hero who breaks the rules of the gods or nature, sometimes maliciously (for example, Loki in the tradition of Norse myth), but usually with ultimately positive effects. Often, the rule-breaking takes the form of pranks or thievery.

Tricksters can be cunning or foolish, and they are often humorous—even when considered sacred or performing important cultural tasks. The trickster is the court jester who gets away with lampooning his master, the comedian who cracks jokes about people in the audience, and the merry prankster who leaves the whoopee cushion on the boss's chair.

○ *Wise Old Man*: Represented by a kind, insightful, older fatherly figure who uses an impressive intellect and personal knowledge to create cautionary tales or narratives of guidance for those who need it. Consiously or unconsciously, most people's construct of God or the Divine coincides with this archetype. Unlike the hero, the wise old man doesn't need physical strength to overcome adversity; rather, he commands respect through his accomplishments and considerable wisdom. Examples of this archetype in popular culture would include Yoda and Obi-Wan Kenobi from the *Star Wars* series, Gandalf from Tolkien's *Lord of the Rings*, and Owl from *Winnie the Pooh*.

Aristotle

Aristotle (384 B.C.E.–March 7, 322 B.C.E.) was born the son of the court physician to the king of Macedon in the Ionian city of Stagira, in Chalcidice. Along with Plato and Socrates, he is often considered to be one of the most influential ancient Greek philosophers to shape Western thought. He studied almost every known subject during classical times, and wrote books about such widely diverse subjects as physics, poetry, zoology, government, and biology.

Aristotle remained in Athens from the ages of 18 to 37 as a pupil of Plato, and distinguished himself at the Academe, where he remained until Plato's death in 347 B.C.E. He then joined a circle of Platonists living at Assos, the area surrounding the ancient city of Troy, under the protection of the tyrant Hermais of Atarneus. He remained at Assos for three years and then moved to Mytilene, on the island of Lesbos. At the age of 44, he accepted an invitation to supervise the education of the young Alexander III (Alexander the Great) at the Macedonian court at Pella, where he spent another three years. Following a five-year stay in his hometown of Stagira, he returned to Athens, where he opened his own school called the Lyceum. After the death of Alexander the Great in 323 B.C.E, the school was in danger of attack from the anti-Macedonian party, which was in Athens. Aristotle sought refuge in Chalcis, one the islands of Euboea, where he remained until his death a year later at the age of 63.

Aristotle's writings are classified into three separate categories: memoranda and collections of material, popular writings, and scientific and philosophical treatises. Unfortunately, none of his popular works and only some of his philosophical works have survived. The only knowledge we have of these works is by proxy, from quotations and references in later pieces by other writers. The largest surviving segment of Aristotle's writings consists of the psychological works *De Anima* and *Parva Naturalia*, which fall into the classification of scientific and philosophical treatises.

According to Aristotle, the goal of psychology is to discover the essence and the attributes of the soul (psyche), commonly referred to by the Greeks as the realm of human consciousness and subjectivity. He developed his doctrine of the soul through three different approaches. These characterized the three separate periods into which his work is usually classified. The most notable characteristic of the first approach was his use of the Platonic concept of the soul as an entity separate and distinct from the body. This approach corresponded with the period of his earliest writings (through 347 B.C.E.) in which he was an enthusiastic defender of Platonism.

The second approach spanned the years 347 to 335 B.C.E. and reflected an increasingly critical attitude toward the teachings of his former teacher. Aristotle's view of the body as an instrument of the soul defined the second period of his philosophical endeavors. Examples of this are found in both his biological treatises and the *Parva Naturalia*.

The final period of Aristotle's thought began around 355 B.C.E. During this time, he rejected the essential principles of Platonic metaphysics and embraced instead pure empirical science. He extended his earlier theory of the body as an instrument of the soul and developed it into the theory of the soul as a form or emanation of the body. Aristotle elaborated this theory in his *Metaphysics*.

In the treatise *De Anima* he presents yet another theory in which he treats the soul and body as constituting a unified substance, standing next to each other in the relation of form to matter. *De Anima* provides a detailed analysis of the faculties of the soul, as well as which hierarchical levels these various faculties occupy. Aristotle felt that it is possible to classify all living creatures according to where each creature falls in this hierarchy. The lowest and most basic level of the soul is the nutritive, or that which exists in every living thing. Just above that, the sensitive soul exists, which is present in all animals and encompasses the sensations of touch, taste, smell, sight, and hearing. Aristotle argued that the sensitive soul also has the function of feeling pleasure, pain, and desire, with the subsequent products of imagination and movement present in most, but not all, animals. The highest faculties of the soul, peculiar to humans alone, are reason and intelligence.

His theories on dreams, as outlined in the three systematic treatises *On Prophecy*, *On Sleeping and Waking*, and *On Dreams*, explicitly delineate the nature of the soul and its relationship to dreams, and come closer than any other ancient writer to modern views. Aristotle felt that the main functions of imagination are the formation of images and the process of memory. The direct consequence of perception is imagination, which operates only after the sensed object, physical or other, has disappeared. Memory is the function of the faculty by which we perceive time, which is impossible without an image. Likewise, dreams are a product of imagination produced during the state of sleep, as well as a by-product of previous sensations. In essence, dreams are impressions produced by our senses that linger in the imagination after the senses have ceased to be active.

In *De Somno et Vigilia*, sleep is described as an inactivity of the primary or "commonsense" faculty. According to Aristotle, sleep, waking, and the close examination of each are indispensable to the understanding of dreams (he felt that sleeping and waking are two states of the same faculty—two sides of the same coin, if you will—with waking on the positive side and sleeping on the negative).

He considered sleeping and waking to be "afflictions" of the soul and body, taken as a whole. While the soul does not exist apart from the body, during the state of sleep it is capable of returning to its original, purely spiritual state. Aristotle also discusses the illusion of sense perceptions in *De Insomniis*. This illusion is due to the improper functioning of the senses, which frees the way for the formation of dreams and nightmares without judgment, evaluation, or correction. In contrast to modern conceptions and explanations of dreams and dreaming, he asserted that the process of dreaming is not affected by actual perceptions or thoughts.

Finally, Aristotle denies that dreams have a divine origin or that their interpretation can shed light on the supernatural world. He suggests, instead, that dreams and nightmares are actions or symptoms of physical bodily disturbances:

> In the same manner during sleep the phantasms, or residuary movements, which are based upon the sensory impressions, become sometimes quite obliterated by the above described motion when too violent; while at other times the sights are indeed seen, but confused and weird, and the dreams [which then appear] are unhealthy, like those of persons who are atrabilious, or feverish, or intoxicated with wine.

(from *De Insomniis*)

Aristotle always maintained that "divination" through the interpretation of dreams is the result of coincidence.

Art

References to dreams in art are as old as literature itself: the story of Gilgamesh, the Bible, and the Iliad all describe the dreams and nightmares of major characters and the their respective meanings. However, the idea of dreams *as* art—without being situated in the context of a narrative or story—appears to be a later development.

In the late 19th and early 20th centuries, popular discussion of dreams reached a new level of public awareness in the Western world due to the work of Sigmund Freud, who introduced the notion of the subconscious mind as a field of scientific inquiry. At about the same time, Symbolism and Expressionism formally introduced dream imagery into visual art. The Symbolist painters unpacked the elements of mythology and dreams in order to create an intensely personal and often ambiguous narrative in their art.

Freud also greatly influenced the 20th-century Surrealists, who combined the visionary impulses of the Symbolists with a focus on the unconscious as a creative tool. This movement's approach paralleled Freud's ideas about the unconscious and the repression of irrational urges by the conscious mind, urges that manifest themselves in dreams. The Surrealists held that dreams that include images or experiences that are fantastic, absurd, or even terrifying subvert the ordinary or normal. In this, there was always an assumption that "irrational" content in art could contain significant meaning, perhaps more so than straightforward, rational content. Like other forms of modern art, Surrealism was an answer to the boundaries of rationalism—the artist's chief hope was to discover new creative possibilities by plumbing the depths of the unconscious.

Likewise, poets and writers have claimed that their work, or inspiration for their work, has appeared to them while in a dreaming state. Dreaming and the act of reading and writing use different areas of our brain; but, even so, it is not inconceivable that many great literary works were inspired by dreams or nightmares. This highlights the importance of the Freudian concept of dreams as messengers of our unconscious, making us aware of thoughts or ideas that our conscious mind refuses to recognize, but are essential in creative expression. Nightmares, and even recurring nightmares, have been reported by such authors as Fyodor Dostoyevsky, August Strindberg, Rene Descartes, Bram Stoker, Andre Gide, Theodore Drieser, Edgar Lucas White, Henry James, Nathanial Hawthorne, Mark Twain, Edgar Allen Poe, and Jack Kerouac.

In European literature, the Romantic movement emphasized the value of emotion and irrational inspiration. "Visions," whether from dreams or intoxication, served as the raw material for this inspiration and were taken to represent the artist's highest creative potential. Similarly, Expressionism—as a literary movement—was evident in the later work of the playwright August Strindberg, who coined the term "dream play" for a style of dramatic narrative that did not distinguish between fantasy and reality.

In the year 1818, the famous horror story *Frankenstein* was published. The book's author, Mary Shelley, claims direct inspiration and content from her nightmares. She is quoted as saying, "I have found it! What terrifies me will terrify others; and I need only describe the spectra which has haunted my midnight pillow." Robert Lewis Stevenson also accredited his classic *Dr. Jekyll and Mr. Hyde* to images remembered from his nightmares. After two days of reflection, he reportedly received "the scene at the window, and a scene afterwards, split in two, in which Hyde, pursued for some crime, took the powder and changed in the presence of his pursuers," delivered to him completely as a nightmare. At the time of his dream, Stevenson was in an extremely critical financial state. Needless to say, the popularity of his book dramatically changed his fortune— and probably his dreams as well.

Numerous other artists have accredited their dreams for inspiration for portions, if not the whole, of their works of art, including music. For example, the composer Giuseppe Tartini attributed his popular "Devil's Trill" sonata to a dream, and Hector Berlioz's *Symphonie Fantastique* was supposedly inspired by an opium-induced nightmare.

The invention of film and animation brought new possibilities for vivid depiction of the bizarre and nonrealistic events of dreams, but films consisting *entirely* of dream imagery have remained an avant-garde rarity. Comic books and comic strips have explored dreams to some extent, including Winsor McCay's popular newspaper installations, and the trend toward confessional works in the alternative comics of the 1980s saw a proliferation of artists drawing inspiration from their own dreams.

Dream material continues to be used by a wide range of contemporary artists for various purposes. This practice is considered by some to be of psychological value for the artist—independent of the artistic value of the results—as part of the discipline of "dream work."

The International Association for the Study of Dreams currently holds an annual juried show of visual dream art.

Artemidorus of Daldis

Dreams and nightmares have captivated the human mind for centuries, and the ancient Greeks were particularly interested in the subject. The largest and most complete compilation of dream lore to survive from the ancient world is the *Oneirocritica* (*The Interpretation of Dreams*) of Artemidorus. As one of the very first individuals to employ an empirical approach to the analysis of dreams, Artemidorus is said to have investigated and analyzed no less than 3,000 dreams for the *Oneirocritica*.

Although Artemidorus inscribed the *Oneirocritica* as "Artemidorus of Daldis," he was actually born in the ancient Greek city of Ephesus. Other than the information derived from the few autobiographical remarks made in the *Oneirocritica*, little else is known of his life except that he authored earlier books on divination. The first three subdivisions of his work comprise a method of dream interpretation intended for the general public. The last two books are addressed to his son, who was aspiring to follow in his father's footsteps.

The *Oneirocritica* is largely a dream dictionary, but it also contains some broader advice on the general interpretation of dreams. Artemidorus interviewed professional dream interpreters and purchased manuscripts from all over the known world in order to familiarize himself with the general conception of dreams up to that point. Unlike most dream dictionaries of today, which are predominately psychologically oriented, Artemidorus's book focuses on deciphering dreams as omens of the future or messages from the gods. Although this view may seem quaint, Artemidorus's approach was in many ways quite sophisticated and nuanced. Like many modern theorists, he was careful to point out that symbolic meanings could vary depending on the culture or personal circumstances of the subject in question. This also holds true as time passes and cultural climates change.

Another notable difference between the *Oneirocritica* and modern dream dictionaries is that the *Oneirocritica* is organized according to categories of images rather than alphabetically. Thus he discusses, in a very literal "head to toe" progression, dreams concerning various body parts. He then moves on to discuss the appearance of gods and deities, also covering types of animals, weather, fire, flying, and many other topics. For the sake of completeness, he committed his third section to random, miscellaneous dreams he could not find a place for in the previous sections.

There were several pieces of information that Artemidorus considered essential for the proper analysis of dreams: whether the events of the dream were natural, lawful, and customary for the dreamer; what was happening at the time of the dream; and the dreamer's name and occupation. It was his belief that the associations evoked by the dream images in the mind of the interpreter were the keys to successful dream analysis. He was also the first to distinguish between dreams that stemmed from everyday life and the present state of the mind and body (the *insomnium*), and dreams that invoked deeper consideration of the dreamer's life at a mystical level (the *somnium*). The second classification of dreams was believed to foretell future events.

It is for his pioneering thinking and his commendably flexible approach to symbolic interpretation that Artemidorus is recognized as a prominent figure linking ancient beliefs about dream interpretation to the modern world. His observations reflect an appreciation for symbolism and an excellent grasp of dream metaphors, making him a worthy forerunner to such modern dream authorities as Freud and Jung. Freud actually named his major work on dreams, *The Interpretation of Dreams*, as a way of indicating his debt to Artemidorus.

Artemidorus believed that dreams were neither good nor bad. For this reason he did not touch on the specifics of nightmares. It is not the symbolism per se of a dream that makes it a nightmare, but rather how those symbols are interpreted and "filtered" through the lens of the dreamer's life circumstances.

(See also *Dream Dictionaries*)

Ashes

After any fire there are ashes—the dirty cinders mark the finality of the destruction of what has been consumed. In a nightmare, ashes can represent the end of the danger and destruction, and the beginning of rebirth and renewal.

Astral Projection

The theory that people consist of seven different "bodies," one for each plane of reality, is a teaching of Theosophist Madame Blavatsky. According to these teachings, the astral body, also known as the *aura*, is the seat of feeling and desire. Astral projection refers to the ability to project one's soul or aura out of the physical body. It is the older term for what has come to be known as an out-of-body experience (OBE). During this experience, it is believed that the astral body separates from the physical body and is free to journey at will to all corners of the universe. The astral body remains the vehicle of consciousness even when it separates from the physical body, and takes with it the capacity for feeling. It is said to be an exact replica of the physical body but composed of subtler elements, ethereal in nature, more of a "life force" than actual physical matter.

Some people believe they can project at will, and there are books available that claim to teach people how to do this. Some also believe that the astral body can spontaneously leave the physical body during sleep, while in a trance or coma, under the influence of anesthetics or other drugs, or as the result of certain kinds of trauma. Although there are many testimonials and vivid anecdotes attesting to the reality of astral projection, it is still not recognized by mainstream science.

The idea of bi-location, the ability to be in two places at the same time, has also been associated with the concept of astral projection. Instead of literally being in more than one place at a time, one possible interpretation of bi-location is that the physical body remains in one place while the astral body is in another. Throughout history, many mystics, monks, and other holy figures have been said to have the ability to bi-locate. Included in this category are famous Christian saints such as St. Anthony of Pradua and St. Ambrose of Milan.

British scientist Robert Crookall is among the many researchers who have given serious scientific study to astral projection. He has compared hundreds of cases in which people reportedly left the physical body and reentered it after traveling unseen in the astral body. Likewise, authors Sylvan Muldoon and Hereward Carrington maintain that there are various degrees of projection, which range from fully conscious projection to unconscious projection during sleep. This is discussed fully in their books *The Phenomena of Astral Projection* and *The Projection of the Astral Body*. Robert Monroe, founder of the Monroe Institute, published several accounts of his experiences with astral projection, including *Far Journeys* and *Journeys out of the Body*, which are considered by some to be the definitive works on the subject.

Psychic or precognitive dreams are often associated with unconscious projection during sleep. One may dream about something happening miles away only to discover later that the events in the dream actually took place. This event may be a specific and detailed conversation, a death, or a natural disaster. A possible explanation for this is that the dreamer unconsciously projected his or her astral body while sleeping and was present when the event occurred. They then remember the experience in the form of a dream, albeit an especially vivid dream. Frightening encounters have regularly been reported during astral projections. If the individual is asleep, these encounters are experienced as nightmares.

One phenomenon that is closely related to astral projection and out-of-body experiences is a near-death experience. Near-death experiences begin as out-of-body experiences when the physical body dies or is in the precarious state of serious trauma. With the help of modern medicine, the body is saved and the soul returns. People who have experienced this particular phenomenon often report floating above their bodies and looking down as the scene unfolds below them.

The prevalence of dreams in which the dreamer is flying is also sometimes attributed to the phenomena of astral projection. Flying is one of a handful of dream patterns that are so common that virtually everyone has had one of them (other common dreams are dreams of falling and public nakedness). It is important to note that flying was a widespread theme in dreams before the advent of airplanes or other modes of aeronautical travel. It was covered extensively in Artemidorus's ancient classic, the *Oneirocritica*. The explanation often put forth by writers of the occult is that during sleep everyone at one time or another travels outside of their bodies. In these experiences, the individual is unencumbered by the laws of physics such as gravity; they then remember the experience as a dream in which they were floating or flying.

(See also *Flying*)

Attic

The attic is arguably one of the two creepiest places in a house (see also *Basement*). Because attics are dark and dusty, and because there may be mice, bugs, spiders, and other vermin (or worse) present, it is one of the least frequented spaces in a house—making the space both mysterious and scary. Attics are traditionally the setting for many ghost stories—the things that go bump in the night often find residence in our attics or other secret, out-of-the-way places. A nightmare set in an attic may indicate that your intellect is exploring distant memories and/or coping with the tribulations and "ghosts" of the past.

Australia

There are more than 500 distinctly different Aboriginal tribes in Australia. Although these tribes have individual customs, they all share common beliefs concerning humanity and its relationship to nature. All believe in a mutual interdependence between the human race and nature. Dreaming plays a central role in the creation myth narrative of these people: according to the myth, the universe dreamed itself into being. The Aboriginal concept of "dreamtime" is similar in many ways to the modern Western concept of the imagination. Dreamtime refers to the dawn of time when mythical beings created the world, a time that somehow also coexists with the present. Humanity and nature exist as a result of the actions of these mythical figures. In Aboriginal cultures, the term commonly used to refer to the mythic past also means "dreaming."

Many Aboriginal ceremonies revolve around the dreamtime myth narrative. Individuals reenact what the mythic figures did in dreamtime because they believe that every meaningful event leaves its mark on the earth, much like a footprint in the sand, and because these figures of the dreamtime also exist in the present. Rites of initiation and other rituals evoke the past, and the actors become vicarious participants in history. By reenacting the dreamtime myth, Aborigines feel that they can maintain a bond with their creators. The past, present, and future coexist through ritual. Life and death are part of a cycle that has both its beginning and its ending in the dreamtime. A person's totem connects him or her to a particular mythic figure.

The Australian Aborigines feel that they can see and communicate with distant people during sleep, even with those who are long dead. During the process of dreaming, physical limitations of space and time are overcome, as they are in ritual, so that it is possible for the ancestors and heroes to relay immediate and practical information regarding past or future events. Nightmares are often interpreted as precognitive, usually an ancestor's attempt to warn the dreamer about tragic events to come. The dreamer

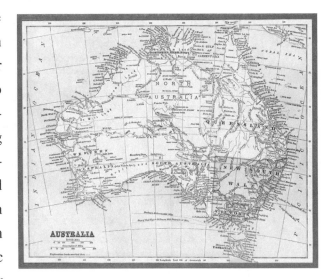

reports these nightmares to the tribal shaman who, if he deems the dream prophetic, provides special instructions to alter the outcome in the nightmare. As in many other undeveloped nations and tribal cultures, it is the telling of a nightmare that diffuses its potential for harm, and prevents it from becoming fully realized.

Automobile Accident

The automobile often represents the ego or an extension of the ego. We generally feel safe in our cars; secure in the protective bubble of metal that insulates us from the outside world. To dream of an automobile accident signifies a loss of control in our lives—things may be running too fast, the road may be crumbling underneath us, the brakes have gone out, and the very thing we've depended on to protect us is now imperiling us. Because the car is an extension of ourselves, to have a car damaged in a dream may mean that we are also feeling personally damaged.

Driving out of Control

Jen Brown is a 36-year-old wife and mother who lives in Santa Rosa, California. When she was 21 years old, she had a nightmare that was so vivid that it has affected her ever since.

The Nightmare:

> My nightmare was quick, but very specific. I was driving down Bennett Valley Road in Santa Rosa really fast. I was driving a light-green Mercedes C190, late-'80s or early-'90s model. I was listening to Night Ranger's song "Rumors in the Air" (though I have no idea why).
>
> The car went out of control, and I flew off the road into a small pond. The car sank, and I was inside trying to roll down the windows to get out, but nothing was working. Then I told myself that it's a dream and to wake up, only I couldn't. I kept saying to myself, "Wake up! Come on, wake up!" but the nightmare went on. Finally I said, "Oh God, I can't wake up!" and I shot up out of bed. I was completely wet with sweat and my heart was leaping out of my chest. I started to cry.
>
> To this day, I will never own a Mercedes or even ride in one, or even a green car—period. And I refuse to listen to any Night Ranger song (no big loss). I also will not drive on that road—ever.
>
> I once had the opportunity to buy a Mercedes, and I almost dared myself to buy it because I thought I was being paranoid about my dream (besides, it wasn't green). I test-drove it for a day and almost got into three accidents just driving for an hour.

When asked if the dream affected her driving habits, Jen said, "Yes, at least for a while, I slowed down. I still avoid that road. It has been years since I drove down it. I have only driven down it once since my dream just to confirm that there was indeed a large pond off to the side of the road where I dreamed it was—I drove *really* slowly over that part of the roadway."

Having had 15 years to reflect since the dream, she said she hasn't had any major automobile accidents like the one in her dream, nor has anyone close to her.

The Analysis:

> The color green is obviously significant, as Jen won't even ride in a green car anymore. And not only does she remember music playing, she remembers which song, "Rumors in the Air." Because of the color green, the fact that she's driving a luxury car, and the word "rumors" in the title, the analysis would lean toward envy playing a factor—perhaps envy of wealth or material things. This sense of envy led her to chase something. She claims she was driving rapidly, which indicates that she was trying to get somewhere or to someone quickly when she lost control and went into the pond.
>
> It sounds as if she got the message her nightmare was sending. She slowed down her driving, and perhaps also her life by a mile per hour or two, and passed on the luxury car when she had the chance.

■　　■　　■

Avalanche

Like a flood or fire, an avalanche represents some source of fear and/or vulnerability in the dreamer's life. Someone who has suffered a traumatic experience of some kind (such as a rape or the death of someone close to you) may endure recurring nightmares that replay the exact experience. But more commonly, the dreams contain more generalized disaster images such as avalanches. Psychiatrist Ernest Hartmann would say that this kind of dream "contextualizes," or provides a metaphorical picture context for, the overriding emotion in the dreamer's waking life. Obviously, the dreamer did not actually experience an avalanche, but his wise and perceptive emotions connect the actual trauma with the avalanche of his imagination. The avalanche then becomes the metaphor that represents the real event, and is no less terrifying for being a metaphor.

(See also *Metaphor*)

Axe

As a tool, the axe is cumbersome, but effective. Its weight and design make it well suited for splitting wood and felling trees. As a weapon, however, the axe is blunt and messy—a weapon used in a crime of passion and not one of premeditated precision. A nightmare about being hacked with an axe may indicate a messy separation, such as the loss of one's job, a breakup, or a divorce.

Bardo Thodol

Sometimes called the Tibetan Book of the Dead, the *Bardo Thodol* is a funerary text that describes the experiences of the soul after death and during the *bardo* (the time interval between death and rebirth). The word literally means "liberation through hearing in the intermediate state." The Bardo is recited by lamas over a dying or recently deceased person, or sometimes over an effigy of the deceased. It has been suggested that it is a sign of the influence of shamanism on Tibetan Buddhism. The *Bardo Thodol* divides the intermediate states between one life and another into three bardos:

○ The *chikhai bardo*, or "bardo of the moment of death," features the nearest approximation of the experience of the "clear light of reality" of which one is spiritually able to receive.

○ The *chonyid bardo*, or "bardo of the experiencing of reality," features visions of various Buddha forms.

○ The *sidpa bardo*, or "bardo of rebirth," features karmically impelled hallucinations that eventually result in rebirth into another life.

Descriptions of the *Bardo Thodol* can be compared to modern accounts of out-of-body experiences as described by people who have nearly died in accidents or on the operating table. These accounts typically entail the experience of a "white light" or divine presence, and of helpful figures that correspond to the person's religious beliefs.

The *Bardo Thodol* also mentions three other bardos: those of "life" (or ordinary waking consciousness), of "dhyana" (meditation), and of "dreams." Taken together, the bardos classifiy the states of consciousness into six broad types, and any of these states further entails an "intermediate state"—a state found between itself and other states of consciousness.

Basement

Along with the attic, the basement or cellar of a house is the place to store items we may no longer have use for, but lack the will power to throw away. That powder blue leisure suit from the 1970s, the parachute pants from the 1980s, or even the *New Kids on the Block* records from the late 1980s are just some of the frightening items we may have tucked away but would rather not discuss or let anyone else see. In our nightmares, a basement is the perfect Freudian repository for unacceptable thoughts, impulses, and feelings. Nightmares set in the basement may indicate the presence of a dirty secret that we may be trying to keep hidden or repressed. Like the abyss or pit, the basement can represent the depths of the unconscious and may signify latent guilt over real or imagined transgressions.

Bats

Bats have long been symbols of darkness and evil. There is something of the uncanny about them: they're blind, yet they can fly and hunt their food with amazing accuracy; and they're nocturnal—living in the night world. In Western

culture, the bat is often a symbol of the night and its attendant anxieties. Bats are closely associated with vampires, ghosts, death, and disease. In popular culture, the bat is the emblem of fictional characters of the night, such as the villian Dracula and the hero Batman. (Interestingly, Batman is a force for good, and appropriates the image of the bat as a *persona* in order to confound his enemies and bring order to society.)

In Finnish folklore, bats are the itinerant souls of the sleeping, enabling the spirit to explore the night world unencumbered by the physical body. In ancient Greece, bats were associated with Persephone, wife of Hades (they ruled darkness together as Lord and Lady of the Underworld). The bat is sacred in Tonga and West Africa, and is often considered the physical manifestation of a wandering soul. Among some Native American peoples, such as the Creek, Cherokee, and Apache, the bat is a trickster spirit. In contrast, Chinese lore sees the bat as a symbol of longevity and happiness. The bat is similarly auspicious in Poland and Greece, as well as among the Kwakiutl and Arabs.

Unfortunately, seeing a bat in your dream is usually regarded as a bad omen, and some say it may warn of death or the ending of something important, such as a relationship.

Battle

Witnessing a battle scene in your dreams usually represents inner conflict. Observing two large groups locked in combat engenders a feeling of helplessness; once underway, the fight must be carried to its logical conclusion. The battle in your dreams may indicate a split or disagreement between your intellect and your emotions: your brain may be battling for one position while your heart is standing in complete opposition. The battle may also be a  metaphor for a real, waking conflict between you and another person. In the case of veterans who suffer from post-traumatic stress disorder, a battle nightmare may simply be a reenactment of the real trauma of combat.

(See also *War*)

Bears

The bear is a large, powerful, and fierce creature that can be highly protective of its territory and especially its young; however, bears generally only attack humans when provoked or when they've been surprised. A nightmare that involves being chased by a bear may indicate a need to change course and watch your step, as forces bigger than what you may be able to handle are lurking in the underbrush. Bears are also one of the threatening or large wild animals that populate the nightmares of very young children (along with horses, cats, snakes, lions, and mythical dragons and monsters).

Bed

The bed isn't always a place of serenity and rest. At times, it can also serve as a place of unrest and even fright. The underside of a bed is a dark, scary place, full of dust bunnies at best, and slimy beasts at worst. A typical childhood fear is "The Thing Under the Bed," sometimes called the boogeyman—that ubiquitous yet faceless monster waiting for a stray leg to hang over the side so it can grab its prey and drag its victim under. It's the same creature that makes children leap

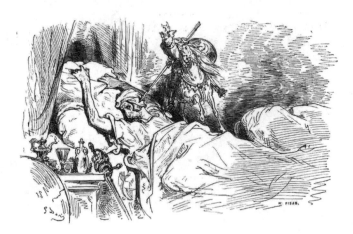

into bed from a few feet away so their ankles aren't within grabbing distance. Many adults carry traces of this fear from their childhood into adulthood.

Some people experience the unsettling sensation of their beds shaking them awake. In earthquake-prone regions, a shaking bed may have a perfectly natural reason, but some people experience this sensation where there are no quakes at all. The shake is usually very slight—more of a vibration than violent shuddering, though in rare cases some people report that they thought an earthquake was in fact taking place. An esoteric explanation for this event is that, during the night, the dreamer's spirit leaves the body (see also *Astral Projection*) and travels to alternate planes. But the spirit is always attached to the living body by a thin cord. If the sleeper's physical body is disturbed, the spirit will suddenly be re-assimilated into the body, which then causes the body (and the bed) to shake. The commonly accepted medical explanation for the "shaking bed syndrome" is that it is either a by-product of sleep apnea or a slight episode of sleep paralysis.

(See also *Sleep Paralysis* and *Sleep Apnea*)

Bedbugs

"Don't let the bedbugs bite" is a little bit of folklore that parents repeat to their children in jest as they tuck them in for the night. In reality, however, there has been a recent resurgence of bedbugs, especially in hotels, airline seats, college dorms, and cruise ships. In many countries, bedbugs are a serious concern. The rust-colored *Cimex lectularius* grows to be a little larger than an eighth of an inch in size and is extremely bloodthirsty. The vermin hide in creases and crannies and wait for their meals to come to them. Their mouths are perfectly adapted with pinchers that can pierce the skin, enabling the bug to gorge itself on blood. Adult females lay two to three eggs per day, and those eggs hatch in less than two weeks, which means that even a few bedbugs can quickly turn into a rampant infestation. People who are victims of bedbugs may not notice the tiny, itchy lesions until several days after the first bites. In some cases, multiple bites and lesions can lead to sleepless nights, as the victim lies itching in bed. Fortunately, they have never been known to transmit any diseases.

Bees

To be stung by a bee or several bees in a nightmare may represent internalized fears from childhood memories of being stung. Metaphorically speaking, you may be projecting anxiety about a business deal, an impending purchase, or some form of financial commitment in which you're feeling apprehensive about getting "stung."

A giant swarm of bees trying to attack you is an image out of a horror movie, especially if you find yourself in an open area with no place to hide. This imagery can represent the buildup of little things in your life that may be "bugging" you and that may eventually completely overwhelm you.

Beheading

A dream of being beheaded may indicate traumatic memories about bad judgments and wrong decisions made. The head symbolizes the intellect, so a beheading may also represent a feeling of disconnect from one's emotions, body, or spirituality. As in amputation, the body part that is severed is usually representative of the abandonment or neglect of talents that are used or symbolized by that body part. If your head is severed in a nightmare, you may be feeling intellectually insecure or stagnant, or perhaps you are regretting the fact that you didn't pursue your education more fully.

(See also *Decapitation* and *Amputation*)

Bible

The Bible is rich in references to dreams and nightmares. A few can be found in the New Testament (most notably in the revelatory experience of St. John on the Isle of Patmos), but they are most prevalent in the Hebrew Scriptures of the Old Testament. Here, examples of dream interpretations, dream experiences, and observations on the function and nature of dreams are common. In general, the Bible presents dreams as the most widely expressed form of immediate and personal divine communication. Personal, face-to-face encounters with God in the Bible are fraught with extreme peril for the individual, so God seems to mitigate this by manifesting his presence in dreams, waking visions, and inspirations. The crucial message conveyed by these dream manifestations is the constancy of God's presence, and the function of dreams as a liaison or means of divine communication to a sleeping consciousness.

The Bible's stance on dreams and their meanings and origin is often ambivalent and sometimes outright contradictory. Therefore, it is difficult, if not impossible, to find a unified theory of dreams and dreaming in the Bible. Numerous examples of dreams and nightmares as important divine revelations are cited throughout both Testaments, but there are also many passages dismissing dreams as worthless and illusive. Some biblical passages present dreams as darkly deceptive and seem to disparage those who would have the audacity of claiming to know God's will through dreams.

The ancient Hebrew community was unique in that it did not believe that dreams originated in the realm of the dead. Rather, they believed there were prophetic messages from the one true God. Consequently, and unlike other surrounding societies at that time, they did not actively seek to induce their dreams. They believed that only their God could be the source of divine revelation, and that he made these revelations only to those who were worthy. The belief was that only someone in the Jewish tradition could properly interpret prophetic dreams. This helped to consolidate Judaism as a unified religious and ethnic entity, and to confirm their sense of messianic calling. Not surprisingly, an entire section of the Talmud is devoted to the systematic analysis of dreams, nightmares, and visions.

It is possible to separate biblical dreams into three discrete categories, although there is some significant overlap among them. The first category is *symbolic dreams*. Examples of this particular type of dream can be found throughout the surviving literature from the ancient Near East, but in the Bible they occur almost exclusively to the gentile rulers and other important political figures. A well-known example of a symbolic dream is the disturbing dream of the pharaoh, as interpreted by Joseph. Here, the pharaoh first dreams of seven fat cows followed by seven lean cows, and then of seven plump ears of corn followed by seven thin ears. Joseph uses these dreams to predict seven years of plenty followed by seven years of famine in the land, thus gaining the pharaoh's respect as a dream interpreter. Joseph does not take credit for his abilities of divination when his prediction comes true, but instead attributes it to the wisdom and power of his God.

The second category of biblical dreams, *symptomatic dreams*, addresses the physical and spiritual health of the dreamer. When Daniel interprets the dreams of King Nebuchadnezzar, he proclaims that the great tree in the dream symbolizes the king himself. Using this symbol and others, he is able to deduce that the king will suffer an unavoidable mental breakdown as long as he refuses to acknowl-

edge God as the one true god. Daniel, like Joseph, also refuses to take credit for his interpretive abilities and accredits them to God's grace and inspiration. This is another example of an Israelite being the only person equipped to discern the divine message presented in a dream.

The third and most highly regarded type of dream recounted in the Bible is the *mantic*, or *prophetic*, *dream*. Joseph is one of the most prodigious dreamers of biblical times. In the beginning of his story, dreams are almost the cause of his undoing but they are also instrumental in his ultimate triumph. Some documents dating from that time refer to him as *Baal Chalomot*, meaning "master of dreams." Demons are also given names beginning with the epithet "Baal," and it is also the name of the primary Pagan deity as well as a Christian symbol of idolatry. Thus Joseph's title may have caused some confusion, but Genesis assures us that his interpretations come purely from divine, and not demonic, influences. The authors of the Bible concede that not all dreams come directly from God himself; the angel Gabriel is given the name "Prince of Dreams" due to his involvement in delivering divine messages through dreams, visions, and even nightmares.

Although the Bible does not use the term "nightmare" directly, not all of the dreams sent by God are pleasant. In fact, there are times when these dreams are extremely frightening to the dreamer and bring a message of warning. Jacob experiences a dream in which he wrestles with a dark, mysterious figure until morning; Abimelech is warned in a dream not to touch Abraham's wife, Sarah; and Job suffers horrible nightmares during his spiritual and physical afflictions. Even the wife of Pontius Pilate, who sits in judgment over Jesus before his crucifixion, suffers from nightmares—one particular nightmare moves her to speak to her husband and petition him to show mercy to Jesus.

The views of the Latin-speaking, Western Christian world concerning dreams and their interpretation was drastically changed in the early fifth century A.D., when Pope Damasus I commissioned Jerome to translate the Bible into Latin. Although legend has it that Jerome converted from being a follower of Cicero to one of Christ due to a dream, it appears that he deliberately mistranslated the Hebrew word *anan*, or "witchcraft." In seven out of the 10 times the word appears in the Bible, he translated the word correctly. The other three times,

when the passage was specifically condemning the practice of witchcraft, he replaced *anan* with the Latin word for "observing dreams." So instead of reading "thou shall not practice augury or witchcraft," the passage reads, "thou shall not practice augury or observe dreams." The fact that he had properly interpreted the word before seems to indicate that the mistranslation was willful. The exact reason for the misinterpretation is unclear; however, the result was that dreams and nightmares would be viewed with much more suspicion in subsequent centuries. Within 200 years following Jerome's "translation," Western Christians were completely discouraged from giving serious consideration to their dreams. In contrast, however, the Eastern Orthodox Church followed the views of the Greek Bible, and their favorable views on dreams have remained much the same.

(See also *Apocalypse*, *Precognitive Dreams*, and *Talmud*)

Birds

A bird in a dream is often seen as a good omen. A soaring bird can represent a triumph over adversity and a sense of freedom and success. In the folklore of certain cultures, birds—real or symbolic—can represent everything from death,

rebirth, and the afterlife to the presence of a deceased loved one's spirit. But what about birds of prey that swoop at you with sharp, outstretched talons and omnivorous beaks? What if you look up and see circling vultures, or find yourself, Hitchcock-style, the subject of many pecking beaks? When birds attack in a nightmare, the imagery can represent your fear of the opinions and judgment of others. In Alfred Hitchcock's movie *The Birds* (1963), the marauding flocks seem to be motivated by revenge (justified by the caged lovebirds carried throughout the film). If you dream of vicious flocks of birds, perhaps there is someone in *your* life who wants payback.

Blindfold

A blindfold is a popular image when depicting a firing squad. Blindfold imagery in a nightmare may represent the execution tableau, or perhaps may be a sign that you feel "under the gun" yourself. The imagery also symbolizes a temporary loss of sight, meaning that you might be lacking insight regarding an important issue.

Blindness

As a dream symbol, blindness can represent lack of self-awareness or insight. Perhaps you are truly unaware of your own emotional or physical needs, or perhaps you are indulging in some "selective inattention" about the importance of the needs of a relationship. Experiencing the loss of sight in a nightmare may indicate that you are willfully turning a "blind eye" to what you don't want to know: a classic example of Freud's idea of symbolization.

Blizzard

Snow squalls and blizzards can create white-out conditions in which a cold, biting wind and the frozen, swirling flakes reduce visibility to zero. Like blindness, blizzards in your dreams indicate a lack of awareness or insight. They may also indicate that certain emotional wellsprings are being closed up and turned off in your waking life, and the experience is creating temporary confusion for yourself and possibly others. Hopefully the snow will settle to reveal the problem, at which point the frozen feelings will begin to thaw.

Blood

Blood in a nightmare can have many different meanings. We have a complex relationship with blood: it is the very essence of life—it runs through our veins delivering oxygen and nutrients to our entire body. We know that we would die without it, yet we generally don't like to see it; some people faint at the sight of the most miniscule amount of blood. Metaphorically speaking, blood is associated with our emotional center. If the blood in a nightmare is the dreamer's own, it may indicate a feeling of being "bled dry" emotionally by a relationship. Blood is also connected to notions of kinship, so dreams about blood may be the subconscious's way of obliquely referencing family issues or problems. To dream of

drinking blood or receiving a transfusion may indicate a need for emotional nurturing or recharging. A woman experiencing menstrual bleeding in a dream may be concerned about fertility issues. For veterans, nightmares involving blood and gore could be a straightforward replay of the traumas experienced during combat (see also *Post-Traumatic Stress Disorder*). General images of bloody violence in a traumatic nightmare may be residue from an earlier life experience. Repetition of this type of nightmare may indicate depression and/or a penchant for doing harm to one's self or to others.

Bomb

A ticking bomb is a cause for real fear. If you can't defuse the device or get away from the inevitable explosion in time, it means certain doom. A bomb in a nightmare may represent potentially explosive situations in your waking life or a devastating secret that you are hiding at all costs in order to protect yourself and others. Alternately, the dreamer may have latent anger or rage that is threatening to come to the surface and explode.

Bones

Bones are a common symbol of death in almost every culture: just think of the Carnival in South America, Dia de los Muertos, Halloween, and other institutionalized and culturally sanctioned ways to cope with death and dying. Dreams of bones and skeletons may indicate a fear of death, or perhaps even the "death instinct" making itself manifest. Bones also represent our inner, hidden architecture, giving strength and shape to our bodies, yet at the same time being incredibly frail and vulnerable to breakage. To see an exposed bone in a nightmare is to have pieces of yourself emotionally vulnerable and open to the world. To see the bones of others in a dream may indicate that someone in your life has made him- or herself vulnerable to you.

Boogeyman

The boogeyman (also spelled bogeyman, bogyman, or boogieman) is perhaps one of the greatest fearsome creatures ever created by folklore. The reason? He can take the form of whatever most frightens or disturbs the dreamer. Dracula, Frankenstein, and the werewolf all have a reasonably predictable "look"—but not the boogeyman. This creature is a shape-changer that is usually bent on mischief and, occasionally, pure evil. According to folklore, the boogeyman will become friendly with young children as a way to gain entrance into a home.

The online resource *Encyclopedia Mythica* traces the etymology of the word from the "bugis," who were fearsome pirates from Malaysia and Indonesia. The English sailors likely brought home tales of these men and warned their children to behave or the "bugismen" would get them. The children would have no visual reference for the bugis, so they were left to create the creature from the darkest depths of their imaginations and most primal fears.

Bosch, Hieronymous

Carl Jung called this late Gothic-era painter "the master of the monstrous...the discoverer of the unconscious." Born Jerome Bosch in 1450, Bosch spent his

career in the Dutch town of Hertogenbosch (from which his name was derived). He was a member of a religious community called the Brotherhood of Our Lady, and for this reason his paintings were mainly centered on religious visions—especially the darker side of biblical prophecy and lore.

One of Bosch's best-known paintings is the triptych entitled *The Temptation of St. Anthony*. The work focuses on the mental and physical torment of the saint who remained true to his faith even in the face of his own execution. The left panel features the physical torment of Anthony, the right panel displays the temptations of food and sex, but the central panel represents the darkest, most nightmarish element: a black mass. A mockery of the Catholic Mass is held in the ruins of a church as demonic creatures look on from outside the ruins. In the skies above the scene, half birds/half sailing vessels float across the sky in a twisted imagery that is so bizarre, yet so well crafted, that the sinister, nightmarish feeling is rendered even more acute.

In Bosch's *Christ Carrying the Cross*, the faces surrounding Jesus as he pushes the cross along seem almost comical, but the eyes betray the evil undertone, and the dark hues of the work turn the comical to horror. Bosch's paintings are worth a thousand fire-and-brimstone sermons about hell from the most impassioned preacher.

Bosch died in 1516, leaving a legacy of horrific religious imagery in his work and giving his audience fodder for their own nightmares.

Breasts

Dreaming of naked breasts could simply be a sexual dream, or it may symbolize the need to be nurtured. A breast being mutilated in a nightmare can indicate a fear of breast amputation due to breast cancer. There are documented cases in which the dreamer was spurred on to get a checkup because of recurring nightmares about breast cancer—a prediction that actually turned out to be true.

"Briar Rose"

The Brothers Grimm (Jacob Ludwig Carl Grimm, born in 1785, and Wilhelm Carl Grimm, born in 1786) began collecting folktales from their homeland of Germany around 1806. They gathered and put on paper the traditional folk stories and myth narratives that had been passed down orally to children and told around campfires for many years. The story of Briar Rose is one of those tales.

"Briar Rose" is the story of a king and queen who long for a child. When they finally have a daughter, the king throws a great banquet to celebrate the event, but as he has only 12 golden plates, he can only invite 12 of the 13 Wise Women from the village. The first 11 Wise Women bestow magical gifts on the child, such as virtue, beauty, and riches. But before the 12th Wise Woman can give her gift, the uninvited 13th barges in and cries with a loud voice, "The King's daughter shall in her 15th year prick herself with a spindle, and fall down dead!" The 12th Wise Woman cannot undo the curse, but she mitigates it by saying, "It shall not be death, but a deep sleep of a hundred years, into which the kingdom shall fall."

When the princess turns 15, she pricks her finger and the kingdom falls into a 100-year sleep. Thorny vines overtake the castle and block everyone out for a century. The story of the beautiful but cursed "Briar Rose" circles the country. Princes come to try and break through the thorns, but none are successful. After a century passes, a prince comes to the castle, ready to try his hand at breaking through the thorns, but suddenly and magically the thorns and vines disappear. The spell is gone, and he awakens the sleeping princess with a kiss.

"Briar Rose" was the inspiration for Disney's *Sleeping Beauty*. For many of us, sleep is a sought-after reward, but a century of sleep truly would be a nightmare.

Bridge

Crossing over a bridge in a dream indicates new opportunities to come or the reestablishment of old relationships with people, places, or things. If a bridge is burning in a nightmare, you may be trying to get away from your past. If the bridge is in flames in front of you, it indicates that you are hesitant to forge ahead to the future. If the bridge is in ruins, it represents a broken relationship that is beyond repair. People who are afraid of heights can have recurring nightmares in which they are on a bridge (or tall building) that is collapsing, or a nightmare in which they are driving or falling off a bridge into nothingness. People who have lost loved ones from suicide may have nightmares about themselves or other people jumping off of bridges.

Burglar

To experience a break-in is to be violated on a personal, material, and emotional level. This is a traumatic violation that causes feelings of helplessness and vulner-ability, and may cause you to lose something of value in the process. Perhaps the dream is a reenactment of a real burglary that you experienced, or perhaps it represents an event beyond your control that took something significant from you, emotionally or tangibly, such as a business deal that cost you not only finances but also a friend. Traumatic nightmares often involve a dark, masked, or otherwise faceless man who is chasing or trying to attack the dreamer.

Burial

A dream about attending someone's burial service symbolizes bidding farewell to old conditions and relationships in your life. If you are being buried alive in a nightmare (and you believe in reincarnation), you may be recalling a past-life experience. Or perhaps you feel the need to get out of a situation in *this* life that is figuratively burying or inundating you.

Burning

(See *Fire*)

Cage

Cages come in many shapes and sizes, and they don't necessarily have to have bars on them to make you feel imprisoned. A dream or nightmare that involves cages signifies a feeling of being held captive or trapped in a job or relationship from which you desperately want to escape. You may feel confined by your responsibilities at work and feel the need to run screaming to the nearest exit, or perhaps you feel oppressed or subjugated in a significant relationship.

Cancer

In general, the dreams of those who are dying often contain imagery that symbolizes the continuation of life after death. This expectation of death as a form of rebirth into another plane of existence is helpful to those who fear dying because it gives them hope that death is more than oblivion. Having some kind of religious faith often helps a person accept the inevitable approach of death. The belief in an afterlife can help to diminish the fear that many feel when examining their own mortality, and by lessening this fear it will decrease the frequency of anxiety nightmares as one approaches death. For example, a patient who was suffering from terminal cancer experienced the recurring dream of a hand beckoning from the other side of a river. Each time she had this dream the river was progressively narrower, until at last she could step over it to the other side. This last dream occurred shortly before her death. It seemed that the river in her dreams represented the river of life, and crossing it in her dream indicated that she was prepared to cross it in her waking life as well.

Dreams that diagnose or predict cancer, or at least inspire us to seek medical advice, are not uncommon. The award-winning author of *Healing Dreams* (Rodale, 2001), Marc Ian Barasch, suffered from a recurring nightmare that centered on his neck area. After a particularly distressing dream in which an iron pot filled with painfully red-hot coals was hung beneath his chin, he decided to seek out a medical opinion. The initial round of tests didn't detect anything, and the nightmares continued. Barasch was insistent that they run more tests. Eventually, doctors detected a hard lump in his neck that turned out to be malignant. He was subsequently treated for thyroid cancer (fortunately, in the very early stages) and was able to beat the disease; however, his prognosis may not have been so positive if his recurrent nightmares had not spurred him on to insist on a second opinion. By prompting early detection, the nightmares were likely responsible for saving his life.

As in the case of William C. Dement, the pioneering sleep researcher and founder of the world's first sleep laboratory at Stanford University, nightmares may also encourage us to break self-destructive habits. At one time, Dement had been a heavy smoker. During this period, he dreamt he had inoperable cancer of the lungs. In the dream, he felt the full force of the diagnosis and suffered the fear of dying. When he woke, the sadness and guilt he experienced when faced with the prospect of losing his family forever made him quit "cold turkey" the next day.

Of course, this kind of nightmare does not necessarily mean that the dreamer has cancer, though it could certainly reflect a fear of cancer. Cancer is often a notoriously sneaky and subterranean disease: people can have cancer for months or even years and not realize it, only to find out the true diagnosis too late. Cancer, especially breast and prostate cancer, has become a permanent fixture in the news and media. Unfortunately, it has become part of the anxiety discourse of our age, so a cancer nightmare could be a response to a celebrity, acquaintance, or loved one who has been diagnosed with or who has died from the disease.

Alternately, we often use cancer metaphorically to talk about threatening conditions that are expanding destructively in our lives, so a dream about cancer could reflect a feeling that something is consuming the dreamer.

(See also *Poison*)

Cannibalism

This nightmare indicates a sense of helplessness and vulnerability at some deep level for the dreamer. Being a victim of cannibalism in a dream may suggest that you feel as if you are being eaten alive by work, a relationship, or some other enmeshing condition in your life. To dream that you are the person eating another's flesh is to literally be devouring their essence, and may indicate that you are a "psychic vampire" in need of a new source of sustenance. For most modern Western people, cannibalism, like murder and incest, represents the definitive forbidden act—the ultimate taboo.

Castration

This type of nightmare usually expresses feelings of emasculation, inadequacy, or impotence (sexual or otherwise) in the life of the dreamer, most likely in a relationship with a partner. The dreamer may feel that his power has been usurped in either his business or his personal relationship, or both. Of course, in psycho-analysis, Freud was the first to posit the term "castration complex" or "castration anxiety," or the fear of losing one's testicles penis. He saw this childhood fear as playing a fundamental role in infantile development. In some cultures, most notably in 19th-century Europe, it was not unheard of for parents to threaten their children with castration—a phenomenon Freud documents several times. Of course, women do not suffer from this kind of anxiety, but may instead feel sexually inadequate or disempowered in a more general way (that is, they are not thin enough, sexy enough, sexual enough, and so forth).

Cats

Cats are often thought to represent the negative aspect of feminine mystique. If

you are being scratched or bitten by an angry feline in a nightmare, it's likely that someone you know (most likely a woman) has issues with you and might be looking for a way to "get her claws into you." According to some folklore, cats have the ability to steal a child's breath during sleep. This is a primitive explanation for **SIDS** (sudden infant death syndrome).

Caves

Dark caves in dreams often represent the womb. As such, the imagery has many sexual implications. Like basements, pits, the abyss, and dark holes, caves may also function as the metaphorical repositories for the unacceptable urges and thoughts residing in the unconscious. To be lost inside of a cave in a nightmare may demonstrate a struggle with guilt over sexual feelings, and a threatening, dark cave may represent anxieties about the sexual act itself. To emerge unharmed from a cave may represent a birth, a rebirth, or a narrow escape. In modern society, a man is thought to have a need to "go to his cave" in order to recharge, to gain some privacy and insulation against the feminine world, and to get back in touch with his machismo. So a man dreaming about a cave may have an unexpressed need to embrace his more masculine side. In addition, Plato's metaphorical "cave" was the place in which the essence of everything and every idea resided.

(See also *Basement*)

Cayce, Edgar

"Dreams are today's answers to tomorrow's questions," Edgar Cayce once said. Born in Hopkinsville, Kentucky, on March 18, 1877, and raised on a farm, Cayce was one of the most renowned psychics in the world. He was an average man by many accounts: never formally educated and married with two children, he was a photographer by trade and a devout Christian. But his psychic abilities brought him celebrity and many followers of his work. He became known in the press as "The Sleeping Prophet" and "America's Greatest Mystic."

He had an ability to lay down on a couch, close his eyes, fold his hands over his stomach, and immediately put himself into a sleep state in which he could meditate and tap into the cosmic mind or "collective unconscious" (as Carl Jung would call it). Once in his sleep state, he would give "readings" as people would ask him questions that spanned a diverse range of subjects, from the mundane ("How can I remove a wart?") to the complex ("What are the secrets of the universe?"). A stenographer sitting near Cayce during his readings noted everything he said. He appeared to work in a kind of sleep-trance or unconscious, guided hypnotic state.

Cayce encouraged everyone to interpret and use his or her own dreams in day-to-day life. During his "dream readings," he would often interrupt his client and offer an interpretation before the dream had been fully recounted, and he would sometimes fill in parts of dreams that the dreamer had supposedly forgotten. Unlike Jungian or Freudian dream interpretation, Cayce did not emphasize the importance of symbols. Rather, he felt that every individual has his or her own unique symbols, and is therefore best suited to interpret his or her own dreams. He encouraged people to keep dream journals and document the imagery for later reference. Cayce claimed that dreams are a source of valuable insight that is always of use to the dreamer. Besides offering practical daily insight into one's life, he claimed that dreams enabled people to communicate with loved ones, dead or alive; remember past-life experiences; predict the future; and experience many other psychic phenomena. He stated that these paranormal abilities were not for the gifted few, but rather were skills that anyone could learn.

The two sources Cayce claimed to obtain his readings from were the subconscious mind of the person asking the question, as well as the so-called "Akashic Record," which is said to be the library of information that chronicles everything that has occurred throughout the entire history of the Earth.

Cayce seemed to receive his insights through dreams while in his meditative dream state, and he believed that everyone has the ability to experience these different levels of awareness in dreams. He felt that dream imagery could help people understand and diagnose their health problems, guide decisions, and even help keep people on a morally upright path. He felt that any important issue that presents itself in waking life would first be alluded to in a dream or nightmare.

Cayce did his readings daily for 42 years until his death in Virginia Beach, Virginia, on January 3, 1945. The Association for Research and Enlightenment, Inc., a group founded by Cayce in 1931, has copies of more than 14,000 of Cayce's readings on file.

Cemetery

Finding yourself in a cemetery in a nightmare could indicate a deep sadness, sense of loss, or unresolved grief in your life. It could also be indicative of a "dead past" lurking in the hidden, secret part of your consciousness. Cemetery dreams also reflects a preoccupation with, and fear of, death and dying.

Chagall, Marc

Marc Chagall (1887–1985) was a Russian-born French painter. He was raised by his Hassidic family and taught the Torah by his grandfather. He lived during a time when he and his family needed a permit to live in St. Petersburg because of the anti-Semitic laws of the day. Closely associated with the Surrealist movement, his work is heralded for drawing upon the subconscious mind and exposing humor, fantasy, and the darker side of ourselves. Chagall's imaginative works reflect the fantasy and irrationality of dreams and dream imagery. During and after World War II, Hitler's Holocaust and the atrocities perpetrated against the Jewish people weighed heavily on Chagall's mind, and some of that imagery made it to Chagall's canvases. Many of his works depict Jewish refugees and persecuted religious leaders. One such painting, his 1938 painting *White Crucifixion*, which depicts Jesus on the cross as the central theme, is said to be a statement about Jewish oppression, the Holocaust, and Joseph Stalin's leadership.

Chains

The sound of rattling or dragging chains has been associated with tormented spirits since before Charles Dickens penned *A Christmas Carol*. Folklore says that spirits are bound to this earth and weighted down by heavy chains as punishment for living bad lives. To see visions of chains in your dreams means you may need to break free from the chains that bind you to conditions in your waking life. Your bondage may be self-inflicted, just like Scrooge's was, or involuntary and circumstantial. Chain imagery may also refer to a complete or whole pattern in a chain of events—a pattern missed by focusing on only one aspect of a problem. The solution may lie in seeing how all of the parts link together.

Chainsaw

The chainsaw isn't a delicate instrument. It is loud, cumbersome, and tears through anything it comes in contact with. A chainsaw-wielding murderer in a nightmare demonstrates a wanton, psychopathic disregard for human life, as there is no remorse and certainly no concern about possible witnesses to the crime. A nightmare that involves chainsaws could also be an indication of repressed anger and even rage that is threatening to make itself known in a not-so-subtle way. The symbolism may indicate that you feel unfairly treated in, or broadsided by, a workplace conflict. Perhaps someone isn't fighting fairly, or perhaps workplace gossip is turning venomous and you feel ill-equipped to deal with the ramifications.

Charon

In Greek mythology, Charon is the ferryman of Hades, the underworld and abode of the dead. Charon takes the newly deceased across the River Acheron if they have an *obolus* (coin) to pay for the ride. According to the myth, those who cannot pay are doomed to wander the banks of the Acheron for 100 years. For this reason, the dead were always buried with a coin underneath their tongues in ancient Greece. Charon is usually depicted as either a decrepit, cranky, skinny old man or a winged demon with a double hammer.

In Shakespeare's play, *Richard III*, Clarence relates a long and terrifying nightmare in which Charon figures prominently:

> O! then began the tempest to my soul.
> I pass'd, methought, the melancholy flood,
> With that grim ferryman which poets write of,
> Unto the kingdom of perpetual night…
> I trembled wak'd, and, for a seaon after,
> Could not believe but that I was in hell,
> Such terrible impression made my dream.

> (lines 44–47 and 61–63)

Chase Dreams

You are walking down a dark street that you realize is unfamiliar to you. Out of the silence you hear steps behind you, following you. As panic sets in. Your pace quickens. The footsteps behind you also increase their tempo, and you now start to run, your fear giving unusual speed to your gait. Yet the menacing presence begins to gain ground nonetheless. By now you are at a full sprint, only to realize that it—whatever *it* is—is right behind you, perhaps close enough to grab you. The next thing you know you are in the safety of your bed, a cold sweat is covering your body, and your breathing is shallow and labored.

Nightmares in which you are pursued by a nameless, faceless, menacing figure are one of the most common types of troubled dreams. While they occur most commonly in children, they can also occur in adults. This is particularly

true after you experience a traumatic incident or are involved in other kinds of stressful situations, although the visions are often more specific and clear when caused by a trauma. The most common emotions that evoke these particular "picture metaphors" are extreme fear, vulnerability, and even guilt.

Chaucer, Geoffrey

Born in London in 1343 (d. 1400) as the son of a wealthy wine merchant, Geoffrey Chaucer was perhaps one of the greatest literary figures in all of medieval England. He learned the ideals of courtly love and chivalry at an early age, when he served as a page at the court of Lionel, Earl of Ulster. Throughout his life he held such varied positions as soldier, government official, justice of the peace, and clerk of the king's works. As a poet, he was heavily influenced by the works of Boccaccio and Petrarch, as well as by the genre of the "dream vision" poem (itself a vehicle for the courtly love poetry of 14th and 15th century English literature). Arguably the best example of this school of poetry can be found in de Lorrris's and de Meun's *Roman de la Rose*, which served as a model to several court poets, Chaucer included.

Among Chaucer's major works are *The Canterbury Tales* and *Troilus and Criseyde*. *The Canterbury Tales* (1387) is a collection of narrative tales recounted by a group of 30 fictional pilgrims traveling from London to the shrine of St. Thomas à Becket. The stories of the pilgrims, who are stock characters of late medieval English society, reflect Chaucer's interest in contemporary attitudes toward religion, love, and marriage. In *Troilus and Criseyde*, which is an adaptation of Boccaccio's *Filostrato*, Chaucer explores the complexity of the love relationship, weaving a story of fate, fortune, and hubris that finally destroys the lovers' search for happiness.

In addition to his translation of the *Roman de la Rose*, Chaucer wrote four dream-vision poems: *The Book of the Duchess, The House of Fame, The Parliament of Fowls*, and the Prologue to *The Legend of Good Women*. The first three of these poems are presented as the narrative of a series of dream visions. The narrative form connects the unreal, visionary dream experience with ordinary reality, and was typical of Chaucer's contemporaries (although it was used before in classical and biblical models).

In the "Nun's Priest's Tale" from Chaucer's *Canterbury Tales*, the priest is asked to tell a story. So he relates the tale of Chanticleer, a rooster who rules over seven hens in a poor widow's yard. His favorite hen, Pertelote, awakens to disturbing sounds—Chanticleer is having a nightmare in which a doglike animal is trying to attack him. When he relates his dream, his beloved taunts him for being afraid. She further asserts that nightmares are caused by overeating, and then offers to make him a laxative.

Chanticleer responds with a lengthy defense of predictive dreams, after which he declares that he is so overjoyed with his beloved's presence that he is no longer frightened by his nightmare. After he flies into the yard and has intercourse with Pertelote, a fox that has been hiding in the bushes tricks the rooster, grabs him, and carries him off. Chanticleer, however, is able to trick the fox in turn, and narrowly escapes up a tree.

Children's Nightmares

The nightmares of children have been noted almost from the beginning of recorded history. Nothing is as potent or terrifying as a child's nightmare. Adults may wake up from a nightmare and quickly calm down after convincing themselves that it was "only a dream." A young child lacks the capacity to understand the idea of boundaries (between reality and unreality, and between sleeping and waking), and also lacks the ability to articulate what has happened and why he or she is so scared.

A 16th-century Belgian doctor made a list naming the 52 most common diseases affecting the children of that time. Nightmares were listed as the ninth most common affliction on that list. Today we know that nightmares occur more commonly among children than they do among adults, and studies have shown that adults who suffer from chronic nightmares often have exhibited these problems since childhood.

Worldwide dream expert and psychologist Dr. Patricia Garfield conducted a study on nightmares involving 120 children, 109 from America and 11 from India; the majority of these children were between the ages of 5 and 8 years old. She managed to collect a sample of 247 dreams, which she classified simply as "good dreams" and "bad dreams." Out of this total, she cataloged 73 percent as "bad dreams." Nightmares with an overarching theme of being chased were reported 77 times. Dreams in which the child sensed danger but was never directly threatened accounted for a significantly lower number of the nightmares, with only 28 reported. Finally, in third place, 26 nightmares were reported in which the dreamer was injured or killed by accidental means. In contrast, there were only 89 dreams with a positive theme reported in this particular study. Thirty dreams were of general good times—for example, playing with friends, trips, and holidays—and 15 dreams involved the dreamer receiving some sort of gift. These two classifications represented 50 percent of the total good dreams. She also took time to offer parents general counsel to help deal with the frequent, recurring nightmares in their children.

David Foulkes, an international leader in the study of children's nightmares, conducted a long-term study of children's dreams. Based on his observations, he concluded that the dreams of young children and young adults do not differ greatly from each other. Contrary to Garfield, he did not find that the dreams of children were predominantly unpleasant, disturbing, or terrifying. He reached these observations based on his initial laboratory studies of two groups of 14 children, but his study came to include approximately 40 in total when additional subjects were added to replace those who dropped out. While Foulkes believed that the only reliable representation of dreams comes from laboratory dreams, his conclusions lacked the benefit of a large or random sample to support them, and they are in disagreement with more current theories.

In general, studies have discovered several traits common in children's dreams. One of the more remarkable characteristics is that children seem to have significantly more nightmares in which they are the victims of violence than do adults. Nightmares in which the dreamer is pursued, whether by monsters, strangers, or wild animals, are the most common type of children's dreams with negative content. There is also a general lack of pleasant exchanges, which seems to hold especially true for boys. Fear and fear-related emotions are twice as frequent in the dreams of young children when compared to the dreams of adults. This may be due, in part, to the fact that children often feel they have no control over their waking lives. They are anxious about to their ability to control external events, and this free-floating anxiety is reflected in the content of their dreams.

One of the leading researchers into the phenomena of nightmares is Ernest Hartmann (you can read his interview on pages 339–342). He developed a theory of "boundaries" regarding the frequency of not only nightmares, but also remembering one's dreams in general. Hartmann maintains that, generally speaking, the nightmares of children stem from their underlying feelings of vulnerability. As a child grows, he or she may develop a stronger defense to the stressors of waking life. Children in this group have what Hartmann calls "thick boundaries," and, because of this, they often cease to experience nightmares as they grow up (except for the same sporadic bad dreams that affect the majority of the population). They also have a significantly lower frequency of remembering their dreams. At the other end of the spectrum are children with "thin boundaries." These individuals often retain a sense of the vulnerability they experienced during their childhood, and thus continue to experience vivid nightmares into adulthood.

A discussion of nightmares in children would be incomplete without mentioning *night terrors*. While some sleep researchers insist that they are not exactly nightmares because they occur during the fourth stage of sleep and not during the REM cycle, the terrifying effect that they have on children is undeniable. A significant difference between night terrors and nightmares is that, in night terrors, the child will wake with no specific memory of what was frightening him; in a nightmare, the content of the dream itself is often recalled, sometimes in great detail. The exact cause and source of night terrors is unknown, but studies have shown that, for the most part, the frequency of night terrors decreases as the child ages. In one study of 23 children who regularly experienced night terrors, 22 had the phenomena stop completely after the removal of their adenoids. The correlation between night terrors and adenoids has not been researched fully, but the original study opened the door for further investigation. Furthermore, if a child has night terrors when he or she is very young, there is a good chance that they will disappear with age. Conversely, night terrors that begin in an older child are much more likely to remain a problem well into adulthood.

(See also *Night Terrors*)

China

Like many early societies, the Chinese believed that many dreams originated from the realm of the dead. The Chinese separated the soul into two distinct forms: there was the *p'o*, which they considered the "material soul," or the physical essence that gives life to the body and then ceases to exist after death, and the *hun*, which is the "spiritual soul" that can depart from the body during dreaming, yet still retains the appearance of the physical body. During its nocturnal journeys, the *hun* often visits the land of the dead, where it communes with the ancestors of the dreamer, as well as with the souls of others who are asleep. As in astral projection, these nocturnal journeys are experienced as dreams.

The recording of dreams and dream interpretation in Chinese history dates back more than 4,000 years. The ancient Chinese almanac, the *T'ung Shu*, contains an important section on dreams, dated at around 1020 B.C.E., entitled "Chou Kung's Book of Auspicious and Inauspicious Dreams." The author's name, Chou Kung, is still associated with dreaming and dream interpretation to this day.

The *T'ung Shu* divides dreams into seven different categories, and it discusses the symbolism of these categories independently of one other. In the section regarding the human body, the author asserts that dreams of one's teeth falling out indicate that one's parents are in danger, whereas dreams about the rising of the sun or moon indicate that the dreamer's family will be prosperous in the future. These and other prophetic dreams are discussed in the sections on the heavens and weather. Animal dreams were particularly relevant in ancient Chinese culture as well; according to the *T'ung Shu*, dreams in which a parrot is calling to you prophesies an upcoming quarrel that has the potential to be quite serious, while dreams of a swallow flying to you presage the visit of a dear friend from far away.

In contrast, the *Lie-tseu* employs the Taoist approach to dream interpretation. Taoist doctrine posits the unity of the universe and the relativity of the material world. In this doctrine, concepts or ideas are meaningless and empty without their contrasting counterpart. The *Lie-tseu* organizes dreams into several different classifications:

○ Ordinary dreams, which are merely random by-products of the mind without any previous emotion or influence.

○ Dreams of terror, or what we would call nightmares.

○ Dreams of thought, or what the dreamer's mind was consumed with the previous day.

○ Dreams of waking, which are the residue of or fallout from the dreamer's actions throughout the day.

○ Dreams of joy.

The *Lie-tseu* exemplifies the Taoist principle of yin/yang (balance) in that it discusses the need for harmony in one's life and how our dreaming mind compensates for the various imbalances in our waking lives. For instance, someone who is hungry in the waking world may dream of having or eating abundant food. In the same way, a person who is materially wealthy may dream of giving to the poor. A dream of crossing water may indicate that the yin is particularly strong in that individual's life, while walking through a great fire of some sort may indicate the yang is of greater strength. The Taoist approach to dreaming also includes the use of astrological factors for explaining the meaning of specific dream symbols.

The Chinese developed a fairly complex conception of energy (Chi), and the practice of acupuncture gave them a more complete understanding of how energy fields functioned in and around the human body. Because of this knowledge, they considered it dangerous to wake a person. When the *hun* is traveling out of the body, the person must wake up according to the soul's timing. If one were to be jarred abruptly from sleep, the consequences could be dire: should the *hun* be unable to return to the body in time, the sleeper would then be susceptible to chronic health problems or even madness. Alarm clocks and other abrupt means of waking the body are seen as violent to the soul and thought to result in a variety of negative side effects.

Dream incubation (the purposeful seeking of dreams and their meanings) was also a widely observed practice in various temples throughout China. Until sometime during the 16th century, Chinese society expected prominent political figures to seek dream guidance periodically in order to maintain their balance and objectivity. The sequence of preparatory rituals required before receiving a dream usually began with the supplicant burning incense as an offering before an image of a specific god. Prayer or some ceremonial chanting often followed, all of which was designed to invoke the favor of the temple deity. Not all dreams were sought in a temple setting, however: in the province of Fu-Kien, for example, people called upon their ancestors for dream revelations by sleeping on a grave.

Regardless of the methods used, if the supplicant received the requested dream, he or she would seek to establish whether or not a god sent the dream. If the dreamer was able to determine that the dream was divinely inspired, she or he was then free to spend time contemplating the symbolic meaning or, as often was the case, seeking out a professional dream interpreter. Once the true meaning of the dream was deciphered, the dreamer was able to decide on a course of action and apply the message to his waking life.

A Christmas Carol

In 1843, Charles Dickens published his legendary tale about the Christmas Eve nightmare of one Ebenezer Scrooge. In *A Christmas Carol*, Scrooge is the wealthy, miserly old man whose heart is as cold as the London winters. He loves nothing but his own money and uses it to distance himself from the suffering and poverty that surrounds him. However, a sequence of dreams and nightmares changes everything.

Scrooge is visited first by the ghost of his former business partner Jacob Marley. Marley is dressed as he did in life, but is covered in chains: "[The chain] was long, and wound about him like a tail; and it was made (for Scrooge observed it closely) of cash-boxes, keys, padlocks, ledgers, deeds, and heavy purses wrought in steel," Dickens wrote. When Scrooge asks Marley why he must wear the chains, the ghost replies, "I wear the chain I forged in life. I made it link by link, and yard by yard; I girded it on of my own free will, and of my own free will I wore it. Is its pattern strange to you?" In this segment of the dream, Dickens's readers don't need to be dream interpreters to figure out the meaning of Marley's chains. It's the same fate that awaits Scrooge unless he changes his ways. Enter the Ghost of Christmas Past.

The Ghost of Christmas Past takes Scrooge on a journey to his own child-hood, where they witness a happy and young Ebenezer. Each scene is a different

Christmas Eve, each scene was a sign of happier times for Scrooge. To dream of childhood memories is a yearning to return to the innocence of youth. In the case of Scrooge, this part of the dream is in stark contrast to his current lifestyle.

The Ghost of Christmas Present invites the present-day Scrooge to witness the life of his employee, Bob Cratchit, and Bob's sick child, Tiny Tim. Scrooge is surprised to find deep inner happiness in the hearts of those with so little. During the Cratchit family dinner, Scrooge watches as Bob Cratchit toasts him as the "founder

of the feast," though Mrs. Cratchit is quick to disparage Scrooge's name. To dream of others in your life is to gain a perspective on yourself. In a way, the Ghost of Christmas Present was holding a mirror up to the dream Scrooge so he could see how the world perceives him, and perhaps illuminate how he sees himself.

The Ghost of Christmas Yet to Come takes Scrooge's dream from an emotionally charged, mildly discomforting experience into a full-blown nightmare. In this, Scrooge witnesses the aftermath of his own death. The business associates who laugh at his expense, who agree no one is likely to attend the funeral services, and who sum up Scrooge's life as a successful one when it came to saving money, but a failure in all other regards—all point to a life greedy, pointless, absurd, and pathetic. For Scrooge, the dream is real. This *is* his death—the death of the man he was. Scrooge finally experiences real self-knowledge and a sense of contrition over the wrongs he has committed. The end of the dream leaves Scrooge in a sorrowful rage over his life, and it is this rage that carries over as he wakes on Christmas morning, spurring him into action to make things right in his own life.

This is a perfect example of how dreams can be instructional and helpful to the dreamer, even if they are unpleasant or downright terrifying.

(See also *Existential Dreams*)

Circadian Rhythm

The circadian rhythm is the body's internal resting/waking schedule over the course of one day and night. No two people have exactly the same circadian rhythm, which explains why some people are "morning people" and some are "night owls." Circadian rhythm can change over the course of a lifetime so that a onetime early riser becomes a night owl later on (or vice versa). Generally, however, people remain active during the day and rest at night.

Influences such as jet lag, night-shift work, alcohol consumption, drug use, medical problems, mood disorders, and even seemingly innocuous lifestyle choices and habits can disrupt the circadian rhythm temporarily. Persistent sleeping difficulties can occur if neurological problems force the circadian rhythm to be out of sync with the normal cycle of waking and sleeping. The discrepancy between when the body craves sleep and what society expects can lead to sleep deprivation. (In modern-day America, for example, the need for sleep is considered a sign of weakness, and some people find it difficult to reconcile their bodies' needs with the needs and expectations of a career, family, and other responsibilities.)

Chronic nightmares can make an individual avoid sleep, and thus bring about a temporary disruption in their normal circadian cycle. A treatment would involve resolving the underlying reasons for the nightmares, which would in turn restore the normal sleep pattern.

Clones

Cloning has been a provocative news topic in recent years. The implications of cloning are as vast as they are frightening: What if something goes wrong and scientists bioengineer a mutated monster? What if everyone began to look alike? What if someone cloned you again and again? What if cloning enabled the proponents of a "genetically pure" race to realize their dreams? This postmodern nightmare reflects an underlying fear of what is to come in the future. The dreamer may feel the world is spiraling faster and faster and they simply can't keep up, and perhaps witnessing multiple versions of one's self is a way of compensating for these feelings of inadequacy. Of course, the reality is that no one can ever keep up with the myriad changes in the world, and the dreamer's task should be to focus on what is most important to him- or herself.

Closet Monster

Young children often ask their parents to close the closet door before they're tucked in at night. When the lights go down in the evening, even a cracked closet door will show the ominous pitch-blackness within. Some children carry this trepidation with them to adulthood, finding themselves closing the closet door before going to bed "out of habit." But the reality is that there still remains an irrational fear in their psyche of that same closet monster—the creature from the depths of our imaginations that we know will come lurching, shuffling, or slithering out of the darkness to attack.

In 2001, Disney/Pixar launched the animated movie *Monsters Inc.*, which took the concept of the closet monster to an entirely different level. In *Monsters Inc.*, monsters enter the world of sleeping children via the closet door. They need to scare children and collect their screams in order to power the monster cities back home. Like real parents, the parents in the movie assume that their screaming children are having a nightmare, and never believe that a real monster came calling.

Clowns

Send in the clowns? Not so fast. Clowns are supposed to be the colorful, clumsy, and capering characters that amuse us at circuses and children's parties. But many young children are frightened by the bright colors and exaggerated proportions of the makeup and costume, such as the oversized shoes; colorful, bushy hair; and large red nose. The face painting, though amusing to a more mature audience, may seem grotesque to a young child. The child is dimly aware that under the costume lies a person, but everything in his mind is telling him "like, yet unlike." This is the essence of what Freud described as the "uncanny," the notion that something familiar and close to home has somehow been rendered different, other, terrifying. Many people carry that fear of clowns into their subconscious and then into their adult lives, and this fear can be expressed in truly terrifying nightmares. The clown nightmare represents a distressing paradox lodged in the dreamer's thought processes—what was familiar is now strange, what was supposed to be funny is now frightening, what was supposed to be harmless now seems malevolent. This imagery taps into the primal fear of the uncanny that young children and adults alike can carry. A clown nightmare could mean that you're sensitive to an issue that others don't seem to have a problem with, or it may represent a deep-seated personal issue that you will need to resolve if you're going to be able to move on.

(See also *Uncanny, The*)

Cockroaches

For many, these genetically adapted insects are associated with filth. They can be small and numerous, or as large as mice, offering a horrific *crunch* when crushed (a sound that is often worse than the sight of the bug itself). To experience a cockroach in a nightmare means you may need to reevaluate the cleanliness of your own kitchen or other place(s) where you take nourishment (physically and otherwise). The bugs could also indicate that you have fallen prey to some suspect ideas or schemes.

Coffin

The coffin is the final stop on our mortal journey. It's the box our remains are squeezed into before being lowered into the ground and out of sight. The image of a coffin in a nightmare may represent a deteriorating or dead situation, or perhaps a feeling of restriction and confinement on the part of the dreamer. Coffin imagery, such as corpses, graveyards, and bones, may also reflect a preoccupation or obsession with death and dying.

Cold

Cold shivers are often associated with fear. A sensation of being cold in a nightmare can signal a fear of being excluded or left out of something (that is, "left out in the cold"), or the inhibition or stunting of certain emotions.

Coleridge, Samuel Taylor

The vivid imagery of nightmares has inspired many great works of art. But in very rare instances, the art takes direct dictation from the dream. In the summer of 1797, poet Samuel Taylor Coleridge was staying in a farmhouse between the towns of Porlock and Linton in England. During an opium-induced nightmare, Coleridge saw in his dream what was to become his most famous poem, "Kubla Khan." The opening lines of "Kubla Khan" read:

> In Xanadu did Kubla Khan
> A stately pleasure-dome decree:
> Where Alph, the sacred river, ran
> Through caverns measureless to man
> Down to a sunless sea.
> So twice five miles of fertile ground
> With walls and towers were girdled round:
> And there were gardens bright with sinuous rills,
> Where blossomed many an incense-bearing tree;
> And here were forests ancient as the hills,
> Enfolding sunny spots of greenery.

Coleridge included a note with the published poem, part of which reads:

> In consequence of a slight indisposition, an anodyne had been prescribed [to the author], from the effects of which he fell asleep in his chair at the moment that he was reading the following sentence, or words of the same substance, in *Purchas's Pilgrimage*: "Here the Khan Kubla commanded a palace to be built, and a stately garden thereunto. And thus ten miles of fertile ground were inclosed with a wall." The Author continued for about three hours in a profound sleep, at least of the external senses, during which time

he has the most vivid confidence, that he could not have composed less than from two to three hundred lines; if that indeed can be called composition in which all the images rose up before him as *things*, with a parallel production of the correspondent expressions, without any sensation or consciousness of effort. On awakening he appeared to himself to have a distinct recollection of the whole, and taking his pen, ink, and paper, instantly and eagerly wrote down the lines that are here preserved. At this moment he was unfortunately called out by a person on business from Porlock, and detained by him above an hour, and on his return to his room, found, to his no small surprise and mortification, that though he still retained some vague and dim recollection of the general purport of the vision, yet, with the exception of some eight or ten scattered lines and images, all the rest had passed away like the images on the surface of a stream into which a stone has been cast, but, alas! without the after restoration of the latter!

This poem is a perfect example of "dream art," in which a dreaming or dream-like imagery has directly influenced the theme or aesthetics of a work.

(See also *Art*)

Colors

Most people (close to 70 percent by some estimates) dream in color. The minority of people only dream in black and white, and a few dream in both color and black and white. Colors have contained a symbolic meaning in and of themselves since the beginning of time. Color even holds significance for many species of animals, such as the verdant plumage of a mating bird.

Colors affect our moods; many believe they have the power to heal; and they are critical to how we express ourselves in almost every aspect of our lives, from clothing, to architecture, to art. Colors also have a nearly universal meaning for millions of people. For example, when driving, green means "proceed," yellow means "caution," and red means "stop." Without these conventions, driving would be quite a dangerous endeavor.

Science has evolved enough to know that all colors reside in the visible light portion of the electromagnetic spectrum. The electromagnetic spectrum encompasses the entire universe of vibrating waves—from radio waves, which are the longest, at one end of the spectrum; to gamma rays, which are the shortest, at the opposite end. The visible light spectrum is only a tiny sliver somewhere near the middle.

In 1810, Johann Wolfgang von Goethe studied color for two decades before publishing his work in *Zur Farbenlehre*, or *Theory of Colors*. Goethe was the first to identify the three primary colors of red, blue, and yellow, and he explored the psychological effects of color on people. He also identified complimentary colors—those colors that go together in harmony. Like music, colors can have harmony as well as discord.

Within the context of a nightmare, sometimes a predominant color is present. In this case, there are general meanings for each color:

- **Black** is the absence of color. It represents the dark and unknown, perhaps a blockage of ideas or possibly ill health. Black is not necessarily evil, but it is the opposite of, and thus the balance for, white.

- **White** is the inclusion of all colors. It symbolizes purity, lightness, and divinity. White is also the color of clarity and can signify healing.

- **Red** is a passionate color, full of vibrant energy, as well as the color of blood. But red is also a color of warning and aggression. Moderation is the message when red becomes too dominant in dream imagery.

- **Orange**, like yellow, is a color of caution, but it also represents the desires of the dreamer's physical body. This may be a sexual desire, but it could also be a desire for food or for exercise. Orange also represents change or a desire for change.

- **Yellow** is a bright, vibrant color—a symbol of caution that demands attention. But yellow also represents creative energy and the intellect.

- **Green** is the color of prosperity and abundance, but also the color of greed and envy. Green is also associated with nature and healing.

○ **Blue** is a tranquil color that signifies peace and serenity, but certain shades of blue can also mean sadness or depression.

○ **Indigo** is often associated with psychic abilities and the spiritual realm. To dream in indigo means spiritual matters are on your mind.

○ **Violet** is associated with power, especially royal or political power, but can also be the sign of an emotional or mental disorder.

Comets

In poet Robert Frost's 1920 poem "Fire and Ice," he writes: "Some say the world will end in fire, some say in ice." According to many astronomers, both may be correct. Somewhere in the vast Milky Way galaxy might just be a comet with Earth's name on it. The killer comet's impact has a potential for mass destruction: first a sea of fire at the site of impact that sends shockwaves around the globe, then thousands of years of ice as the atmosphere fills with debris from the impact and blocks out the sun.

The comet nightmare is a doomsday dream. It may also express the dreamer's anxiety over surviving a major life disruption, such as the loss of a job or the end of a relationship.

(See also *Apocalypse*)

Computers

As technology has become fully, and permanently, integrated into every part of our lives, it has also become a fixture in our dreams. For a growing number of people, the computer represents how they make their living, how they get their entertainment, even how they form and keep relationships. The computer may even store our financial records, our prized family photos, our calendar, and our address book. Not surprisingly, many people often report feeling that their computers are an extension of themselves. The computer represents the left side of our brain—the rational, "objective" part of us. Something going wrong with our computer, such as a virus or hard drive failure, can create a living night-mare in our waking lives. To dream of computer failure symbolizes a feeling of vulnerability. Data loss means the loss of power, which makes us feel weak and ineffectual. It's time to make "backups," to take extra care to study the subjects in which we are less than proficient. To dream of electric failure during a critical moment on the computer is a sign that perhaps the rational side of our brain is overworked and needs to shut down, or, conversely, that the creative side of our brain is insisting on having a say.

Contamination

Choking air, poisoned food or water sources, or a contagious disease that's been turned loose are all causes for alarm. This is an especially potent image for persons earning their wages from factories that poison the air, food, and water supply. These are the people who would most likely suffer from nightmares of toxic contamination, perhaps brought on by a conscious or subconscious sense of guilt over the ecological effects of their employer's factory. People who are germ phobic may also suffer from anxiety nightmares in which they have been contaminated or infected in some way. In general, dreams of contamination may be indicative of latent guilt over some real or imagined transgression.

Control of Nightmares

If nightmares, especially recurring nightmares, have become intrusive and problematic in someone's life, dream analysis is the first and most important step in trying to control or treat the problem. Analysis allows for the discovery and "excavation" of the emotions that are the driving force behind the dream. Once the dreamer acknowledges the negative emotions from her or his waking life that are triggering the nightmares, they loose the power they hold in the subconscious and are no longer manifested as a terrifying force. By seeking professional help with the analysis of dreams, the dreamer is able to freely discuss the specifics of the nightmares in a safe environment, which enables the dreamer to confront the fearful, repugnant, or undesirable aspects of his or her subconscious. The ability to face fears head-on often results in the growth of self-esteem and self-reliance; it also will commonly end, or diminish the frequency of, the occurrence of the nightmares themselves.

It is the belief of many dream researchers that dream analysis can enable the dreamer to more readily attain the state known as *lucid dreaming*. Lucid dreaming takes place when dreamers are aware of the fact that they are dreaming without waking up, and are then able to control the imagery or narrative of their dreams. One of the first steps to controlling the nightmare is the rehearsal of pleasant dream imagery during waking hours. All that is used in this technique is the power of imagination to change the elements of the dream environment or to "re-narrate" the entire negative experience. Once the dreamer is able to call upon pleasant images or scenes at will, he or she will then be able to start actively influencing the content of the nightmares. By taking an active role in the themes and plotlines of the nightmares, the dreamer is able to manipulate an outcome that is neither stressful nor terrifying. When someone who suffers from nightmares is able to develop a plan of action and then take steps toward its implementation, it greatly enhances confidence and a sense of agency and control, which can be a very empowering experience indeed. This technique has also been found to be useful in the treatment of some cases of insomnia, because it eliminates the reoccurrence of the same nightmares in the same night and thus fosters a more restful, uninterrupted sleep experience.

Recording details from a nightmare in a dream journal can also be very useful in the control and treatment of nightmares. It is useful at any time after the dreams have occurred, but the sooner a nightmare is written down, the more details are likely to be remembered. Thus it is generally most effective to write everything down immediately after waking. The journal is useful as a reference when interpreting the dreams later, but there have been cases of the nightmares stopping altogether by the mere act of recording them.

Cooper, Alice

In 1964, lead singer Vincent Furnier and four of his high school friends formed a band called Earwigs. They had some initial local success but knew they needed to relocate to a larger market if they were going to hit it big. In 1967, the band moved to Los Angeles and finally settled on the name "Alice Cooper" for their band—the idea being the shock value of an all-male band with a woman's name.

Soon after, Furnier changed his name to Alice Cooper to push the shock value even higher. By 1970, the band moved to Cooper's hometown of Detroit, where they found an audience for their raucous sound and wild stage show. In 1972, they released "School's Out," which propelled the group into an even bigger spotlight with the number one hit.

The music and lyrics were hard-driving and sometimes dark, but the stage show was often even creepier. Alice Cooper and his band came on stage in full makeup, and the show included dramatic and nightmarish theatrics such as a guillotine, whips, mannequins, hatchets, blood, giant teeth and dental drills, smoke machines, and snakes. All of this quickly garnered a reputation for horror and perversion for the band. In 1975, Alice Cooper released the album *Welcome to My Nightmare.* The lyrics of the first song, eponymously called "Welcome to My Nightmare," read:

> Welcome to my nightmare
> Welcome to my breakdown
> I hope I didn't scare you
> That's just the way we are when we come down
> We sweat and laugh and scream here
> 'cuz life is just a dream here
> You know inside you feel right at home here

Alice Cooper still performs today, bringing his "nightmare" to audiences around the world.

Corpse

A dead body in a dream may represent feelings that have had the life sucked out of them. Perhaps you are being micromanaged at work and have lost your ability to be creative or think freely in the workplace, or perhaps a psychic vampire in your life is feeding on your vitality and energy. A lifeless corpse in a dream may also indicate a feeling of enervation, such as what one experiences when adhering to a lifeless routine. Dead bodies in your nightmares can also represent an unhealthy preoccupation with death and dying.

Critical Incident Debriefing (CID)

The aim of CID is to minimize the psychological distress in the aftermath of a traumatic event by allowing someone to vent his or her impressions, feelings, and reactions. This technique helps people make sense of the experience by creating a better general understanding of the nature of traumatic incidents, and by educating them about the absolute normalcy and predictability of their reactions (that is, "I am not alone"). Also, this allows the sharing of feelings and reverses the natural tendency of traumatized people to "bottle things up." Sometimes CID also employs group therapy in order to reduce tension and stress, reinforce normalcy, and reduce feelings of isolation and being "different." People with shared traumatic experiences can commiserate with people who were there, who helped during or after the event or events, and who "understand."

CID helps traumatized people by enabling them to:

O Discover and raise awareness of all available personal, group, organizational, and other resources.

O Prepare for the eventuality of future reactions by initiating the process of normalization and education, by providing a central source of information, and by raising awareness of the options available should additional help be needed.

O Examine future needs for themselves, their family, their peer group, and their larger social milieu.

CID is also very effective for the prevention and treatment of intrusive traumatic nightmares. The efficacy of this treatment is in its immediacy: the sooner a traumatized person can get into treatment the better. Someone who suffers from post-traumatic stress disorder, however, has already had time to build up the thick psychological "walls" and tenacious boundaries that discourage commiseration and treatment in the first place.

Crushing

To dream of being pressed by a heavy weight is an indication that an issue is "weighing heavily" on your mind. Anxiety and panic increase in direct proportion to the amount of pressure we experience—this is an issue that must be dealt with before it completely crushes you. Perhaps you have a high-pressure job situation, or perhaps there are expectations in a personal relationship that are squeezing the life out of you. Some people also experience a crushing sensation during sleep paralysis (also known as "Old Hag Syndrome") in which they partially wake to find that they can't move or breathe.

(See also *Sleep Paralysis* and *Old Hag Syndrome*)

Dagger

A dagger is traditionally viewed as a symbol of male power or as a phallic symbol. Alternatively, it may be a symbol of hostility, as in the expression "she had daggers in her eyes." Nightmares involving daggers or knives may indicate that you are experiencing anxiety in your relationship with a significant male figure, or that you are involved in an overtly hostile conflict with someone. If you are a woman, you may fear sexual encounters with men.

Dali, Salvador

Salvador Dali (1904–1989) was one of the best-known surrealist painters of the 20th century. His style is instantly recognizable for both its detail as well as its bizarre, dreamlike imagery (Dali's 1931 *The Persistence of Memory* featuring melted clocks hanging over a tree branch, on the edge of a block, and on the ground is arguably his most recognizable work). Dali described the idea behind his approach to art as "critical paranoia," which may explain some of the haunting and grotesque imagery in his work. In his 1940 painting *The Face of War*, Dali portrays a browned, decomposing face in the desert surrounded by many snakes poised to strike. Inside the face's mouth and eye sockets are more faces, each in a further state of decay than the larger face before it. The image is haunting at first glance; but upon closer examination of the detail, the ugliness of death is further exposed in the nightmarish image. War is the subject of several of Dali's more horrific paintings. For the surrealists in general, dreams—especially dreams with fantastic, absurd, or even terrifying imagery—functioned primarily as inspiration for the content of their art.

Dam

A dam holds back great quantities of water—the structure itself represents man's triumph over and subjugation of nature. Metaphorically, the water represents the deep wellsprings of emotions (positive and negative) in our unconscious, and the dam signifies a lack of openness and emotional availability to others. The dam is the figurative wall we've been putting up to others as a defense. To experience a dam breaking in your nightmare may mean that the feelings you've been holding back want out—*badly*. Remember that a huge quantity of water like this can be a destructive force, so be careful if and when you decide to "let go."

Danger

Any kind of feeling of danger in a dream may be a realistic warning signal for the dreamer to be more cautious in his or her waking life (for example, more cautious in their driving, handling of sharp objects, or walking alone after dark). An overwhelming feeling of danger in a dream is typically seen as a harbinger of trouble in the near future—it's time to be alert. The fight-or-flight response and its attendant emotion, fear, are the most common emotions experienced in a nightmare.

Daniel, Book of

The Book of Daniel contains the most detailed and fascinating exploration of dream interpretation found in the Old Testament. Although the actual historical person Daniel remains something of a mystery, the Hebrew Scriptures read that he lived under foreign oppression during the Jewish exile in Babylon, when the Jews were struggling against the oppression imposed by Antiochus Epiphanes in the second century B.C.E. The Scriptures depict him as a prolific dreamer as well as a great dream interpreter in his own right. He often suffered apocalyptic nightmares of a four-headed monster.

Perhaps the most famous instances of dream interpretation in the Bible are the stories of Daniel's interpretation of the dreams experienced by King Nebuchadnezzar. In one story, King Nebuchadnezzar suffers from insomnia and frequently complains of portentous and disturbing nightmares, but he can never recall specific details about the dream's content or narrative. In order to remedy this he first consults the palace soothsayers, and when they are unable to help him, he has them executed. When Daniel is finally faced with the opportunity to disclose the meaning of the king's dreams, he goes one step further and describes the elusive details of the dream content that the king cannot remember. Insisting that the dreams are prophetic, Daniel describes the first one as a city of magnificent metals that has been broken and crushed. He interprets this to signify the impending division of the kingdom, claiming that the only kingdom that is indivisible or unconquerable is the kingdom of God. (This may correspond with the fall of the city of Nineveh.) The second series of dreams consists of a tall tree, with branches reaching toward heaven. In this dream, Nebuchadnezzar receives instructions from God to cut the tree down and let it weather for seven years. Daniel boldly asserts that the symbolism of this dream corresponds to the king's great pride—he himself is the great and arrogant tree, and if he does not remove himself, God will. Nebuchadnezzar fails to heed these warnings, and is afflicted with a great madness, probably what we would describe as lycanthropy (he devours human flesh because he thinks he is a wolf). His psychosis lasts for seven years, paralleling the seven years foretold in the dream.

(See also *Bible*)

Darkness

Darkness can be frightening even in our waking world—when the lights go out, the familiar becomes instantly unfamiliar. Darkness can signify evil, death, a fear of the unknown, ill health, or simply a feeling of being lost. Any dark place in a dream (for example, a hole, cave, or pit) can also signify the unconscious, with all its unacceptable thoughts and urges. To dream of light fading in your dreams usually relates to work situations and can mean you're going to need help with the project or task that is giving you trouble, or that you're losing your focus for the task at hand. Like blindness, darkness in a nightmare can also signify a lack of sight or insight. Perhaps there is something troubling you and you don't know what it is—if you have the courage to look into the darkness and not away from it, you might find out.

Deadlines

Our lives are run by deadlines. The morning alarm clock alerts you that your sleep time is over and your waking deadline is here. In our jobs, deadlines are everywhere—from small projects to large, everything has some kind of due date.

Authors experience deadlines when they submit manuscripts or articles, and the pressure to meet them can be so great that some authors fall apart. Deadlines can be represented in dreams in a number of ways. In some dreams, the deadline is experienced simply as a nagging feeling that the dreamer has an important event coming up and must hurry to accomplish the tasks at hand. A common deadline nightmare is one in which the dreamer is late for an appointment, exam, or social obligation, but has no idea how to get there or what the meeting is all about (similar to the unprepared nightmare). Imagery symbolizing deadlines could be doors or windows closing, axes falling, alarms ringing, or books closing.

Death/Dead

Sleep and death have long been linked in various cultures. Sleep may be a metaphor for death, or it may be a conduit for the dreamer to visit deceased ancestors. According to Carl Jung, death dreams are linked to the universal theme of transfiguration and personal transformation. In this, death becomes a means to a new self, a new life, or an entirely new plane of existence.

Dreams about the dead are not usually portents of the death of the dreamer, as some people would imagine. Depending on the context of the dream and the circumstances of the dreamer's life, a death dream could simply mean the end of something in your life. To have a dream about a loved one who has already passed on may signify that you have unresolved feelings, such as guilt over arguments you may have had, or even anger at the person for leaving you. A death dream can also reflect anxiety about, or a preoccupation with, death. Violent death in a nightmare may in fact just be the repressed aggression and anger that the dreamer feels in her or his waking life.

(See also *Corpse*)

Decapitation

Nightmares of being beheaded can have a variety of meanings, from losing control of your emotions (as expressed in "losing one's head"), to a split or disconnect between your mind and body. This dream may also indicate unpleasant feelings or anxiety having to do with punishment or being punished.

(See also *Beheading*)

Demons

The belief that malicious entities in the spirit world lie behind natural disasters, illness, madness, and other unpleasant aspects of human life is very old, but the notion is still alive and well in many traditional societies. Before the advent of scientific discoveries that proffered more neutral explanations for the irregularities of nature, it was not unreasonable to postulate that such beings were responsible for unexplainable natural disasters and diseases. While scientific explanations have gradually supplanted metaphysical explanations, demons and devils presently survive in the archetypes of Carl Jung's collective unconscious (for example, the shadow self), as well as in other schools of psychology that interpret evil forces and hallucinations as projections of human fears and anxieties.

While often the two words are used interchangeably—*devils* from Greek *diaballo*, or "to throw across" (that is, the accuser); *demons* from Greek *daimon*, or

"spirit"—their meaning evolved through the centuries and in different religious traditions. Devils have always had the negative connotation of evil forces, whereas demons could be either good or evil, depending on their individual nature. *Daimones* in ancient Greece were semi-divine tutelary spirits with either good or evil tendencies.

In the early stages of Judaism, demons did not have a big impact on the religious belief system. During the first diaspora, when the Jews were in contact with the dualist vision of Zoroastrianism, Judaism developed a more defined role for demons, particularly in the *aggadah* that reflected the popular rabbinic beliefs. These mythological figures found their origin in the indigenous pagan beliefs (such as the *shedim*) and were believed to be creations of God or the offspring of Lilith, the first wife of Adam. In the Kabbalah during the Middle Ages, evil forces took a more definite form with names and roles, although the idea of these forces was never really fully accepted into Orthodox Judaism.

The *daimon* of the Hellenistic world entered early Christian writings with the negative connotation of an impure spirit. The Judeo-Christian tradition elaborated the concept of the devil as the fallen angel who brought sin and suffering into the world, and who was thus forever banished from Paradise and with who there will forever be enmity with God. Christian literature also drew upon neighboring belief systems in the depiction of the Apocalypse, with demonic figures that recall Jewish, Persian, and Mesopotamian myths.

In the transmission of the texts of the Scriptures, the devil (in Hellenistic Greek, *diabolos*) came to be identified with Satan (the name used in the Hebrew bible to indicate adversary). The belief in evil powers as the source of all suffering for humans is found in all the early Christian literature, and Christian theology acknowledges evil as necessary for the fulfillment of free will. From its early history, Christianity developed the practice of exorcism to expel evil spirits that had taken over control of human individuals. In medieval Europe, the belief in the existence of demons came to be associated with witchcraft and contributed to the development of the practice of exorcism and witch hunting that died out only after the introduction of the religious skepticism of the Enlightenment.

References to demons and their association with nightmares are frequent. Christian theologians often attributed dreams or nightmares with any sexual content to the influence of Satan and his demonic minions—this concept traces its roots to Macrobius. Macrobius, who lived circa early fifth century c.e., is considered by some to be one of the earliest philosophers/authors to influence Christian theology with his writings on seductive demons. Macrobius's work, the *Saturnalia*, is a collection of books covering his thoughts on psychology, philosophy, and mythology. In his thesis on dreams and nightmares, he included categories of apparitions and nightmares that were not previously covered by Aristotle; this included, but was not limited to, references to the nature of incubi, succubi, and the demon Lilith. The third-century Christian theologian Tertullian portrayed demons as the most common cause of nightmares in *A Treatise on the Soul*. In this, he assured that any sins committed while dreaming were not the fault of the dreamer, because these types of dreams were merely the attempts of various demons to lead the faithful astray. St. Thomas Aquinas also acknowledged the direct or indirect influence of demons in particular dreams and nightmares.

When considering the emphasis that the Western Christian world placed on celibacy, it is clear why demons were blamed for sexual dreams. It was not common for the clergy of this period to acknowledge their internal demons (lust). Instead, they just redoubled their efforts on controlling and eliminating the external demons that, they asserted, were to blame.

It is possible to find just as many pre-Christian references to demons as well. In ancient Mesopotamia, demons were included as instigators of nightmares, along with evil spirits and the spirits of the dead. For example, a demon that resembled a goat was the cause of erotic dreams. The female demon Lilith was associated with sexual dreams that any person, regardless of gender, experienced while sleeping alone, because Lilith could change her physical form and presumably her gender as well. Lilith's sister, Namaah, and Igrath were both female demons responsible for nocturnal emissions.

Nightmares where demons appear can represent evil or torment, or repressed and unacceptable urges and thoughts. Demons in dreams can also represent a wanton, unabashed sexuality (as in the common expression "you devil you"), or even a preternaturally cunning intelligence (as in being "devilishly clever").

(See also *Incubi and Succubae* and *Macrobius*)

Dentist

Many people fear a visit to the dentist for the simple reason that it can mean

discomfort at best, and terrible pain at worst. The dentist's defense for the pain is usually something along the lines of: "If you took better care of your teeth and flossed regularly, these visits wouldn't hurt." But in a dentist nightmare, we know better. The dreamer knows the dentist takes sadistic pleasure in inflicting pain on his victims/patients.

A nightmare involving a dentist may signify a fear of painful situations in which one has no control. It may also be an indication that the dreamer should be mindful of what he or she says in delicate situations. Any nightmare that involves teeth may also represent issues regarding power and sexuality.

What kind of nightmares do dentists have? A recurring theme seems to involve every patient coming in for a cleaning after having just eaten a tuna fish sandwich and Oreo cookies.

(See also *Teeth*)

Descartes, Renè

The rationalist philosopher and mathematician, Renè Descartes (1596–1650 C.E.) was born in Tourine, France. His mother died in childbirth a year after he was born, and his father, Joachim des Cartes, was a counselor in the parliament of Rennes and spent half the year away from home when the courts were in session. The frequency and duration of these absences led to a somewhat estranged relationship between father and son, which was even more tragic because of the early death of his mother. At the age of 8, he left home to attend La Fleche, the Royal Jesuit College in Anjou, and his relationship with his father deteriorated even more.

At the age of 16, Descartes moved to Paris, where he studied music, mathematics, and philosophy. While he was in Paris, he fathered a daughter, who

later passed away at the age of 5. Historians indicate that during his time in Paris he began to exhibit manic-depressive qualities as well as symptoms indicative of schizoid personality disorders. His lack of affection and feelings of attachment are common among individuals who have lost their mothers at a young age, and it's likely the estrangement from his father only served to exacerbate the problem.

In 1618, Descartes left France and went to Holland to serve in the army of Maurice of Nassau. He also traveled throughout Germany, Poland, Italy, and Hungary. The first substantial work attributed to Descartes was the unfinished treatise *Regulae ad Directionem Ingenii*, first printed in 1701. This work shows Descartes's preoccupation with method as the key to the advancement of science.

Among other things, Descartes is remembered for his method of systematic doubt as the most dependable means to discover truth. By critically reviewing his own beliefs, he hoped to answer the basic question, "What can I know?" He often cited the false judgments we make as a result of the tricks of our senses as well as our dreams (which seem to be real, but are illusions) as evidence for why a "methodology of doubt" was so important. In his work *Meditations*, Descartes dismissed anything he felt had the slightest grounds for doubting, even the existence of the physical and spiritual universe, God, the past, and the truths of mathematics. Descartes's systematic doubt led him to conclude that the only fact he could not doubt was that, as the thinker/doubter, he must exist: "I think, therefore I am."

The questions posed by dreams presented a difficult obstacle for Descartes. He wondered how one could definitively determine that the perceptions occurring in dreams were false when they were often as vivid as the ones experienced when awake. He concluded that dreams are merely a result of the activity of the dreamer's sense organs in response to waking experiences and desires. Thus, he used the abstract form of dreams to cast doubt on the authenticity and reliability of sense perception. Descartes claimed that because we cannot conclusively distinguish between the perceptions of dreams and those of waking life, we also cannot regard information derived from our senses as providing a stable foundation for the expansion of knowledge. This seems to fly in the face of the scientific method itself, which relies solely on empirical evidence gathered through these senses.

Despite the fact that Descartes used the abstract form of dreams to cast doubt on the reality of sense perception, he experienced some important personal dreams in which he put great faith. He had always been in the habit of recording his dreams in his journal, which he referred to as *Olympica*. At some point during the 17th century, this journal was lost, but the contents are known today because of the efforts of the Abbè Adrien Baillet: He had access to the *Olympica* before it was lost, and he published a paraphrased, biographical version, *La Vie de M. Descartes*, in 1691. It is through this record that we have knowledge of Descartes's more private life. The following is an account of the Abbè Baillet's version of the events that unfolded in a three-act dream Descartes experienced on November 10, 1619, as described in *La Vie de M. Descartes*:

> After he fell asleep he imagined he saw ghosts and was terrified by them. He felt a great weakness on his right side, and, believing he was walking through streets, was forced to lean over to his left side so as to be able to continue his journey.
>
> Ashamed to be walking in this way, he made an effort to stand up straight, but he was foiled by a violent wind that spun him round three or four times on his left foot.

With great difficulty he managed to drag himself along, fearful of falling at every step. Then, seeing a college that was open, he entered it hoping to find some respite from his affliction.

He was surprised to see that people who had gathered 'round the man in the quadrangle to chat with one another were able to stand firmly upright on their feet, whereas Descartes had still to walk crookedly and unsteadily, even though the wind had abated.

At this point he awoke in pain, fearing some evil spirits were trying to lead him astray. Having fallen asleep on his left side, he now turned over on to his right side. He prayed to God to protect him from all the misfortunes that might threaten him as a punishment for his sins. He recognized that his sins were grievous enough to call down on him the wrath of heaven, although in the eyes of men, he had lead a relatively blameless life. He lay awake about two hours, pondering the problem of good and evil, and then once more fell asleep.

In the first part of Descartes's dream, filled as it was with anguish and terror, he was forced to lean heavily on his left side, which corresponds with the unconscious, to be able to continue walking. This was due to the fact that his right side, which corresponds with the conscious, was so weak that it could no longer support him. In this dream, the higher significance is given to the left, or subconscious, side. The dream reminded Descartes of the importance and necessity of his non-rational, or intuitive, side.

The last part of the dream continues, as Descartes comes across two books that he does not recognize. The first book is a dictionary and the second is an anthology of poetry, entitled *Corpus Poetarum*, that contains small portraits engraved in copperplate. Two phrases stand out in this dream more than any of the others. The first translates as, "What is the path to the way of life?" The second is *Est et non*, or "To be and not to be." The dictionary in the dream represents "all the sciences gathered together," and the anthology signifies the value of emotion and imagination. For Descartes, the two books taken together seem to represent a happy union of philosophy and wisdom, the rational and the "irrational," science and art. These are no longer mutually exclusive terms that are hostile to one another, and this seems to have constituted the answer Descartes sought in his philosophical endeavors.

The first part of Descartes's dream/nightmare is a unique and illustrative example of the existential dream, a dream—often a nightmare—that involves intense emotion at the end (usually some combination of distressing feelings such as discouragement, agony, guilt, anger, shame, or sadness), but which can actually help the dreamer in some way in waking life.

Desert

The desert is one of the harshest and least forgiving environments on earth. The scenery is desolate and sandy, often void of vegetation and with little or no water. If one is equipped for the journey, the desert can be a peaceful and even beautiful place. But the scorching heat of day and the chill of night can be deadly for those caught unprepared. Interestingly, the desert has traditionally been a place of spiritual awakening, renewal, or insight/vision. In a nightmare setting, the desert may indicate that you are feeling a void or going through a spiritual dry spell. The extreme feelings of dehydration and thirst may indicate that you desire higher knowledge or sense of purpose in life. A desert is also a place of loneliness and isolation, so desert imagery could indicate that you are feeling unloved or abandoned.

Diet

Various folklore traditions and "old wives' tales" usually try to demonstrate a correlation between a person's diet and the types of dreams he or she experiences as a consequence. For example, it is commonly believed that eating spicy food before bed will cause vivid or disturbing nightmares. There is also the conception that eating anything at all right before bed will result in nightmares. In reality, eating before bedtime (spicy foods or otherwise) may or may not "cause" nightmares, but it can certainly result in indigestion, which in turn may disturb sleep patterns and thus trigger nightmares.

Overindulgence or gluttony has often been associated with nightmares as well as "false dreams" (dreams that are thought to offer misleading or untrue predictions). Many of the ancient writers claimed that such nightmares were demon-induced and harbingers of negative incidents in a person's future, while the ancient Roman philosopher Macrobius insisted that these nightmares were indicative of the dreamer's present state of mind and did not relate to his or her subconscious or future at all. Macrobius always maintained that such dreams were of no use in theological inquiry. (See also *Macrobius*)

The early Christians believed that fasting would create optimal conditions for true divine visions. They hoped to please God and, thus, invite his presence through the humiliation of the human body. This is reflected in both the purposeful, voluntary fast of the biblical Daniel and the forced fast of Perpetua. Those who intentionally fasted for extended periods hoped to prevent natural dreams in general; this way, they could be sure that any dreams that did occur were sent by God.

Modern research has shown that a sharp decrease in daily calorie intake results in a decreased sexual interest while a person is awake. This also causes fewer nocturnal emissions in men and a decrease in the sexual themes of dreams for both genders. The sleep patterns of individuals who suffer from anorexia nervosa differ drastically from those with healthy eating habits. In general, anorectics sleep much less than the average person, and the sleep they do get is light and fitful, as they wake repeatedly throughout the night. They also experience a proportionately larger amount of REM sleep, although they remember substantially fewer dreams than do their healthy counterparts. However, after anorectics recover and return to healthy eating habits, they also return to their original sleep patterns, sleeping more often and more soundly.

Digging

Digging or excavating is rich in symbolic meaning. In a dream, the earth may represent our unconscious; our family of origin; or long-buried emotions, thoughts, and desires. It is critical to understand the purpose of your digging in the dream in order to understand the meaning behind the symbolism. The task contextualizes the symbol and gives it meaning. Are you burying something in a nightmare? If so, you may be trying to cover up a mistake, indiscretion, or transgression. If you're creating a tunnel, you may be trying to find a hidden way out of a relationship or other situation. And if you're looking for something (an artifact?) that is already buried, it may indicate an uphill battle you are currently facing. Digging in a dream may also be your psyche's way of indicating a need to dust off and revisit long-buried issues.

Many ancillary problems can arise during this dream, bringing the images and narrative well into the nightmare realm: For example, if water starts filling in around you as you dig, it indicates that you are probably losing that uphill battle. A cave-in may indicate that the issue represented by the task is taking over your life and may have potential for great emotional harm or breakdown if it's not dealt with.

Dinosaurs

Dinosaurs are some of the many "monsters" that may invade a nightmare. But these monsters are real, as they roamed the Earth millions of years ago. We've seen their bones in museums and watched artists' renderings in documentaries and Hollywood blockbusters, such as *Jurassic Park*. To have a nightmare about dinosaurs may indicate that a huge, unwieldy issue is weighing on you, though it's likely an "extinct" issue—something that has already been brought to some resolution. Dinosaurs are also some of the "monsters," along with dragons and werewolves, that populate the nightmares of very young children.

Dirt

To dream of dirt or filth may reflect an impropriety or transgression somewhere in your past. You might be feeling "dirty" in a sexual, moral, or legal sense. If you have a nightmare in which you are covered in filth and people can see you and are mocking or reviling you, this probably means that there is a part of you that wishes you could jettison the feelings of guilt and "come clean." Dirt is also a part of fertile soil, and as such represents the possibility for growth and new life. Perhaps a confession of the deed will wipe the slate clean and enable you to get a fresh start.

Dismemberment

Dreams involving dismemberment are usually accompanied by strong emotions of fear and anxiety, which may reflect significant disintegration in the dreamer's waking life. This nightmare may be telling you that, like an initiation, one part of yourself is being destroyed so that a new self can emerge. The stress and grief surrounding a death or divorce, in which the dreamer feels that he or she is being torn asunder, can also be reflected in this kind of imagery. If you are watching someone else being dismembered in a nightmare, there may be some latent hostility or rage percolating under your surface.

Ditches

Ditches are the inevitable potholes on the road of life. If you fall into a ditch in a nightmare, you are experiencing a setback in a personal or work relationship.

Divination

Dream divination is the practice of interpreting dreams and nightmares in an attempt to find meaningful, predictable patterns in everyday life, and, especially, predictions or omens for the future. The most important tradition of dream divination existed in ancient Mesopotamia, where more interest was shown in divination than in any other known civilization. This ancient culture was the first to set down divinatory lore in writing; a number of cuneiform tablets dealing with divination have been found, and some of them treat dreams and make predictions based on the contents of these dreams. To properly evaluate the role assigned to the dream in Mesopotamian civilization, it is necessary to place the dream omens in the context of the full range of the diviner's art.

The Mesopotamian heritage of oneiromancy (divination by means of dreams) was imparted both to the Hellenistic world and to Islamic civilization. Oneiromancy is the oldest form of divination in Islam, where the influence of its pre-Islamic past is remarkable. The *Oneirocritica* of the second-century Greek Artemidorus represents the basis of a popular tradition of dream classification and interpretation. According to Artemidorus and those who followed him, the analysis of dreams is based on the observation of the commonality of daily experience rather than on the belief in the existence of a divine spirit. Islamic civilization took over the Greek tradition of dream interpretation, which survives to this day in Muslim countries.

Dream divination plays a fundamental role in many contemporary traditional cultures. For instance, the power of Temne (a West African tribe) diviners depends upon active accomplishment in dreaming. They derive their abilities from an initiatory dream in which they establish a contractual relationship with a patron spirit, whereas most ordinary people are passively acted upon in their dreams and nightmares by spirits, ancestors, or witches. During divination, diviners do not merely pronounce on the meaning of a client's dream, they may also ascribe a specific dream to a client who, until then, had been unaware of having dreamed it.

Dream divination can play a significant political role in traditional cultures, especially in societies where succession to leadership or other political status is determined by dreams. Dream divination can be used as a way of deciding upon one claim or candidate rather than another, sometimes even effecting the selection of a successor from among those who had not previously claimed candidate status.

Dog Attack

In the wild, dogs are pack animals that hunt, like wolves, with their "alpha male" at the lead. To dream of being attacked by a pack of dogs can be especially horrific, especially if the dreamer has already experienced a dog bite or attack in waking life. Examine your own life for an alpha personality (probably a man) whom you regard as scrappy, underhanded, or vicious. This alpha may be leading a hungry pack your way. Stop/appease the alpha, and you'll stop the others as well.

A nightmare involving a single dog chasing you may indicate that you're feeling a loss of control or a sense of vulnerability in your own life. Someone or something in your life may be pushing you around in subtle ways.

Doors

In dreams, a door can simply be a passageway, or it can be something more ominous. Do you know what or who is waiting on the other side? Which side of the door are you on? Are you on the outside wanting in, or the reverse? A door is a break in a boundary, an open space that allows entry into what was once closed. For some, this relates to sexual desire. Front doors represent the side of yourself that the public sees (often your *persona*), and back doors are the private self that almost no one sees.

In a nightmare involving a door, you might have a great fear of opening it and passing through because of the unknown. This may be symbolic of a boundary in a personal relationship that you are considering crossing with great trepidation.

Dragons

"Do not meddle in the affairs of dragons, for you are crunchy and taste good with ketchup!" so the bumper-sticker wisdom says.

Dragon legends go back as far as the earliest written records, and the folklore involving these giant mythical creatures dates back significantly further. The ancient Sumerians wrote about monsters that were fought by gods. Before the ancient Greeks gave the monster its moniker of "dragon," other cultures also wrote and spoke of these fantastic creatures. The ancient Chinese were captivated by the dragon, and in almost every part of the world there is lore about giant creatures walking the land. In medieval legends, brave knights went off to slay dragons and save villages.

Today, dragons are more a part of our fantasy world than our history. But they remain as popular as they ever were. To dream of a dragon signifies a major issue in your life that must be dealt with. Only large and important issues will take the shape of dragons, and defeating the beast, and the issue, will be no small feat. Children especially have nightmares involving dragons and other large and threatening mythical beasts. In any case, nightmares of being chased by such creatures are most likely anxiety dreams.

Drains

Many children don't like to take baths. It may be that they like to be dirty, or they don't like it when soap gets in their eyes, or they dislike the water itself. But there's another reason: the drain. Many children fear they will be sucked down the drain to the black abyss of the pipe below. This is a fear many people carry into adulthood. Some germ-phobic people may fear drains because of the myriad of bacteria and other germs that may be growing in there.

To dream of being sucked down a drain means you may have a sense of losing grip on the world around you, or you may have given up on a problem or relationship in your life. This imagery is a sign of surrender.

Dream Catchers

Dream catchers originated with the Native American Ojibwe tribe (also known as the Chippewa), who lived in the region that is now Minnesota, Wisconsin, and Ontario, Canada. Frances Densmore was the first to see these devices in the early 1900s when he was researching the culture of the Ojibwe people. Densmore described her findings in the 1929 book *Chippewa Customs*. In her book, she described a wooden hoop with a diameter of about 3-1/2 inches, strung like a spider's web with nettle-stalk cord that was dyed red. She observed the strange item hanging from young children's cradleboards. The Ojibwe called this item *bwaajige ngwaaggan*, which means "dream snare."

According to Ojibwe oral tradition, the dream snare came into being at the very beginning of the Ojibwe Nation, when they lived on Turtle Island. Turtle Island was the land formed when the Earth was entirely covered in water, and only the muskrats could swim to the bottom, scoop up a paw full of dirt, bring it to the surface, and pile it on the back of a giant turtle to form land. In the very beginning of time itself, Asibikaashi (also known as "Spider Woman," and traditionally the protector of children) helped bring the sun to the Ojibwe. When the Ojibwe left Turtle Island to populate North America, Asibikaashi had difficulty traveling to all of the cradleboards across the vast land. So the women of the Ojibwe Nation began weaving magical webs into circles that represent the sun and hanging them on the cradleboards to prevent the bad dreams and evil spirits from entering the sleeping infant. A feather was placed at the center of the dream snare to represent air or breath. The dream snare offered the Ojibwe baby a toy to play with, a feather to watch dancing in the breeze, and a lesson in folklore and heritage from the earliest age.

Today, many other Native American cultures have made dream catchers to sell to tourists, and the idea lives on in New Age and craft stores around the world that sell kits on how to make your own. Like any magic item, dream catchers work when the person who is being protected (and the people doing the protecting) has faith in the object's power. Today, dream catchers are mainstream and can be found in homes everywhere.

Dream Dictionaries

The average person spends about one-third of his or her life sleeping, and during this time he or she experiences the phenomena we call dreaming. While not everyone remembers all of their dreams (and some people don't remember them at all), it is the rare person who has not awakened from a particularly vivid dream or nightmare and felt certain that there was a message hidden somewhere in its content. As not all of us are dream analysts, dream interpreters, or psychologists, we need help interpreting our dreams. This is where a dream dictionary proves useful.

Dream dictionaries are not a modern phenomenon. For example, the *Oneirocritia* of Artemidorus of Dalis in the second century is an extensive, ancient dream dictionary. Smaller collections also exist in Egyptian and Mesopotamian literature. The dominant approach of these texts is to view dreams, including nightmares, as omens and as messages from the divine.

Although the basic understanding of some dream symbols have remained intact through the ages, the influence of modern psychology has given a distinctly psychological slant to the interpretations found in today's dream dictionaries. Contemporary dream dictionaries present themselves as more of a starting point for interpretation, and thus are less rigid than the ancient texts. It is up to the dreamer to discover what particular meaning is represented by considering the circumstances of his or her waking life.

Despite the psychological cast of modern dream dictionaries, professional psychotherapists generally remain highly critical of them. This is partially because symbolic meaning is such a nebulous concept: the meanings can vary depending on the larger context of the dream or nightmare, as well as the context of the dreamer's life circumstances. Providing any kind of definitive meanings for dream content and symbols is problematic at best, but a good dream dictionary will convey this complexity and nuance to its readers. Some even suggest keeping a personal record of what specific symbols mean to the individual dreamer. A personalized dream dictionary, when cross-referenced with a standard dream dictionary, may help the dreamer to interpret the dream more correctly. The goal in consulting a dream dictionary should be to provide a springboard or guide, which the dreamer can then use to enrich his or her own creative response and interpretation.

(See also *Dream Interpretation*)

Dream Interpretation

In modern-day dream interpretation, context is everything. For example, if you have dreams about water, some dream analysts might say the water represents your innermost feelings or emotions—gentle water, such as a still pond, can mean serenity; violent, tumultuous ocean waters might signify fear or rage. But what if you're a marine biologist and your job requires you to be around water and aquatic life all day? In this case, water in your dreams might have an entirely different meaning. A marine biologist would need to look for out-of-the-ordinary elements within the water and dream imagery to find meaning in the specific dream.

As we go through our daily lives, our brains are processing images, language, sights, sounds, tastes, smells, as well as creating memories. One theory of dreaming is that we are experimenting with possibilities and problem-solving. If this is true, then a nightmare is your subconscious mind's attempt to get the full attention of your conscious mind. You may not remember an ordinary dream in which you are simply walking down the aisle of a grocery store, but if there is someone chasing you with a chain saw and canned goods are flying off the shelf at you as you try to run away, you would probably wake up terrified, short of breath, and wondering what just happened. As with any dream, every element of a nightmare needs to be seen within the context of your life as a whole, especially your dominant emotional state at the time of the dream. If you work in a grocery store, are you having issues with your supervisor or some other authority figure? If you don't work in a grocery store, is it possible that you have food issues or an eating disorder? If you don't work in a grocery store and you don't have an eating disorder, maybe the dream represents some kind of breakdown in your life. Grocery store shelves are usually lined with products in a neat and orderly fashion; to have them fly off the shelves, and to be chased by a chain-saw–wielding maniac, could signify chaos in your life. If you figure out what the threatening figure chasing you represents in your own life, you'll find a satisfactory meaning for your dream.

The only way to understand a specific dream is to explore the details of the waking life of the dreamer. There is no better person to interpret your dreams then yourself. By keeping a dream journal, you will not only increase the number of dreams you remember, but you can also reflect back on past dreams in order to better understand your current dreams. The dream journal will also help you find and connect the patterns of the ideas and images your unconscious mind explores—waking or sleeping.

Dream Journal

Many dream analysts recommend that people keep a dream journal to document their dreams. To be truly effective, the journal (and a writing instrument) should be kept next to the bed, so that whenever the dreamer awakes the first thing he should reach for is the pen and paper to record whatever he can remember from the dream. Waking up naturally in the morning, without the assistance of an alarm clock, often produce results that have the most clarity of memory, though in today's fast-paced world this isn't always practical or feasible. By noting the date as well as the content of the dream, over time dreamers tend to remember more of their dreams, and even tend to take on more active roles within their dreams, an effect known as lucid dreaming (see also *Lucid Dreaming*). The dream journal is also a critical analysis tool that can help one interpret the meaning of the dreams and compare the narratives to events in their lives.

Dream Sharing

Dream sharing is a common practice in many societies throughout the world. In traditional civilizations, people would often share bad dreams in hopes of negating or avoiding the negative effects prophesied by the visiting spirit or ancestor.

In the Hopi culture, this practice is necessary to keep good dreams hidden. Holding them in the heart enables the positive outcomes seen in the dream to come to full fruition. In the same way, bad dreams are shared and "confessed" with the group in order to dispel their negative energy. The Aguaruna of Peru share similar philosophies regarding their nightmares. Conversely, the Quiché believe that *all* dreams must be shared, regardless if they are deemed good or bad, as dreaming is regarded as a universal phenomenon. Rastafarian societies often discuss dreams, and the elders of a given group often authenticate their tutorial role in the society through dream sharing. In Senoi culture, dreams are thought to have a purpose beyond the understanding of the dreamer's consciousness, and dream sharing plays an important role in the education of the Senoi children.

Dream sharing can be highly ritualized, or it can be an informal event that can occur at any time. The Kagwahiv share their dreams at any time, whether it be during the night when they are awakened or during the day. Likewise, the Raramuri of northern Mexico have been known to get up periodically during the night in order to analyze their dreams and nightmares as they happen, and these dreams are frequently the topic of everyday conversation. The Sambia people of Papua, New Guinea, have developed private and public dream-sharing rituals. The household members will often discuss their dreams in informal gossip sessions or in public and secret storytelling sessions. Dreams are also recounted during healing ceremonies, initiation rituals, and community hunting and trading trips.

Within the last few decades, dream sharing has gained considerable popularity in contemporary Western societies. Montague Ullman was a psychoanalytically trained psychologist who founded the Dream Laboratory at the Maimonides Medical Center in New York during the 1960s. He was very interested in developing ways of making psychiatric services available to communities that did not have access to them. Ullman felt that "dream appreciation" should be a focus of community mental health services. In Sweden, he was able to obtain government funding to support his community dream-sharing groups. Ullman believed that sharing dreams and nightmares in a group setting was helpful to the dreamer because it provided much-needed support and enabled others to offer different perspectives on the meaning of the dream symbolism.

Ullman developed a five-step process that he found to be effective when sharing dreams in a group setting. The first step entails the initial recounting of the dream, which is followed by group reflection on the dream's content. This includes the emotions, thoughts, and desires they believe are represented by the dream imagery. During this second step, the dreamer does not comment on the group's opinions, but responds later and without further commentary from the group in the third step. The fourth step involves actual dialogue between the dreamer and the group. The final step allows the dreamer to reflect in solitude on the meanings discussed by the group. These steps are covered more extensively in the book *Working with Dreams* (Delacorte Press, 1979), which Ullman wrote with Nan Zimmerman. In the book, Ullman emphasizes that it is only after the five steps of the dream sharing are completed that the dreamer's job really begins.

Jeremy Taylor is another leader in modern dream-sharing therapy. A Unitarian Universalist minister, he held his first formal dream-sharing group during a seminar in which he hoped to raise consciousness on racism. He asked those present at the seminar to discuss any dreams they had of African-Americans. The following is an excerpt from his book, *DreamWork* (Paulist Press, 1982):

> The energy for growth and transformation of personality and unconscious attitudes and fears that were released by this work was truly astonishing, even to me. The dream work was effective in bringing deep-seated unconscious ambivalences to light, and the work was further effective in transforming them, because each of us was forced to "own" both the negative and positive images of black people in our dreams as representations of aspects of our own personalities.

It is Taylor's belief that the invaluable aspect of dreams and sharing them with a group is found in the way the group is able to enrich the range of possible meanings while providing the opportunity to explore multiple meanings. He suggests that a group of six to 12 people, with one person serving as the facilitator, is the optimal size and will yield the most positive results. He also recommends that the group meet in a quiet place and have a "touch-in," in which everyone discusses how they are doing in waking life before starting the process of sharing dreams. After the group greets one another in this way, each member then proceeds to share one dream, and the group members choose the one they would most like to discuss. They are then able to offer comments, ask questions, or suggest meanings that are relevant to that one particular dream; this may take anywhere from 15 minutes to a few hours, but Taylor asserts that it is best to discuss more than one dream per meeting.

Taylor's dream groups use the "if it were my dream" method when commenting on the dreams of others. This means that instead of definitively saying, "Your dream means...," they begin their comments with, "If it were my dream...." This serves as a reminder to the group that the dream ultimately belongs to the dreamer, and it fosters a respectful, non-confrontational tone. By considering these factors, the dreamer has more of an opportunity to reflect on what the dream means to him, while taking the suggestions of the group into account. The ultimate goal of Taylor's dreamwork is to help individuals overcome personal barriers such as race, age, gender, and socioeconomic status.

The modern "dreamworking" movement today, a rapidly growing grassroots movement designed to enable people to communicate and compare their dreams in an informal setting, is another way to dream share, with the goal of learning about ourselves through the distorted yet fascinating "mirror" that our dreams provide.

Dreamscape

The 1984 film *Dreamscape* (directed by Joseph Ruben) is the story of a young psychic named Alex Gardner (played by Dennis Quaid), who agrees to participate in a government-funded experiment to see if he can project himself into the dreams of others. The ultimate objective is for Gardner to be able to project himself into the dreams of the president of the United States, whose nightmares about a nuclear holocaust are prompting him to end nuclear proliferation and the Cold War. But of course there are those in the government who want Gardner stopped, and the president killed. Another psychic with bad intent, named Tommy Ray (played by David Patrick Kelly), is hired to stop Alex by those in the government working against the president. The battle ensues within the dream realm, where both Gardner and Ray create a nightmare landscape for each other. The movie takes the concept of lucid dreaming to significantly higher levels.

(See also *Lucid Dreaming*)

Dreamwork

According to Freud, this is the censoring process by which the dreamer's mind disguises dream content so that sleep is not disturbed by disturbing images. Freud's main theory of dreams is that they are simply wish fulfillment, allowing us to indulge in thoughts, emotions, or desires that are somehow unacceptable or undesirable, and dreamwork is the way in which these unacceptable impulses (what he called the *latent content* of a dream) are coded and disguised (into *manifest content*). This censoring process involves the processes of displacement, condensation, symbolization, projection, and secondary revision.

Of course, this theory failed to account for nightmares, for, as everyone knows, nightmares are by definition already disturbing and upsetting.

Drowning

Water often represents emotion, so drowning can mean that you are overwhelmed by feelings, especially repressed feelings. Water is also an initiatory symbol that emerges during a crisis—for example, a divorce, the loss of a loved one, or the loss of a job or home. People who suffer from sleep apnea often report a sensation of choking or drowning before they wake.

Drugs

There have been numerous studies done on different drugs and the ways they affect sleep patterns, but there have been significantly fewer studies on the effects of drugs on dreams and their contributions to nightmares. Most of the studies concern the impact of drugs on REM sleep, which is the phase of sleep most conducive to dreaming. Studies of alcohol and dreams indicate that the quantity of REM sleep decreases, while the fourth and deepest stage of sleep increases. This creates the impression that one has slept more soundly under the influence of alcohol. Alcoholics who are in withdrawal (as well as those who are in withdrawal from barbiturates) often report an increase in dreaming and nightmares. (See also *Alcohol*)

Some over-the-counter allergy medications have been shown to cause dreams and nightmares that are so intense or unusual they are now mentioned as a possible side effect of taking the drugs. Nicotine patches and even melatonin, an over-the-counter sleep aid, are reported to increase the vividness of dreams and nightmares. The nicotine patch, in particular, is said to intensify dreams to the point of distraction, often causing the dreamer to awaken.

The impact of many prescription drugs on dreaming has also been studied. Drugs that are used for regulating the endocrine system, for controlling blood pressure, and in the treatment of neurological disorders can wreak havoc on the form, content, and frequency of dreams. "Alpha-one blockers" that are used in the treatment of hypertension are among the drugs recognized for causing nightmares. This category also includes anti-Parkinson treatments such as L-dopas, bromocriptine, and selegeline, which have also been known to cause psychosis. Selective serotonin reuptake inhibitors (SSRIs) such as Prozac, Paxil, Zoloft, and Celexa increase the frequency and intensity of vivid dreams in the non-REM stage of the sleep process. Although the effects of these drugs on dreams are profound, it must be noted that suddenly stopping their intake will also cause a sudden occurrence of the vivid dreams and nightmares that are normally associated with REM rebound (the body's attempt to catch up on REM sleep by staying in the REM stage longer than normal). Obviously, weaning yourself off any drug is not recommended without the approval of a doctor.

The influence of illicit drugs on dream content is also a topic of interest. LSD floods the nervous system with serotonin and results in hallucinations involving all the senses—visual, auditory, olfactory, gustatory, and tactile. In terms of a biological response, it is the closest thing to a dreamlike experience a person can have without being asleep.

The link between hallucinogenic drugs and dreams has been recognized since the time of the oldest societies. Belladonna was the drug of the ancient oracles of Delphi, used to induce trances and dreams. The early Persians used Haoma for the same general purpose. The use of drugs is common in almost all ancient societies for the purposes of dream incubation and/or for more easily achieving a dreaming state or a dreamlike trance.

Dynamite

Nightmares can be release valves for feelings of explosive and destructive anger and aggression, and dynamite is a natural symbol for these feelings. It is wise to pay attention to a nightmare such as this, as it can be a warning of a person—you or someone you know—or situation that is about to explode.

Earthquake

The Earth represents the material basis of life, so an earthquake in a nightmare may signify an impending upheaval in your financial security, or a physical illness on the horizon.

Eating

Eating is usually an enjoyable experience in waking life. In dreams, eating can mean literally or metaphorically filling oneself with some kind of nourishment, whether it is with a sense of acquiring knowledge or experiences, or with real calories. But sometimes the things we eat are bad: the taste of food may be repugnant, and the stomach may sour as the food is ingested. To dream of eating rotten food may signify that you are "fed up" with being treated badly in a work or personal environment. To dream that you are stuffing your face to obscene proportions may indicate that you are trying to fill an emotional void. Or it may simply be that you are hungry!

Egypt

Ancient Egyptian civilization has a history reaching back as far as 4000 B.C.E. and continued virtually uninterrupted up to the time of Alexander the Great's conquest of Egypt in 332 B.C.E. Information about the beliefs of this culture were lost to the world and remained hidden until the 19th century brought the first systematic excavations and the translation of hieroglyphs. The ancient Egyptians, like the Mesopotamians, viewed dreams as messages from a wide variety of divinities and utilized dreams for divination (predicting the future).

From about 3000 B.C.E., the official religion of Egypt recognized the pharaoh (the king of Egypt) as the offspring of the sun god, Re, and therefore as a god himself. Thus the dreams of the pharaoh held more significance than those of an ordinary person, because it was thought that the gods were more likely to speak to a fellow divinity. One of the more famous of

E

Egyptian dreams was that of Thutmose IV, who, around 1400 B.C.E., encountered the divinity Hormakhu in his sleep. In the dream, Hormakhu proposed a covenant with Thutmose in which he promised the kingdom would be united and that Thutmose would be wealthy if he promised to uncover the Sphinx (at the time, it was already partially buried in sand). It seems that both sides fulfilled their promises, and Thutmose had a stone column erected in front of the Sphinx on which the story of his dream was recorded.

The myriad of gods and goddesses in the Egyptian pantheon ruled domains that spanned everything from natural phenomena such as air (the god Shu) to cultural phenomena such as writing (the goddess Safekht). The Egyptians even had a male god of dreams, Serapis, who had a number of temples devoted to his worship. There is a particularly significant one located at Memphis that dates from circa 3000 B.C.E. These temples were the homes of professional interpreters of dreams, who were referred to as the "learned ones of the library of magic." People came to these temples to sleep with the intention of receiving a dream from the gods that would provide an answer to a vexing question (a practice referred to as *incubation*, which was widely practiced in the ancient world). As in the later dream temples of Aesclepius, the dreamer fasted and engaged in other rituals before lying down to sleep. In cases where the temple was too far away from the person seeking dream guidance, a surrogate could be hired to undergo the rituals and seek a dream *in absentia*.

Along with the other divinities associated with dreams, the jovial midget god Bes was assigned the job of protecting households from nightmares. His likeness was often carved on the headboards and headrests of Egyptian beds. The ancient Egyptians also engaged in rituals they believed could prevent or undo misfortunes predicted in inauspicious dreams.

What we know about ancient Egyptian dream lore comes mostly from two collections of dream *omina* that have survived to modern day. The earliest of these dates from the 12th dynasty, which spanned 2050–1790 B.C.E. The collection is known as the Chester Beatty Papyrus III, in honor of Chester Beatty, who donated it to the British Museum. We do not know who compiled this collection of dreams originally, as the *omina* is incomplete at both ends, but the cursive style of hieroglyphs indicates that it was written by a priest. Because of this conclusion, it is classified as *hieratic*. The complete section consists of 143 good dreams, 91 bad dreams, and their respective interpretations. This section is followed by a list of protection rituals that would supposedly guard the dreamer against the evils portrayed in the bad dreams or nightmares.

The second of the dream *omina* that we have today was recorded by public scribes, and is thus categorized as *demotic*. Unlike the Chester Beatty Papyrus III, which dates from an early period and contains almost purely Egyptian dream lore, the second *omina* dates from the second century C.E. and was heavily influenced by Mesopotamian concepts of astrology and astronomy. The original version of this *omina* consisted of 250 entries, but the passage of time has damaged about 100 of them past the point of recovery. One of the most unusual qualities of this *omina* is that it contains a section devoted to the dreams of women; up until this point, women's dreams were apparently largely ignored in near Eastern cultures.

Electric shock

Energy flowing in a dream is tied to the creative impulse. To dream of being shocked may signify creative overload, so it may be time to get back to a predictable routine in order to complete some of your creative projects before taking on new ones.

Elevator

Elevators in nightmares may signify everything from the fear of death to the raising or lowering of consciousness or life station. Elevators are often seen as threatening and dangerous because, like airplanes, they

confine and engender a sense of helplessness or loss of control. A plunging elevator in your nightmare may indicate that you feel as though your life is spinning
out of control. Being trapped in an elevator could indicate claustrophobia, or
simply a sense of confinement in a personal or work situation.

Emptiness

Mood and setting is everything when it comes to dreams. For one person, standing in a wide-open expanse of land brings a sense of peace and unbridled freedom. For an urban-dweller, this same setting may create feelings of isolation. As
always, the dominant underlying emotion that accompanies the dream imagery is
paramount in interpretation. To stand in an empty building or house with an
accompanying feeling of dread or solitude may indicate feelings of abandonment
or loss. The empty building may also represent potentiality: perhaps you have yet
to find a sense of belonging or purpose in life.

"Enter Sandman"

In August of 1991, the heavy metal band Metallica released their sixth album, the
self-titled *Metallica*. One of the album's singles, "Enter Sandman," written by
James Hetfield, Lars Ulrich, and Kirk Hammett, and spent 20 weeks on the *Bill-
board* charts. "Enter Sandman" is a tale about tucking a child into bed for an
evening of nightmares. The song's title is a nod to the original concept of the
Sandman from the 19th century. (See also *Sandman*)

A part of the song's second verse reads:

> Dreams of war, dreams of liars
> Dreams of dragon's fire
> And of things that will bite
> Sleep with one eye open
> Gripping your pillow tight
>
> Exit: light
> Enter: night
> Take my hand
> We're off to never-never land

Epilepsy

There are certain neurological diseases that are sometimes associated with nightmares. Some sufferers of epilepsy will have extremely vivid and disturbing nightmares as a kind of harbinger that immediately precedes seizures during the night.

Eruption

Geysers, volcanoes, or even puss breaking through the surface of the skin can indicate a forceful breakthrough of unconscious material, such as repressed thoughts, feelings, and urges. Alternatively, this can represent an upheaval in life of the dreamer.

(See also *Volcano*)

Escape

Trying to escape something or someone in a nightmare is usually an anxiety dream. Very often the thing or person from which you are trying to escape remains unknown. A dream such as this may indicate that you are being forced to face an issue that you have been trying to hide or ignore, hoping it would just go away. This nightmare may also indicate that you are placing yourself in a dangerous or compromised situation, and you need to remove yourself from it quickly.

Eskimo Shamanism

Dreams are an integral part of the Eskimo shaman tradition and are closely associated with "calling" (dreams of dismemberment, death, and rebirth are thought to be a calling to the dreamer to become a shaman). In some instances, the dreamer is called by an animal spirit that possesses the dreamer, after which the dreamer awakens and proceeds to

wander naked through the wilderness, grappling with the spirit for control of the body. Eventually, the dreamer gains control over the spirit—a victory marked by the ritual of making a drum—and the dreamer then returns to the community and starts training as a shaman initiate.

In 1976, Joseph Bloom and Richard Gelardin conducted a study on the dreams of the Eskimo people in which a ghost or a spirit appeared. They noted this occurred most often when the dreamer was just falling asleep or just waking up, but they were unaware of the widespread occurrence of hallucinating while in a state of semi-arousal and sleep paralysis (see also *Hypnagogic* and *Hypnopopic Hallucinations*). They recognized the Eskimo experiences as nightmares, but they linked Eskimo sleep paralysis to such amorphous conditions as "Artic hysteria."

Evil

The concept of conscious, inherently evil demonic forces or beings has tradition-ally served as a means to explain suffering, illness, natural disasters, and other mysterious and unpleasant aspects of life. Almost every religious tradition has some concept of evil or force that is in opposition to man and to the divinity. Before the development of contemporary scientific explanations that offered more "neutral" explanations for disaster, floods, famine, plagues, and the like, demonic entities and evil spirits were generally believed to be responsible for the other-wise unexplainable natural disasters and disease.

Considering the almost universal nature of these beliefs, the idea that de-monic involvement is responsible for nightmares is quite understandable. This explanation was so widely accepted that it is common to find prayers and cer-emonies in ancient dream texts specifically intended to protect the vulnerable sleeper from malevolent demonic forces. In ancient Mesopotamian cultures, it was thought that bad dreams were caused by the invasion of evil spirits that had access to a body from which a guardian spirit was absent. When sex and sexuality was regarded as evil during the European Middle Ages, erotic dreams were at-tributed to specific demons, such as incubi and the succubae. Some medieval churchmen even went so far as to proclaim that all dreams and visions were created by the Devil.

Examinations

Like nakedness dreams and chase dreams, taking an examination in a dream is so common that the imagery has made its way into popular discourse. The typical examination or test nightmare often begins with the dreamer beginning to take a test, at which point he realizes that he is unable to complete the exam. Sometimes the questions on the test are incomprehensible, or the allotted amount of time is insufficient, or the subject matter is completely alien to the dreamer, or the dreamer's pen or pencil does not work. Regardless of the reason, the dreamer is unable to pass the test. Other variations of this theme include the dreamer arriving late or being unable to find the location where the test is being given.

Sometimes examination dreams include scenarios in which the dreamer is supposed to be speaking in front of a large group but is struck mute, or is in a play but forgets or doesn't know the lines. All examination dreams share the common theme of being scrutinized and judged by authority figures or peers. These dreams most often occur during times when the dreamer doubts his or her abilities and/or is in a state of high stress or anxiety.

Excrement/Feces

Excrement is a waste product that serves as a fertilizer for enriching the soil, enabling it to grow new vegetation. This symbol in a nightmare may represent the "garbage" or old issues that you no longer need to hold on to, or it could reflect the feeling of being in a "crappy" situation. Freud linked toilet training to issues of control—someone who is "anal retentive" is hyper-controlled and uptight; someone who is "anal expulsive" is thoughtless and has no self-control, tending to figuratively "crap" all over other people.

Existential Dreams

According to psychologist Don Kuiken (professor of psychology at the University of Alberta), an existential dream is a type of "impactful dream" (a dream that has a significant and lasting emotional effect, such as a nightmare) that has "intense emotion at the end of a dream, usually a grouping of distinctive distressing feelings, including discouragement, agony, guilt, anger, shame, and sadness."

Dreams like this typically leave the dreamer upset and confused upon waking, but oddly this can have a beneficial effect (such as motivating the dreamer to sort through a problem or crisis, or presenting alternative ways of thinking about things). René Descartes was said to have experienced a nightmare such as this, which ultimately served to enrich and expand his theories of knowledge, science, and art.

Explosion

An explosion in your nightmare may mean that something hidden and destructive wants to make itself felt. The explosion could be a symbol of destructive anger or rage. Perhaps there is some unresolved anger in your life that needs to be brought out and dealt with. Look closely at your personal and business dealings for a ticking bomb—you may want to diffuse it before it's too late.

Eyes

Did you ever have the feeling you are being watched? Sometimes another person's gaze can have real power over us: a stern look can make us feel vulnerable or guilty, and a hateful gaze can make us feel frightened and small. The "evil eye" supposedly has the power to effect a curse or jinx. Angry, disembodied eyes are a comic cliché in children's cartoons, but can be truly frightening in our dreams. The eyes are the doorway to the soul, so eye imagery in dreams may be a reflection of ourselves. If the eyes seem angry, you may be feeling upset with yourself over an event in your life, and if the dream eyes seem scared, the image may reflect your own internalized fears and anxieties. People who are painfully shy or socially disordered may dream of groups of hostile eyes watching and judging them.

Falling

In the same way that there are fundamental, universal anxieties, there are also universal dream motifs arising from these anxieties. Falling dreams, flying dreams, nakedness dreams, and examination dreams are some of the most common themes and motifs, and almost everyone has experienced one or more of these dreams at least once.

Some social biologists suggest that our fear of falling comes from inherited fears from our distant ancestors' practice of sleeping in trees to avoid predators (which would play into Carl Jung's idea of a collective unconscious). However, some psychologists have theorized that our fear of falling arises from the uncertainties and hurt we encountered as toddlers when we first attempted to walk. This theory, if true, speaks to the impact of childhood experiences on adult psychology.

Whatever the origin of falling fears, the dominant emotion present in the dreamer's life will contextualize the dream and give it meaning. Feelings of guilt or discouragement, or a sense that one has failed or "fallen down" in life, may thus find expression in a falling dream. For example, a woman brought up with conservative sexual mores may dream of falling after an erotic encounter because she fears that she has become a "fallen woman." Dreams of falling also occur during times of high stress and anxiety, when one feels completely overwhelmed and/or out of control, such as during a divorce or the loss of a job.

Falling dreams are not necessarily symbolic. For example, Ann Faraday, author of *The Dream Game* (HarperCollins, 1976), recounts how she once noted that the guardrails on the balcony of her new seventh-story apartment were rickety. At the time, she was so preoccupied with the other aspects of moving that she did not fully register the dangerous condition of the railing. That night, she dreamt of falling off the balcony, which caused her to pay attention to the poor state of the guardrails the next day. Faraday also counters the widely prevalent idea that people who do not wake up before they hit bottom will die. She asserts that this is simply a superstition, and totally unsupported by actual dream experiences.

A final perspective on falling dreams cites the "jolt" that wakes us up from such dreams. According to some traditions of occult lore, our consciousness may wander away from the physical body during dreams (see also *Astral Projection*). When something happens that causes us to wake abruptly, our spiritual self "snaps" back into the body. This "rough landing" results in our being jolted into wakefulness, and is registered in our dream consciousness as a fall.

(See also *Myclonic Jerks* and *Bed*)

Fear

Along with anger, fear or outright terror is one of the most common emotions cited in bad dreams or nightmares. As such, it is difficult to assign to it a specific meaning. Fearful dreams can reflect everything from subconscious, repressed anxieties to real, concrete fears in one's waking life. As in any dream or nightmare, the dreamer needs to identify the context of his or her dominant emotional state at the time of the dream, which will then provide clues to the meaning of the symbols and narrative that is causing the fear in the dream.

Fence

A fence is a boundary and an impasse, but it can also provide protection. If you encounter a fenced-in area in a dream, you'll need to analyze which side of the fence you're on in order to interpret the meaning. To be on the inside may indicate a desire to keep others out of your business, or it may indicate a feeling of being trapped or ensnared in a personal or business arrangement. To be stuck on the outside means something you desire is out of reach or off limits. Fences in dreams may also signify social boundaries that we're unwilling or unable to cross.

Fever

Febrile dreams are often surreal and incredibly bizarre, more so than "normal" dreams. Fever is one of the leading causes of, or contributors to, night terrors, sleepwalking, and nightmares. During a fever, the body is in "high gear," operating at a higher than normal temperature. The immune system is working overtime, and the body likely isn't getting the productive sleep it needs to heal and regenerate. Because of these factors, doctors often recommend extra rest to help fight an infection. Febrile dreams often include frightening imagery, and are especially distressing for children (who tend to get much higher fevers than adults).

Fighting

Nightmares about fighting are common, and may reflect outer or inner conflicts. Stress, conflicting demands, misinformation, unfairness, incompetence, lack of integrity, and broken agreements may all result in a feeling of "not wanting to take it anymore." People who have experienced the trauma of being attacked or raped may have nightmares in which they are unable to fight or resist their attacker, or, if they have worked through the trauma, in which they do manage to fight back.

Finley, Caroline

Caroline Finley was a medical doctor who received decorations for her achievements as a surgeon during WWI, and who is still recognized for her research into the physiological, or biological, causes of dreams. Her findings on the effects of pituitary and adrenal hormones on dreams and dreaming represented a radical departure from the Freudian theories that were in vogue at the beginning of the 20th century.

In the first half of her study, she administered daily doses of a pituitary gland extract to a middle-aged influenza patient. After a week and a half, the subject started to experience vivid dreams that were extremely pleasant. When the same patient was given extracts of the adrenal gland on a daily basis, within a few days the subject recalled a decreased number of his dreams, and the ones that could be remembered were stressful nightmares. The nightmares contained far less color than the previous pleasant dreams, and the predominant emotions were fear and anger. These results led Finley to conclude that the causes of dreams, nightmares, and their content are physical in origin.

Fire

Fire imagery in dreams can have a wide range of meanings, such as passion, anger, purification, transformation, spirit, illumination, or destruction. Some theorists say that the fires started by pyromaniacs have a significant sexual compo-

nent. The particular meaning of this symbol for the dreamer needs to be informed by other cues in the dreamer's waking life, as well as in the nightmare landscape. Maybe you are all "fired up" with intense emotion about an idea, a project, or a new love affair. This nightmare may be telling you how all-con-

suming the situation is, suggesting that you proceed more cautiously lest you get burned. If you see a house on fire or see a fire at a distance, it could be telling you to get your blood pressure checked and/or to stay cool about emotional upsets. If you are rising, phoenix-like, from the ashes of a fire, the image speaks to regeneration and renewal.

Firing Squad

There is a horrifying finality to the image of being tied to a post, blindfolded and helpless, with your last view being that of a group of rifles bristling at you. To know the searing hot bullets will be coming at any moment is a thought more than most humans are equipped to bear. A nightmare about being in front of a firing squad means the dreamer is feeling scorned, condemned, or judged by his peers. You may have committed some real or imagined transgression that you think deserves some punishment, but in the nightmare the punishment is no longer commensurate with the crime. The inevitability of death represents a punishment as well as reprieve—only at death will the pain (and derision) end.

If the dreamer is the one taking aim, the dreamer may be harboring judgmental feelings for the person between the rifle's crosshairs.

Flashback

A flashback is the replaying of a traumatic event or events while one is awake—almost a waking nightmare, in which the initial precipitating event is reexperienced, often in great detail. Flashbacks can be triggered by mundane sensory data, such as sounds or smells, that somehow remind the victim of the initial trauma. A flashback experience is often so intense and "real" that the sufferer fails to identify it as "only" a memory. Flashbacks often accompany recurring traumatic nightmares in post-traumatic stress disorder sufferers.

(See also *Post-Traumatic Stress Disorder*)

Flood

Water is often a symbol for the unconscious. Experiencing a flood in a nightmare may indicate that your repressed thoughts and urges are threatening to encroach on your waking, conscious life. It could also indicate that life circumstances beyond your control may be overwhelming you and are hampering your ability to stay calm and composed. Flooding imagery is also often related to finances: perhaps the dreamer has lost or spent too much money (as in "he goes through money like water"). People who are suffering from traumatic nightmares often encounter flood or tidal wave imagery in their dreams. A flood may also represent an uncontrollable sexual urge.

Flying

There are some dream motifs that are so universal that they deserve separate treatment and investigation in their own books. These motifs include such common dream scenarios as falling, flying, nakedness, and unpreparedness or exam dreams. Such shared dreams arise from experiences and anxieties fundamental to the human condition.

Flying is one of these shared motifs, but it is difficult to clearly identify the source of the flying experience. It is easy to see that other shared dream experiences are rooted in certain common experiences (for example, falling dreams appear to reference our first steps as toddlers). But from what shared experience does the flying dream arise? Some occult-metaphysical writers contend that during sleep we sometimes project ourselves (our spiritual selves, or astral bodies) outside of our physical bodies and travel through space unencumbered by such physical limitations as gravity. These out-of-body experiences are then remembered as flying dreams.

Whatever the origin of flying dreams, they probably symbolically express both our hopes and fears. Flying dreams can thus reflect a sense that one is

"flying high" (like Icarus), or that one has "risen above" something. Flying also represents freedom and joy. Freud associated flying with sexual desire, while psychologist Alfred Adler, founder of the school of "individual psychology," associated it with the will to dominate others. Carl Jung saw it as a manifestation of the desire to break free of restrictions. Contemporary research tends to support Jung's perspective. Flying dreams that are frightening may indicate that you have broken free from someone or something, but the experience, while liberating, is also causing some anxiety.

Fog

Fog is the misty, smoky substance that rolls in to shroud low-lying areas in mystery. Fog can be slight and add an ethereal overtone to the landscape, or it can be thick, limiting visibility to just a few inches. Even those who are familiar with a terrain can find themselves lost in thick fog. Nightmares in which fog figures prominently may indicate that important issues are being obfuscated—they may not be immediately obvious until you walk right into them. Though you may fear the unknown that might be lurking in the fog, the reality is usually that the fog blankets what you already know is there.

Folklore

Different cultures all have their informal, anecdotal beliefs about dreams and nightmares. Contemporary Western culture is no different. A few of the more common legends surrounding common dream motifs are:

○ *If you dream you are falling and do not wake up before hitting the ground, you will die.* Many of us have heard and probably repeated this item of urban myth. The fact is that while most people wake up before they hit the ground, some do manage to land safely in their dreams. An obvious problem with this bit of pseudo-information is that none of us know anyone who has died in a falling dream who was then able to report that a falling dream was his or her last experience before death.

○ *It is dangerous to wake someone who is sleepwalking.* This is a poetic notion that finds its origin in the ancient belief that the soul leaves the body during sleep. The idea is that suddenly waking a person will cut off the soul from the body, causing illness, a heart attack, or insanity.

This is patently false. It is also thought that sleepwalkers will do nothing to hurt themselves. This is also incorrect, as sleepwalkers have been known to walk through glass doors and fall down stairways. It may be *difficult* to awaken sleepwalkers, so a more effective course of action usually is to guide them back to bed.

○ *Some people do not dream.* Modern research has proven that everyone dreams, though some people do not remember their dreams.

○ *You will dream of your future spouse if you sleep with a piece of wedding cake under your pillow.* A romantic bit of folklore, but probably about as effective as throwing birdseed at a wedding to ensure the couple will have many children. Moreover, who actually goes to sleep with a piece of cake under their pillow?

○ *Placing a knife under the foot of your bed will ward off nightmares.* The belief that demons caused nightmares may have inspired this practice; if conscious entities are attacking victims in their sleep, then sleeping with a weapon to fend them off makes a certain kind of sense. However, the sense of security that a person might feel by keeping a weapon close by may make sleep more peaceful.

Other bits of folklore about dreams and nightmares are quasi-verifiable. For example, it has been said that eating spicy food before going to sleep will induce nightmares. This is inaccurate, though spicy foods may cause indigestion, which will then disrupt sleep patterns and dreaming.

Forest

The woods can be a very serene place, but it can also be fraught with danger and pitfalls. It's easy to get lost in an unfamiliar forest: when you've been walking a long time, all the trees begin to look the same, and people who have been lost can walk in circles for days. To dream of being lost in a forest may bode of dissatisfaction in your work, or it may indicate that you are feeling overwhelmed by, and unprepared for, life events.

Frankenstein

Mary Shelley claimed that she received her inspiration for this epic horror story while visiting with Lord Byron (the brother of her future husband, Percy Byron Shelley) at his Swiss villa in 1816. At the tender age of 18, she experienced an extraordinary nightmare following a "ghost story" session in which she had participated along with Percy Byron Shelley, Lord Byron, Byron's mistress, and a local doctor. Lord Byron, inspired by the stories shared in the group, suggested that all present should attempt to write a horror story. Mary Shelley had a nightmare that night, which she recalled vividly enough to base her novel on. The following is part of her account of that nightmare:

> My imagination, unbidden, possessed and guided me, gifting the successive images that arose in my mind with a vividness far beyond the usual bounds of reveries... I saw the pale student of unhallowed arts kneeling beside the thing he had put together—I saw the hideous phantasm of a man stretched out, and then, on the working of some powerful engine, show signs of life, and stir with an uneasy, half-vital motion... He would hope that, left to itself, the slight spark of life which he had communicated would fade; that this thing which had received such imperfect animation would subside into dead matter, and that he might sleep in the belief that the silence of the grave would quench forever the transient existence of the hideous corpse which he had looked upon as the cradle of life... Swift as light and cheering was the idea that broke in upon me. "I have found it! What terrifies me will terrify others; and I need only describe the specter that had haunted my midnight pillow." On the morrow, I announced that I had thought of the story.

> (Text excerpted from: *http://etext.lib.virginia.edu/etcbin/brose-mixed-new?id= SheFran&images=images/modeng&data=/texts/ English/modeng/parsed&tag=public*)

Also known as *The Modern Prometheus*, the novel was published in 1818. The novel is based, in part, on Luigi Galvani, a scientist who concluded through a series of experiments that electricity was the secret of life. He believed it was actually possible to reanimate a corpse by using an electrical stimulus.

In *Frankenstein*, Shelley tells a tale of scientific terror in which Victor Frankenstein creates a living being out of the parts of decomposing corpses. Shelley describes the monster as being a living travesty of death, comprised of the pieces of the recently buried dead. Despite a horrific appearance, however, the Frankenstein monster of Shelley's creation is an intelligent being who has the abilities of speech and reason. The "monster" possesses sophisticated reading capabilities and all the facilities of knowledge, but his weakness or hubris is the objectionable irrationality of his temperament.

The monster's struggle and antipathy with Victor parallels, in some ways, the biblical struggle of the Devil with God. In the end, the monster is triumphant, but he exhibits feelings of remorse, regret, and self-hatred. His acknowledgement of the emptiness of retribution shows a sense of compassion and empathy that is absent in most villains. In the end, the creature vows to destroy itself, but the story concludes with it disappearing into the snowy darkness.

In 1931, James Whale directed a film based on Shelley's novel. Some still consider this the best of all the Frankenstein movies ever made. He made the film as if reenacting a ceremony, staying more or less true to the tone of the novel, if not to every detail. In Shelley's version of the story, her creature is complex: he is not evil by nature, but rather his malice is a result of rejection and abandonment. But Whale's monster is just that, a monster. Physically he resembles a Neanderthal man, and he is endowed with the brain of a murderer. Thus, there is a potential for evil present at the very instant of his reanimation. This primitive Frankenstein monster could only snarl, and possessed little or no emotional facilities. At the end of the movie, unlike the novel, the creature is overcome by the mob of townspeople, signifying the triumph of humanity over the forces of evil.

Freud, Sigmund

Sigmund Freud (1856–1939) was the founder of psychoanalysis and arguably one of the great thinkers in history. Dream interpretation was one of his primary tools for identifying and diagnosing mental disorders.

As a practicing medical doctor, Freud became interested in the role of the mind in disease. Partially as a result of his work with patients afflicted with hysteria (a neurotic, psychosomatic illness), and partially as a result of his training in hypnosis under the brilliant French neurologist J. Martin Charcot, Freud ended up specializing in psychological disturbances. His early theorizing about the sexual origins of mental illness was scandalous to contemporary Victorian society, and it was many years before he was able to persuade his medical colleagues that his discoveries contained some truth. Although few, if any, current analysts adhere to "orthodox" Freudianism, certain fundamental Freudian notions, such as the idea that we are all influenced by unconscious motivations, are widely accepted among psychotherapists.

Freud's theory of human nature (what contemporary psychologists would call Freud's *personality theory*) presents a highly unflattering picture of what it means to be a human being. According to Freud, people are basically self-interested animals driven by aggressive urges and the desire for pleasure, and they only learn how to get along in society when they mature and learn to repress these animal impulses. However, the primitive self is never completely conquered or eradicated. Freud called this animal self, the self that constitutes the core of the psyche, the *id*. Freud said that the other aspects of the psyche, the *ego* and the *superego*, are later developments that arise from the need to adapt to, and survive in, the surrounding social environment. The ego is the rational, reasoning part of the psyche that undertakes the task of adjusting our inner urges to the demands and restrictions of society, whereas the superego represents the internalized rules and mores of society that provide us with a moral compass.

As one would imagine, the superego is frequently in conflict with the id, and the demands of external reality also tend to conflict with certain id drives. Thus, the psyche is a battleground in which the various components of the personality are engaged in an ongoing struggle. Freud felt that the denial of unacceptable urges, the urges that people would rather not admit are part of themselves, could lead to mental illness. For instance, the wish to have intercourse with the parent of the opposite sex (termed *Oedipus complex* in men and *Electra complex* in women) is so taboo and beyond the bounds of what our society regards as proper that we repress our awareness of the urge, and so it remains unconscious. Mental illness comes about when such desires become too strong or potent for the normal coping process.

Freudian therapy involves a discovery of the repressed urge or urges causing the dysfunction. Once the patient is confronted with her or his real desires, and accepts and integrates them as part of her- or himself, a cure is effected. The psyche no longer needs to go to extraordinary lengths to hide the "terrible truth" from the conscious mind. Freud initially hoped that hypnosis would be a useful tool for accessing the unconscious, but soon gave that technique up in favor of free association and dream analysis.

He came to feel that the analysis of dreams was one of the most powerful avenues for uncovering repressed desires, even referring to dreams as the "royal road" to the unconscious. Freud's principal work on this subject, *The Interpretation of Dreams*, was first published in 1900 and went through eight editions in his lifetime. At one point he wrote that *The Interpretation of Dreams* "contains even, according to my present-day judgment, the most valuable of all the discoveries it has been my good fortune to make. Insights such as this fall to one's lot but once in a lifetime." Despite many minor revisions, his basic theory of dreams remained remarkably unchanged after its initial formulation. In Freud's view, the purpose of dreams is simply wish fulfillment—they allow us to satisfy, in fantasies, the instinctual urges that society sees as unacceptable. In the process he called *dream-work*, the part of the mind that Freud called the *censor* transforms the impulse or impulses into certain dream content (*manifest content*) so as to disguise its true meaning (*latent content*), thus preventing the ensuing strong emotions from disturbing or waking us.

Freud explicitly identified five processes brought into play during dreamwork: displacement, condensation, symbolization, projection, and secondary revision (see also *Dreamwork*). In *displacement*, we repress an urge that is then redirected to another object or person. If, for example, a person dreams that he murdered his parents (a repressed urge), the strong emotions evoked by the dream would wake him up. Thus, instead of killing his parents, he might displace his aggression and dream instead that his parents' automobile was being crushed by a train. *Condensation*, as the word implies, is a process that disguises a particular thought, urge, or emotion by contracting it into a brief dream event or image, the deeper meaning of which is not readily evident. In *symbolization*, the repressed urge is acted out in a symbolic manner. For instance, the act of inserting a key into a keyhole could have a sexual meaning in a dream. *Projection* refers to the tendency of the mind to project our repressed desires onto other people. Thus instead of dreaming about having sex with a forbidden sexual partner, we might, for example, dream about a sibling of the same gender (which in a dream can be a projected symbol of ourselves) having sex with that partner. *Secondary revision* is Freud's expression for what he regarded as the final stage of dream production. After undergoing one or more of the other operations, the secondary processes of the ego reorganize the otherwise bizarre components of a dream so that it has a comprehensible surface meaning, a superficial meaning that it would otherwise lack. The process of dream interpretation in psychoanalysis involves a "decoding" of the surface (manifest) dream content to discover the real (latent) meaning of the dream.

The notion of dreams as wish fulfillment led Freud to largely ignore nightmares. Nightmares, especially vivid nightmares that tend to awaken the dreamer, fly in face of his view that dreams are the "guardians of sleep." Freud approached nightmares as unpleasant experiences grounded only in the manifest dream content—experiences that, upon closer investigation, would reveal the latent content of wish fulfillment. He did, however, acknowledge the existence of "counter-wish" dreams, which resulted from fear or anxiety. He posited that these negative emotions also existed at only the manifest content level and usually stemmed from the dreamer's masochistic tendencies.

As the idea of aggressive urges became more dominant in his theorizing, Freud came to assert that nightmares were "an expression of immoral, incestuous, and perverse impulses, or of murderous and sadistic lusts." However, he realized that this did not adequately account for trauma-induced nightmares. So he put forth the idea that traumatic dreams, which were characteristically recurrent nightmares, arose from a "repetition compulsion" to recreate unpleasant experiences (again, due to a masochistic tendency on the part of the dreamer).

In his book, *The Interpretation of Dreams*, fifth edition (Franz Deuticke, 1918), Freud offers analysis of one of his own dreams that appears at first to be a premonition regarding the death of the Pope:

> In another dream I similarly succeeded in warding off a threatened interruption of my sleep which came this time from a sensory stimulus. In this case it was only by chance, however, that I was able to discover the link between the dream and its accidental stimulus and thus to understand the dream. One morning at the height of summer, while I was staying at a mountain resort in the Tyrol, I woke up knowing that I had had a dream that *the Pope was dead*. I failed to interpret this dream—a non-visual one—and only remembered as part of its basis that I had read in a newspaper a short time before that his Holiness was suffering from a slight disposition. In the course of the morning, however, my wife asked me if I had heard the frightful noise made by the pealing of bells that morning. I had been quite unaware of them, but I now understood my dream. It had been a reaction on the part of my need for sleep to the noise with which the pious Tyrolese had been trying to wake me. I had taken my revenge on them by drawing the inference which formed the content of the dream, and I had then continued my sleep without paying any more attention to the noise.

Though many modern psychologists have dismissed most of Freud's theories, his studies did lay the groundwork for many future psychologists to follow, and dream analysis is still a vital aspect of psychoanalysis for many modern practitioners.

Frying

Frying: good for chicken, bad for human flesh. Ours is a fast-food culture, and the sounds and smells of something cooking in hot oil means we're in for a high-calorie, high-fat treat. As obesity continues to be one of the major causes of significant health problems, and our obsession with foods and yo-yo diets carries on, food and cooking are also going to invade our dreams simply because these things are on our minds. Dieters and people with eating disorders are especially prone to food dreams. But sometimes, in nightmares, we may in fact become the food. To dream of being cooked or fried indicates self-esteem issues. This may be our guilty or shamed subconscious telling us that we might as well be cooked alive and become part of the fast-food chain so that others can share in our misery. This dream imagery indicates it is probably time to repair our diets and the way we feel about ourselves.

Funerals

Real funerals have very little to do with death or with the deceased; the ceremonies and rituals are in place to help the living mourners find support and closure. To attend a funeral in your dream could signify your issues with death and dying: you may be preoccupied with death, or you may have recently lost someone close to you and the funeral scenario is simply replaying in your dreams. Funerals in dreams may also mean the end of something—a bad habit, a friendship, or a work alliance. Investigate the instances in your life in which you might need to put something, or someone, to rest and move on.

Fuseli, Johann Heinrich

In 1781, Swiss-born Johann Heinrich Fuseli painted *The Nightmare*. The painting is one of the more recognizable works from the Romantic period; in fact, the painting adorns the cover of this book.

The painting depicts a ghoulish, gargoyle-like creature with a brooding countenance, resting on a reclining woman's stomach. The creature seems to be pondering what terrible vision he should impart to the sleeping woman. The victim, dressed in pure white linen, is clearly unconscious and completely at the mercy of the specter. On the far left of the painting, the dark, disembodied head of a horse looks on (perhaps in reference to the Scandinavian etymology of the word *nightmare*).

Those who have studied the folklore surrounding sleep disorders believe Fuseli's painting is the perfect depiction of the phenomena called "Old Hag Syndrome." The work is also an excellent example of dream art, in which the subject or aesthetics of the work are inspired or informed by dreams and dreaming.

(See also *Old Hag Syndrome*)

Gabriel

In the Bible, the archangel Gabriel is one of the holy messengers of God, and is also considered the archangel of childbirth, emotions, and dreams. The idea of a spirit or divine presence being responsible for dreams, especially prophetic dreams, is not a new one. In the Old Testament, in the book of Daniel, Gabriel comes to Earth in human form to interpret Daniel's visions. In the New Testament, Gabriel is mentioned in Luke 1:19, where he visits the elderly Zacharias and heralds the impending birth of the apostle John (who would go on to become the evangelist, John the Baptist). His name is also mentioned in Luke 1:26, when he visits the Virgin Mary in

Nazareth and tells her about her forthcoming pregnancy. Some biblical scholars feel that Gabriel makes other appearances in the New Testament (though he's not named specifically): perhaps it was Gabriel who gave Joseph the prophetic dream to take Mary and the infant Jesus to Egypt to escape King Herod, or who met with Jesus in the Garden of Gethsemane the night before the crucifixion.

G

Although he is ostensibly a "good" spirit or angel, Gabriel's presence is nevertheless always terrifying, and his messages are almost always prefaced by the assurance of "fear not."

Gaiman, Neil

In 1988, Neil Gaiman published his first in a series of graphic novels called *The Sandman* with DC Comics's Vertigo line. *The Sandman* revolves around the adventures of Dream, a character who is the personification of sleep-time imagery. Dream has six siblings: Death, Destiny, Desire, Despair, Delirium, and Destruction, and the entire family is known as The Endless. Gaiman has been heralded as one of the top postmodern writers, and his *Sandman #19* was the first comic to ever be awarded the World Fantasy Award in 1991. In the first collection of the 10-book *Sandman* saga, *Preludes and Nocturnes*, the King of Dreams is imprisoned by a mystic for 70 years. When he finally escapes, his nocturnal kingdom is a landscape of ruin and horror, and he must traverse the land in order to rebuild.

In 2003, Gaiman published the children's book *The Wolves in the Walls* (HarperCollins). The author told the *Pittsburgh Post-Gazette* that the work was based on nightmares that his then 4-year-old daughter was having about wolves living in her bedroom walls. Gaiman said in the *Post-Gazette* interview, "It was one of those 'sticky' dreams that stay with you. So I started making up stories about wolves and walls to cheer her up." The book's heroine is a young girl named Lucy, and no one in Lucy's family believes that there are actually wolves in the walls until it's too late and the wolves make their way out of the walls and force the family to flee into the walls themselves.

Gang

A nightmare about being in a gang may represent an unconscious desire to achieve things through force and intimidation, or it may be an indication that the dreamer has a deep need to belong or be accepted into a group. Being threatened or attacked by a gang may indicate that you're feeling "ganged up" on in your waking life.

Garbage

Garbage represents the unwanted and discarded pieces of our lives. To be surrounded by the putrid stench of rotting trash in a nightmare may indicate that you're feeling rejected or unloved by those you care about.

Gestalt

Gestalt (meaning "whole") is the psychological theory or school of thought that phenomena should be interpreted as a distinct whole that is greater than the sum of its parts. In 1890, the philosopher Christian von Ehrenfels first coined the term to describe experiences that required more than the five senses to comprehend. The Gestalt movement first entered the language of psychological inquiry in 1912, when German theorists Max Wertheimer, Wolfgang Köhler, and Kurt Koffka incorporated the concept into psychology as a rejection of the predominant methods of analysis of the time, methods that were more focused on examining the disparate pieces of disorders and issues. Critics of the Gestalt method feel it is unscientific to try to make sense of the big picture without first looking at the details.

The Gestalt method of dream analysis involves viewing all parts of the dream as emanations of subconscious aspects of the dreamer. The method asserts that the mind is able to organize the dream experience into a comprehensible whole, even if the sensory information available is incomplete. The focus of Gestalt dream therapy is to discover the emotional "holes" that have been glossed over by the subconscious or repressed by the conscious mind, and then reintegrate them into the larger psychological whole. All dream imagery is viewed as a message in and of itself relating to the dreamer's present situation. This view differs from that of Freud, who asserted that dreams are simply wish fulfillment, as well as Jung, who believed that dreams are a foreshadow of things to come. If one dreams of a tree, with the Gestalt approach, the person would say, "I *am* a tree," and then describe the details of tree in the first person; for example, "I am a tall oak with big, green leaves and several low-hanging branches that swoop toward the ground and then outward, but one branch seems to be broken and dying." This self-analysis leads to the person's greater understanding of how the imagery relates to his own life and how he sees himself. The objective is for the dreamer to understand their own dream and do their own analysis. Frederick Perlz, the founder of Gestalt therapy, once said of dream analysis, "Any interpretation by the therapist is a therapeutic mistake."

(See also *Perlz, Fritz*)

Ghost

The concept of ghosts exists in every culture around the world. Theories as to why ghosts might stick around after they're dead include: they don't realize they're dead, they have unfinished business, or they're merely a kind of psychic impres-

sion or echo left behind. In a nightmare, you need to ask what your ghost represents. If your ghost doesn't realize he or she shouldn't be there, it may indicate that there is a "dead" issue in your life that you're not relinquishing. If your

ghost has unfinished business, then you may need to examine an issue from your past that needs some kind of resolution before you can move on. And if your ghost is a psychic impression, this symbolizes what has gone by and is no longer attainable, as in the expression "I don't have a ghost of a chance."

A ghost in a nightmare may represent the "shadow self," or the darker side of the self—the immoral thoughts and impulses, and shameful actions that are suppressed in the dreamer's psyche. The "ghost" is then communicating the unmentionable and the unutterable. It is speaking because the dreamer's psyche cannot or will not acknowledge this side of himself.

Haunted House Dreams

Brian Leffler is a 40-year-old paranormal investigator who lives in Keewatin, Minnesota. From August 2001 to June 2003, Brian lived in an actual haunted house in Chisholm, Minnesota. While living in the home, he experienced a recurring nightmare related to the haunting.

The Nightmare:

I didn't have this dream nightly, but it was a theme that presented itself on several occasions.

This house in Chisholm had many supernatural occurrences over the time that I was there: doors that were difficult to open would pop open with nobody else around; there were strange shadows and voices that we could see and hear on many occasions; and our normally quiet springer spaniels would begin barking at something we couldn't see, then yip and go cower under a table. That was all shocking at times, but not necessarily scary. This dream, on the other hand, made me sit straight up in bed and have to wipe the sweat from my brow.

In the nightmare, I am sound asleep in my own bed, but by myself. My girlfriend at the time was not there. The night was very clear and contained a very brightly lit moon. I began to feel like someone was there, watching me sleep, but it didn't feel uncomfortable in the least. In fact, it felt quite the opposite. I soon realize I'm watching myself sleep, and after awhile I seemed to meld into the version of me that was sleeping and I started seeing things through my dream version's eyes. I wake up calmly in my dream to see a beautiful young blonde woman floating in through the bedroom window. She is wearing a bright white flowing gown and approaching me very sensually. She drifts very slowly over the top of me, and just when I am thinking that this couldn't get any better, she turns on me and begins to scratch the heck out of my chest, drawing blood. It hurts, but I can't move. I then feel her start to scratch at my legs, drawing blood there too. Then I feel her grabbing my ankles and pulling me. She is pulling me so hard that she is beginning to pull me off of the end of the bed. Amazingly though, I

*don't fall to the floor. But instead, I begin to go out the
window with her. It is at this point that I would wake up
soaked in sweat.*

Brian had this same dream three times, and only while living in the
house in Chisholm. His take on the imagery is likely different than most
peoples' ideas on what nightmares mean. For Brian, this dream represents something more significant. "I definitely think it was spirit contact
in the dream," he said. "There was an occasion when I heard a female
voice in the house." Perhaps that same female spirit was making contact?
But for what purpose?

Through investigating his home with a team that included people who
are psychically sensitive, Brian believes the female spirit in the house had
a problem with men. "I guess I really didn't think about much until I
started having the dream," he said.

The Analysis:

In typical nightmares, ghosts represent something the subconscious might be trying to communicate to the
dreamer—part of the inner spirit trying to come to light
within the dream. Because of Brian's unique background
as a paranormal investigator, and because he claims to
have been living in a haunted house, the ghost imagery is
likely more literal. Even if one doesn't believe in ghosts,
the ghostly woman in the dream represents the personification (albeit, *spirit* personification) of the haunting issues he was having in his home. Living in a haunted house
may make one feel as if they are in a sense under siege. In
Brian's dream, the representation of the haunting was
making herself known to him in more profound ways than
she was during the daytime with a few disembodied voices
and doors opening by themselves. It is worth noting that
the dreams have stopped since he left the house—that
ghost is no longer an issue in his life.

■   ■   ■

Gilgamesh

The area surrounding the Tigris and Euphrates Rivers in modern Iraq was once
the locale of a group of ancient civilizations that together are referred to as
Mesopotamia (or "between two rivers"). The first urban Mesopotamian culture
predated the high culture of Egypt by thousands of years.

The Mesopotamians wrote in *cuneiform* on clay tablets, many of which have survived to the present day. *The Epic of Gilgamesh* is humankind's oldest recorded hero tale, dating from at least 2000 B.C.E. Gilgamesh was a legendary king who ruled the city-state of Uruk around 2600 B.C.E. Son of the goddess Ninsun and King Lugalbanda, he was said to have divine blood running through his veins. As he still remained mortal, however, the central theme of the epic is his quest for immortality.

The first part of the epic begins with Gilgamesh's dream that predicts he will find a friend whom he will "embrace as a wife." Because the dream message is expressed in symbols, Gilgamesh seeks out his mother, who interprets the dream for him. Gilgamesh eventually meets and befriends the formerly savage Enkidu, and together they travel off and slay Humbaba, the giant of the pine forest. On the way to the forest, Gilgamesh has what he feels may be an inauspicious nightmare, but Enkidu acts as interpreter and predicts instead a favorable outcome to their quest.

The triumphant Gilgamesh is so attractive that the goddess of love herself, Ishtar, proposes that she and the young king become lovers. Gilgamesh responds by recounting the bad ends her partners have met, and rejects her proposal. Unused to rejection, Ishtar is so offended that she persuades the Bull of Heaven to come down from the sky and punish the city of Uruk. Gilgamesh and Enkidu, however, make short work of the Bull.

Unfortunately, the slaying of the Bull of Heaven evokes the fury of the gods, who decide that one of the two friends must die as punishment. Enkidu has a bad omen dream in which he learns that the gods have chosen him for this fate, and he later sickens and eventually dies. Gilgamesh is distraught by the death of his best friend. But, as a result, he also begins to consider his own mortality. According to Mesopotamian religious thought, the gods create people out of clay to be their servants on earth; humanity is not endowed with a soul per se, and what afterlife there is remains only a pale shadow of earthly life, much like the Jewish Sheol or the early Greek Hades. Before he dies, Enkidu dreams about the other world, and offers the following description:

> There is the house whose people sit in darkness; dust is their food and clay their meat. They are clothed like birds with wings for covering, they see no light, they sit in darkness. I entered the house of dust and I saw the kings of the earth, their crowns put away forever....

(Excerpted from *www.aina.org/books/eog/eog.htm*)

Like other cultures that buried the dead in the ground, the Mesopotamians conceived of the afterlife as being a dark, dusty, unpleasant underworld.

With this frightful vision before him, Gilgamesh resolves to set out on a quest for immortality. He hears that the mortal man Utnapishtim, the Mesopotamian equivalent of the Christian Noah, was granted immortality by the gods. To discover how Utnapishtim has obtained such a favor, Gilgamesh undertakes an arduous journey. Upon their meeting, Utnapishtim relates how the gods, in a fit of anger, destroyed all of humankind in a great flood. Only the wise divinity Ea had the foresight to warn Utnapishtim, who built a great boat in which he and his family survived. The gods quickly realized the error of their ways, but only after the fact. They discovered that human beings are not only servants, but also "food" for the gods; without humanity, they would starve. After the flood, Utnapishtim makes the appropriate offerings and the gods are able to eat. Out of gratitude, they bestow immortality to him and his wife. In order to determine if Gilgamesh is worthy to be crowned with immortality, Utnapishtim challenges him to stay awake for a week. Gilgamesh promptly fails the test, and sleeps for a week instead. Regardless, Gilgamesh is given a "consolation prize," a plant with the powers of rejuvenation (the next best thing to immortality). Unfortunately, on his journey home, a snake eats the plant, and Gilgamesh arrives home empty-handed. (This is probably in reference to the fact that ancients believed that snakes were wise because the shedding of their skins demonstrated an almost limitless capacity for rejuvenation.)

Gilgamesh reflects the fact that dreams were highly regarded in ancient Mesopotamia as omens of the future, and were valued as a conduit between parallel realities (as when Enkidu gets a preview of the afterlife during a dream). In *Gilgamesh*, dreams also function as a literary device, foreshadowing events that had not yet occurred.

Gloves

Dreams involving gloves may indicate that you are trying to avoid getting your hands "dirty," or that a situation requiring the utmost diplomacy will call for the putting on of "kid gloves." Additionally, boxing gloves could indicate a situation in which the dreamer feels the need to "duke it out" with an aggressive delivery.

Goya, Francisco

Francisco Goya began painting decorative tapestries, and then moved on to become a professional portrait artist. He lived during a troubled period of European history, surviving Napoleon's devastating invasion of Spain. The symbolic expressionism of his later work would serve as inspiration for later generations of artists. His depictions of nightmares, violence, and human suffering are considered to be forerunners of the Romanticism of the following century.

Goya is particularly remembered for the nightmarish works of art he produced during the later half of his life. In the painting

Saturn Devouring His Son, he shows the god in the midst of an appalling feast; somehow, Goya manages to convey the deity's amazement with his own participation in this cannibalistic ritual. His work *The Sleep of Reason Produces Monsters* represents a fear that the freeing of the imagination may result in the free reign of the unmanageable and undesirable aspects of the human psyche. Goya was also known for his depictions of the inmates in a madhouse in Saragossa, Spain, and of scenes of witches' sabbaths.

The nightmarish quality of Goya's waking world was probably what enabled him to realistically portray frightening dreams. He had a habit of "pointing" the bristles of his brush with his mouth, and because of this he began to exhibit the symptoms of what we now recognize as lead poisoning (probably brought on by the lead in the paint he was unwittingly ingesting). The illness progressed to the point at which he was constantly battling intermittent paralysis and deafness, as well as tremors that affected the paint strokes of his work, especially toward the end of his life.

Grave

A grave in a nightmare represents the end of the line for a relationship or situation. If you experience yourself in a grave, you may be "in over your head" and facing grave issues that will require deep inquiry before you can resolve them, such as a business deal. Grave symbolism may also indicate a preoccupation with, or fear of, death and dying.

Grim Reaper

The concept of death as a personified, sentient being with human characteristics is millennia old. This idea has found expression in many mythological, artistic, and, especially, religious texts. The Bible and Koran contain many references to a dark, mysterious creature that delivers a soul from the world of the living to the world of the dead. Over time, the idea of death evolved from an invisible, more general "force" to an incarnate, humanoid form. "Death" as an image gives shape to an abstraction and helps humans better understand the great mystery of death.

In the 1400s, "death" took on the shape of a dark, hooded-robed figure, often as a skeleton underneath the robe, carrying an hourglass to indicate the fleeting passage of man's time on earth and a large scythe used to harvest the "crop" of fresh souls for the afterlife.

The Grim Reaper, or Angel of Death, in a nightmare almost always signifies change—like death itself, there will be the end of one thing and the beginning of another. It may also represent a distressing and fearsome element in your life lurking in the shadows. The Grim Reaper is reviled and feared, but the figure's purpose is to help people make the transition from one side to another. This imagery in a dream could mean the loss of a job, a friendship, or an endeavor, but it could also show that there is a part of your psyche that will be able to remain strong and aid you through the crisis.

Growing

To find oneself growing to enormous proportions can be a good omen, meaning you feel strong, capable, and on top of the world. However, like Alice in her Wonderland, growing too large could be disconcerting at best, and horrifying at worst. But there is no place for giants in our waking world, so this vision is usually tied to an ego that may need to be checked before the giant becomes unwieldy or destructive. To witness another person becoming a giant has similar meaning: one may admire the giant's power before realizing the destructive force that surely comes with such power. A frightening colossus in a nightmare may be a symbol for how we view someone's behavior and overblown ego.

Guilt

Real or false guilt can carry over into sleep and induce anxiety when we experience it in our dreams. *Survivor guilt* often surfaces in the dreams of military veterans and in civilians who have survived a traumatic accident when someone close to them did not. Survivors question their being "singled out" for life when someone else lost theirs or was seriously injured. There is often a feeling of culpability ("If only I had done x, then this wouldn't have happened") even though they are not responsible for the event. These guilt feelings are often carried over into the dream state and, in many cases, the dreamer replays the details of the event over and over in vivid detail. Sometimes the subconscious will modify the dream so that the survivor takes the place of the victim. These kinds of recurring nightmares are a major symptom of the anxiety neurosis caused by a deep emotional trauma. The guilt experienced in these dreams is often accompanied by grief and anger.

Sexual feelings, particularly sexual desires that are at variance with social norms (for example, incest), can also cause the guilt that leads to anxiety dreams. In dreams or nightmares, sex often represents something that is more complex than simply our attitudes about and our desires for the physical act of sex. In other words, the sex act or even sexually charged scenes in dreams and nightmares can be symbolic of other relational issues, and don't always represent a clear-cut desire or impulse.

Guilt can also be manifest in dreams when the "shadow self" is making itself felt. Our shadow is the dark, neglected, and subterranean part of the psyche that often contains disturbing or unacceptable thoughts and desires. According to Jung, a personality is not fully whole until the shadow self is met, understood, and integrated. The fear of confronting the shadow self may stem from insecurities about how we are viewed by society and how we might not fit into the mold of what is acceptable or "normal." The rejection of the "shadow self" can foster the creation of a sort of "dual personality," in which the unacceptable or dark side is hidden. However, the shadow can insistently make itself heard and felt in dreams. In such dreams, the dreamer may be a double agent, a criminal, or find him- or herself in other circumstances where it is necessary to conceal the identity of someone or something. These guilt dreams of a "false self" are most common when dealing with repressed personalities.

Gun

This is a symbol of aggression as well as protection. Freud saw guns as phallic symbols and symbols of aggressive male sexuality, so to dream of a gun may

indicate that you feeling anxious about the sex act. Weapons in dreams may indicate feelings of vulnerability and fear, or, conversely, feelings of anger and hostility. As always, the dominant emotional state of the dreamer provides the much-needed context that will provide the clues for meaning.

Being Chased and Shot

In 2001, Chloe Chandler was a 15-year-old living near Birmingham in England and attending school. She and her closest friends liked to hang out in the music room of the school, which was also the setting for her recurring nightmare.

The Nightmare:

It started in the music rooms of my school, where I spent most of my time then with my three best friends. Two of them were laughing and talking away at the piano at the back of the room, and I was talking with the third friend (who I think I may have had deeper feelings for, but at the time was more confused than anything) while sitting on some desks halfway down the room. Sometimes the dream was set in a practice room, and I would be talking with that one friend at the back on the tables against the wall, while the other two were laughing and talking around the piano by the door. Even though we were usually locked in these rooms so that we wouldn't be disturbed, a man none of us knew opens the door as though it weren't locked, looks around, and spots me. He aims a gun and shoots—aiming for the heart (I always assumed), but hitting my shoulder. He's surprised at missing, and so he reaches out and grabs the friend that I'm talking to, puts the gun to her head, and drags her out of the room. I stand up and follow. He then

*shoots me in the stomach when he sees me following, and
as this doesn't stop me, he shoots me in the ankle and then
the knee. By this time we're out of the building, at which
point he throws my friend to the floor and runs around the
corner. Just as he's out of sight, another guy comes around
the opposite corner, looks perplexed at me and my friend on
the floor, and then follows the other.*

*I had that dream rather frequently, and began noticing
the two men in my other dreams as well, though usually in
the background. In all of the dreams involving the two men,
the one was always menacing, while the other always seemed
to protect him in some way.*

Versions of this dream continued for approximately one year, with a
frequency of two to three times per week in the beginning, then no dreams
for a few months. Then, seemingly out of the blue, they would start up
again. When asked to describe the two men in her dream, she said they
were taller than she was and with dark hair. Otherwise, they were always
vague images.

The Analysis:

Chloe was struggling with some deeper feelings for one of
her friends while at school. Being 15 years old is a time of
many changes—leaving childhood behind, entering adulthood, starting to date—and acceptance and friendship
with peers is critical. The dream begins in a location that
is comfortable and familiar to Chloe—her music or practice rooms—and the people present are those closest to
her. The room is supposed to be safe and secure, yet a
mysterious, dark, and threatening figure enters the room
and begins shooting Chloe and abducting one of her
friends. Because the figure is dark and vague, it represents an unknown and harmful issue that is coming between Chloe and her friend, or possibly Chloe and her
feelings for this friend. Even though Chloe is being shot
repeatedly, she still pursues the abductor in an effort to
save her friend. Being shot signifies the pain Chloe may
have been going through in the friendship/potential relationship that is being torn apart in front of her by a force
outside her control. During the time of the nightmares, it
appears as though Chloe was willing to go to any lengths
for this person, even if the effort would hurt her.

■   ■   ■

Hades

Hades refers to both the ancient Greek abode of the dead as well as to the god of that underworld. The word originally referred to just the god. *Haidou*, its genitive, was short for "the house of Hades," and eventually the nominative came to designate the abode of the dead. Christians often use the word "Hades" as a euphemism for hell.

(See also *Hell* and *Sheol*)

Hair

As it did for Samson in the Bible, hair can denote strength, health, sexuality, and virility. A lack or loss of hair in a dream may indicate a fear of growing old. Long hair is a sign of traditional femininity, white hair signifies wisdom and knowledge, and unkempt hair signifies unpreparedness and confusion. In myth, Medusa's "hair" represents the malevolent, uncontrollable feminine, whereas the short "buzz" cuts of the military are associated with male discipline and restraint. The exact meaning of hair in dreams must be measured in the context of the dreamer's dominant emotional state.

Hallucinations

If you have ever had a dream that was so vivid that it seemed physically

"real," only to discover upon waking that it was not, you are not alone. Almost everyone has experienced this phenomenon at least once in their lives. The sense of dislocation this experience creates is most dramatic after nightmares, when the dreamer awakens to discover that the frightening imagery has evaporated seemingly into thin air. Dream images are sleeping hallucinations in that they have no basis in the physical world, and many waking hallucinations have a familiar dreamlike quality. Waking hallucinations often resemble a hypnagogic experience, in that they are induced by drowsiness and experienced just before falling asleep or as one is waking up.

The boundary between dreams and hallucinations is a blurry one. The majority of dreams are creations of the mind that do not depend upon immediate sensory input for their existence. The phenomena commonly known as "hallucinations" is a bit of an anomaly in modern science. While some hallucinations are highly dependent on sensory input, such as in the case of a drug-induced hallucination, at other times they seem to arise from a completely separate source of sensory data.

Hamlet

Shakespeare wrote the eponymous tale of the King of Denmark's son in 1601, and, like many of Shakespeare's works, this play is full of deception, murder, twists of plot—and dreams. In Act 2, Scene 2, Hamlet is the first to mention dreams in the play:

> O God, I could be bounded in a nutshell, and count myself a
> king of infinite space, were it not that I have bad dreams.

Here, the young Hamlet, Rosencrantz, and Guildenstern are discussing the nature of Denmark and how it serves as a prison for Hamlet. To Hamlet's comment about dreams, Guildenstern replies:

> Which dreams, indeed, are ambition; for the very substance of
> the ambitious is merely the shadow of a dream.

To which Hamlet replies:

> A dream itself is but a shadow.

Hamlet's line reflects the way Shakespeare uses dreams in many of his plays. A dream *is* a shadow for Shakespeare. Only a real thing can cast a shadow, so the dream images are based on and comment on something very real in the narrative.

Shakespeare doesn't require his audience to do too much interpreting of his character's dreams, as, most often, the dreams spoken of are quite literal.

In Act 3, Scene 1, Hamlet delivers the play's most famous monologue that begins:

> To be, or not to be, that is the question:
> Whether 'tis nobler in the mind to suffer
> The slings and arrows of outrageous fortune
> Or to take arms against a sea of troubles,
> And by opposing end them? To die, to sleep—
> No more; and by a sleep to say we end
> The heartache, and the thousand natural shocks
> That flesh is heir to, 'tis a consummation
> Devoutly to be wish'd. To die, to sleep—
> To sleep! perchance to dream—ay, there's the rub;
> For in that sleep of death what dreams may come,
> When we have shuffled off this mortal coil,
> Must give us pause: there's the respect
> That makes calamity of so long life:
> (lines 55–68)

Sleep and dreams, and how they relate to death, are a significant theme in Shakespeare's work. As Hamlet's mind unravels, Shakespeare ponders the big question of what comes with the eternal sleep of death. If nightmares await us, there is no waking up and no escape.

Hammer

Hearing the pounding of a hammer may mean the dreamer is trying to "hammer out" the details of his life, while being pounded by a hammer may indicate that the dreamer feels put upon, anxious, or beaten down by life.

Hands

Dream hands can be of kindness or cruelty. If hands in a nightmare are choking you, or grasping or touching you in a way that frightens you, you may have been traumatized at an early age by physical or sexual abuse. Hand imagery may also be your "shadow side" showing you your rejection of, or guilt over, carnal appetites. This dream could also indicate that you need to get a handle on problems or issues that have been ignored.

Hanging

When a person is executed by hanging, the end can come blessedly quick if the neck is broken, or horrifyingly slow if the trachea collapses and the victim suffocates. To have a gallows nightmare, feeling the rope tightening around your neck, may represent feeling smothered in a relationship. Like other execution dreams, you also may feel as though you are "on the block" in life—there is a lot at stake and you fear failure. Additionally, there may be guilt feelings in the subconscious that are arising and "punishing" the dreamer through this imagery.

Hartmann, Ernest

The psychiatrist Ernest Hartmann is well known for his research on dreams and nightmares. His father, Heinz Hartmann, was also a psychiatrist and was a pupil of Freud (the senior Hartmann is sometimes referred to as "the son of Freud"). Dr. Ernest Hartmann directs the Sleep Disorders Center at Newton-Wellesley Hospital in Boston, Massachusetts, and is professor of Psychiatry at Tufts University School of Medicine. (*For more information on Dr. Hartman, and for some of his insights on dreams and nightmares, see the interview on pages 339–342.*)

One of the first studies on nightmares that Hartmann conducted consisted of 38 adults who suffered at least one nightmare a week for six months or longer. Most had been plagued by chronic nightmares since childhood. Each subject went through an extensive interview process in which the general nightmare history, as well as the specific content of the nightmares, was thoroughly documented. Eleven subjects from the original group were observed in sleep laboratories for a period of four nights. Hartmann was not satisfied with the results of this approach because he felt that the findings were "tainted" by the synthetic environment of the sleep laboratories.

A second study group was assembled that comprised three subgroups: the first group consisted of individuals who suffered from frequent, lifelong nightmares; members of the second group reported having vivid dreams, but no significantly recurring or terrifying nightmares; and the third group had no dream recollection at all. Psychological tests and in-depth interviews were conducted, and the content of the subjects' dreams were examined. After the experiment, Hartmann concluded that, while the subjects of the nightmare group did not share an inordinate number of traits with the members of the second or third groups, they did greatly resemble the personality profiles of the members of the original study. All of the nightmare sufferers had careers in "creative" fields such as the arts, and none of them fit within society's standard, defined gender roles.

Using the information he gleaned from these studies, Hartmann went on to develop his well-known theories concerning the "boundaries" of the mind. He felt that the development of a person's boundaries is intricately related to the early childhood development of mental structures and faculties. These faculties are what make the person able to distinguish between opposites, such as self and others, inside and outside, and fantasy and reality. Those who suffered from chronic nightmares were categorized as having "thin boundaries," and shared the characteristics of unusual openness, vulnerability, and difficulties with certain ego functions. Hartmann felt that thin boundaries could be beneficial in life, in that they make the individual more aware of their inner feelings and the feelings of those around them, as well as make them more inclined to artistic pursuits. However, these same characteristics also make them painfully sensitive, not only to the threats of the outside world, but also to their own desires and impulses. A person with "thick boundaries" has stronger defenses to the outside world and to their own unconscious fears and impulses, and hence is much less likely to experience the intrusion of nightmares.

Haunted House

According to a June 8, 2001, Gallup poll, 42 percent of Americans believe houses can be haunted. For thousands of people, hauntings are a reality and can be quite frightening. People who have experienced a haunting often report a sense of be-

ing violated, as though an uninvited person or burglar has broken in and decided to stay. Other feelings are, of course, fear and awe at the idea of living with proof of life after death. Some typical phenomena reported at haunted houses include mysterious "cold spots" (pockets of air that are noticeably cooler than the surrounding area), disembodied voices and sounds, strange smells, doors and cabinets opening and closing on their own,

and even the classic apparitions with recognizable features. Living with a haunting can certainly affect your dreaming life. Experiencing a ghost has implications that require abstract and creative thinking on the part of the "hauntees." Some of the confusion and fear experienced by the occupants may be made manifest as nightmares, as the dreamers struggle to comprehend the idea of ghosts.

(See also *Ghosts*)

Many Haunted Houses

Kyra Beck is a 34-year-old mom who lives in a Cleveland, Ohio, suburb. In her late teens, she had a haunted house nightmare—one that still recurs to this day.

The Nightmare:

> *The dream varies locations and specifics, but it always involves an evil or threatening ghost/spirit that is menacing*

me in a house. So far, the locations of this dream have been my grandparents' house (which was a safe haven for me as a kid); a house that I lived in from the ages of 5 to 12; and some new house that I haven't seen before the dream, but one that my husband and I have either just bought or are thinking of buying.

Everything usually starts out fine; however, I gradually become aware that there is a presence in the house. Most times, I am the only one who is able to perceive this. Things begin to escalate quickly, with the ghost/spirit screaming, moaning, chasing me, throwing things, slamming doors, etc. If there were others present with me, they seem to disappear at this point and I am left all alone. I am never able to see the entity; I can only hear it, see it manipulating objects, or feel it rushing past me in a gust. The feelings are of pure terror. Usually, I am desperately trying to get out of the house, but am having a hard time doing so. Or, as in one variation of the dream, I had gotten out of the house (one that my husband and I were looking at and thinking about purchasing) only to discover that I had left all the lights on and the doors unlocked, and I needed to go back in to shut all of the lights off and get the keys to lock the doors. I had such a feeling of absolute terror at the thought of having to go back in there, but then I wake up before I do.

The dream is always very unsettling, and I usually feel somewhat "off" for the whole day afterwards, replaying the dream in my mind and thinking of it over and over again.

Kyra and her husband have lived in the same house since 1997, though she says they have been hoping to move for the last few years but haven't found the right time to do so. When asked if she felt if either her current house or her childhood house may have been haunted, Kyra said, "There have been a couple of small, strange occurrences in our current house, but they weren't undeniably paranormal to me. So, I can't say for sure. There may have been something odd going on in the house that I grew up in from the ages of about 5 to 12. I would awaken in the middle of the night to use the restroom without a scary thought in my head, but then I would suddenly be afraid to return to my bedroom. I don't really know what I was afraid of. I would just be scared to death to go back in there. I would be so afraid that I would sleep at the foot of my brother's bed or even on his hardwood floor just so that I wouldn't have to go back in there. My Dad drank heavily and was very abusive to my mother while living in that home. They have since divorced and he does not drink nor treat his current wife the same way. When he drank, it was almost as if he became a completely different person. His face even looked different— mean, almost evil. Also, there had been wallpaper on my bedroom walls for most of the years that we lived there. However, my parents wanted to repaint the room when my little sister was born when I was about 10, so they removed the wallpaper. Underneath the paper were frightening paintings of a vampire woman with blood dripping out of her mouth; an eyeball with blood dripping out of it; and a strange, sun-like object. There was also the word 'moon' written forwards and backwards on all the doorframes. So, who knows what that was all about. All in all, I have really eerie feelings about that place and some very unpleasant memories. That house really could have been haunted. If not by a spirit, then it was definitely 'haunted' with negative vibes and emotions."

The Analysis:

A home is more than just four walls and a roof. For most people, it's the largest single purchase they'll ever make in their lives. It's also the "nest"—the place to nurture their closest relationships and to build their families. In Kyra's dream, the house represents the family, and the ghost seems to be the "unfinished business" kind. This spirit seems to be coming directly from her childhood— meaning the fearful emotions she had in regard to her father when he was drinking, as well as the scared feeling she had in her bedroom.

Kyra mentions that she and her husband have been thinking about the purchase of a new home for several years now, which in and of itself can be a haunting task. The recurring nightmare represents Kyra's fear of settling into a home that is anything like the home/living conditions from her childhood. The more intense the ghost activity becomes in her dream, the more the people around her vanish until she is left alone to deal with it. This further suggests that the issue is from her own past as opposed to someone else's.

■   ■   ■

Hawaii

For the Polynesian tribes of the Hawaiian Islands, as with many traditional tribal societies, dreams represent a way to communicate with the gods and the ancestors. Among these peoples, dreams are known as *moe'uhane*, or "soul sleep," in which the soul is able to exit and enter the physical body through the tear duct, or *lau'uhane*, meaning "soul pit." After leaving the body, it is believed that the soul travels through the earthly and spiritual realms, and, as in the idea of astral projection, these travels are experienced by the conscious mind as dreams. This belief is reflected in the sharing of dreams, in which the dreamer uses the expression "my spirit saw…" rather than "I saw.…"

Traditional Hawaiian beliefs suggest that nightmares are caused by spirits entering the body during the night when the soul is absent. Because of this, it is also possible for a mortal to have sexual relations with a spirit; such spirits are often referred to as a person's "husband of the night" or "wife of the night." When these spirits deliver negative predictions about the future, they are often prayed to for mercy and intervention. Even if the unhappy prophecy cannot be avoided entirely, the spirit is still thought to have the ability to mitigate its negative effects.

Kahunas, or traditional Hawaiian shamans, would sometimes investigate dream content in order to devise cures for illness. If the information acquired proved to be true, and the cure was deemed effective, the shaman would incorporate it into his medical system. Like the Kahunas, the head of a household could also pray for insight in the form of a dream; the dream could provide information on anything—from where to find the best place to fish, to the best name for the newest member of the household. If the supplicant was deemed worthy, the spirits would condescend to answer his questions.

Dreams that required outside interpretation were rare. In these instances, the dreamer would seek out a recognized dream interpreter. Such interpreters may or may not have been a part of the regular priesthood. It was much more common to see family groups sharing their dreams and discussing them within the household community each morning. Such informal discussion was avidly sought when the dreams pertained to the welfare or future of the family.

Hawk

A hawk is a regal messenger as well as a vicious bird of prey. A hawk's keen vision may symbolize insight, or it may portend suspicion and doubt. Perhaps there is a situation in the dreamer's life where someone or something needs to be watched "like a hawk." A hawk's message in a dream seems to be one of caution.

Head

The head is traditionally the symbol of wisdom, intellect, and political power. A nightmare involving harm to the head may indicate that you are feeling unprepared for an intellectual challenge, or that you don't have agency or control in your life. Perhaps you have been "losing your head" over a relationship, or perhaps you are getting a "swelled head" over your ability to exercise power and control over others.

(See also *Decapitation*)

Heart Attack

To witness someone having a heart attack is a frightening experience that will be burned into the witness's memory forever. As obesity and its attendant health problems continue to plague modern, instant-gratification-obsessed society, heart disease and heart attacks continue to kill at increasing rates. To dream of having a heart attack may mean health issues are on the dreamer's mind. The heart also symbolizes the emotional center, so problems with the heart in a dream may also presage the onset of relationship turmoil. To witness another person having a heart attack in a dream may indicate that you are the cause of the emotional suffering of another person.

Hecate

In Greek mythology, Hecate is the goddess of witchcraft and sorcery. One of the less-mentioned deities, she was the only child of the star-goddess Asteria. She's described as having three heads: one of a horse, one of a serpent, and one of a dog. Her presence is usually accompanied by the sound of barking dogs, and two phantom canines are said to faithfully follow her as servants. In more modern times, those of Wiccan faith have adopted Hecate into their worship and ritual because she is also considered the goddess of women's religion and of childbirth.

Height(s)

Nightmares in which the dreamer experiences a profound fear of heights are common in people who actually do suffer from acrophobia. Such people will often find themselves at the top of a bridge, cliff, mountain, or tall building in their dreams, feeling terrified and helpless to save themselves. Symbolically, heights can symbolize lofty ideals or attainments, but they are also often places of great isolation and precariousness. At the "height" of one's profession, there's only one way to go, and that's down. Such a dream may indicate that you are uncomfortable with or fearful of your success, preferring instead a safer, albeit mediocre, environment. Not surprisingly, fear of heights often goes hand in hand with the fear of success.

Hell

Over the last two millennia there have been many attempts to describe heaven, though the religious scholars, poets, and preachers who make the descriptions are usually rather vague. "Paradise," "the pearly gates," "eternal light," "streets of gold," and "a choir of angels" are some of the pleasant, though vague, descriptions given. But speculation about the nature and appearance of hell are much more specific. Some of the greatest and most vivid literature of the last several centuries has embraced hell as its focus.

In the Bible, there are several references to eternal damnation that employ extremely vivid imagery:

> **Matthew 25:30** "And cast ye the unprofitable servant into outer darkness: there shall be weeping and gnashing of teeth."

> **2 Samuel 22:6** "The sorrows of hell compassed me about; the snares of death prevented me."

> **Revelation 9:2** "And he opened the bottomless pit; and there arose a smoke out of the pit, as the smoke of a great furnace; and the sun and the air were darkened by reason of the smoke of the pit."

Revelation 21:8 "But the fearful, and unbelieving, and the abominable, and murderers, and whoremongers, and sorcerers, and idolaters, and all liars, shall have their part in the lake which burneth with fire and brimstone: which is the second death."

Throughout the history of literature, other poets and writers have tried their hands at describing a place that is a cornucopia of all things horrible and paradoxical. Hell is full of damned souls, yet it is also a place of total isolation. It is a pit of fire and brimstone that burns for eternity, as well as a lake of ice and darkness. In 1306, the Italian Dante Alighieri penned his famous *Inferno*, the story of the narrator's journey through all of the many layers of hell. He describes how each layer is a repository for a certain kind of sinner, and what kind of torture they receive as punishment for their particular sin or sins. "All hope abandon, ye who enter in!" Dante writes of the sign atop Hell's entrance.

In the Mandelbaum translation of Dante's *Inferno*, in Canto XVIII, Dante describes the eighth circle of hell where the fraudulent and malicious reside:

> The bottom is so deep, we found no spot
> to see it from, except by climbing up
> the arch until the bridge's highest point.
>
> This was the place we reached; the ditch beneath
> held people plunged in excrement that seemed
> as if it had been poured from human privies.
>
> And while my eyes searched that abysmal sight,
> I saw one with a head so smeared with shit,
> one could not see if he were lay or cleric.

In the mid-17th century, John Milton began working on his epic poem *Paradise Lost*, which was finally published in 1667. Milton begins his epic stating his objective, which is "to assert eternal providence/And justify the ways of God to men." As poet and philosopher, Milton called on all his powers to provide one of the most compelling descriptions of heaven, and hell, in all of literature.

Milton's poem begins in the Garden of Eden, with the fall of man and the very loss of Eden. Book I then covers Lucifer's fall from heaven with the other fallen angels, and the regrouping of "General" Satan and his army. Satan declares that the war against God is not over, but will instead be fought in the theater of the world of man. Though Satan is meant to represent the embodiment of evil, the ultimate malefic vision, some literary scholars believe that Milton meant for his readers to have some sympathy for the Devil.

In Book I of *Paradise Lost*, Milton offers a description of hell and Satan's minions:

> There stood a Hill not far whose griesly top
> Belch'd fire and rowling smoak; the rest entire
> Shon with a glossie scurff, undoubted sign
> That in his womb was hid metallic Ore,
> The work of Sulphur. Thither wing'd with speed
> A numerous Brigad hasten'd. As when Bands
> Of Pioners with Spade and Pickax arm'd
> Forerun the Royal Camp, to trench a Field,
> Or cast a Rampart.

Along with the Bible's brief descriptions, the modern, popular conception of hell is derived mostly from these two works, and the images of eternal suffering have influenced us all.

In a nightmare, the dream "hell" may symbolize the dreamer's own limitations and frustration, or it may signify latent guilt over real or imagined transgressions. Whatever it is that oppresses the dreamer in the waking world is represented in the fire and torture of the hell dream. As psychiatrist Ernest Hartmann put it, "it is hell that should remind us of our nightmares and has been built around nightmares" (*The Nightmare*, p.177).

Hitler, Adolph

Hitler is among the powerful political figures in history who have experienced precognitive dreams or omens. While sleeping in a bunker during World War I,

Hitler had a nightmare in which an avalanche of earth and molten lava buried him alive. Awakened from his sleep by this bad dream, Hitler left the dugout in a trance-like state, seeking fresh air to clear his head. He proceeded to wander into the open area close by, which was the battlefield. This was an extremely dangerous venture, but Hitler later insisted that he was acting in response to a will that was not his own. He remained in a semiconscious state until the sudden burst of enemy fire brought him to his senses. Immediately recognizing the danger, he turned around and sought the relative safety of his bunker only to find that there had been a direct hit on the dugout and all of his comrades were dead. Hitler interpreted this event to be an affirmation of his destined role as a great leader to his people, attributing it to a force that would protect him so he could carry out that role. Because of this "assurance," he felt that he was invincible. Modern-day analysts who review this dream remain skeptical that it was an unequivocal sign of divine election. However, some maintain that it could have been prophetic in nature, predicting his destiny when he died in an underground bunker at the end of World War II. The psychoanalyst Carl Jung cited Hitler's dream as an example of "synchronicity."

Hole

If you find yourself deep in a hole in a nightmare, you may have dug a metaphorical one for yourself in waking life and are wondering how to get out. Frightening dreams about being trapped or buried in holes probably indicate anxiety or a sense of feeling overwhelmed, as in "digging one's self out of a hole." Holes can also symbolize the unconscious, with all its repressed unacceptable desires and thoughts.

Holocaust

A holocaust is the mass murder of human beings on a horrific scale. The most infamous holocaust was, of course, during World War II in Nazi Germany. It's unclear exactly when Adolf Hitler, the leader of the Nazi party, began harboring his deep hatred of Jewish people, but the outcome was clear: the execution of Jews was a priority for him during his rise to power. In Hitler's 1925 memoir, *Mein Kampf* ("My Struggle"), Volume I, he wrote:

> Was there any excrement, any shamelessness in any form, above
> all in cultural life, in which at least one Jew would not have been
> involved? As soon as one even carefully cut into such an abscess,
> one found, like maggots in a decaying body, often blinded by the
> sudden light, a kike.

In his speeches, conversations, and writings, Hitler blamed the Jews as scapegoats for Germany's social, economic, and political problems. As Jewish persecution became the law of the land during the Nazi hegemony, Jews were interred in concentration/death camps and gassed to death, shot, starved, and tortured. The Nazis murdered more than 6 million Jews—along with other prisoners of war, homosexuals, Russians, Poles, Jehovah's Witnesses, and Catholics—by the end of World War II.

Those who survived the living nightmare of Hitler's concentration camps often suffered from post-traumatic stress disorder, survivor's guilt ("Why did I survive when so many others did not?"), and the intense grief of losing loved ones and friends. A part of PTSD is recurring nightmares of the precipitating event or events.

For most people, holocaust nightmares, involving a sea of torture and death, indicate a feeling of isolation and rejection. The dreamer may feel that he doesn't have a place in society, or that he is an outcast and/or a tortured soul. If this imagery is recurring, depression is likely a factor.

Horns

Horns are the pointed defensive structures protruding from the heads of powerful animals, such as bulls, rams, and steer. But these horns can also be used for offensive strategies, such as displaying dominance over others in the herd, and can serve as a visual warning sign

for other aggressive animals. In a dream, the horn is a phallic symbol and is a sign of sexuality and/or aggression.

Horse

If you are on a scary, unpredictable runaway horse in your nightmare, this could indicate a feeling of a lack of control or agency in life circumstances. Perhaps the dreamer has recently been disempowered through a divorce, job loss, or other major life-changing event. A lack of mastery, or a feeling of helplessness and vulnerability, would probably be the dominant emotional state of the person having such a dream.

Hospital

Many people fear hospitals because of the atmosphere of sickness, pain, suffering, and death—a reminder of our own mortality and human frailty. Others fear hospitals in a more immediate sense because of the potential pain, shots, and surgical procedures that may be necessary to fix what's broken. Nightmares set in hospitals may signify health concerns of the dreamer or a person close to the dreamer, but the setting can also mean the dreamer has a fear of change because change is almost always painful. But because hospitals are also places of healing, that change is usually for the better.

"Hotel California"

Recorded in 1976, *Hotel California* went on to become a Grammy-award winning album for the Eagles. Their hit single from the album, also called "Hotel California," has spurred a lot of debate over the meaning of the lyrics. Some have speculated the song is about a drug rehabilitation clinic; others have said the song represents the materialistic and obsessive nature of Americans; still others think the entire song is a metaphor for hell. Don Felder, Don Henley, and Glenn Frey wrote the music and the surreal, often dreamlike lyrics and imagery:

> Her mind is Tiffany twisted
> She's got the Mercedes bends
> She's got a lot of pretty, pretty boys
> That she calls friends
> How they dance in the courtyard
> Sweet summer sweat
> Some dance to remember
> Some dance to forget
> You can check out any time you like
> But you can never leave

On an audio clip on the fan site *www.eaglesmusic.com*, Glenn Frey said of the song: "When we thought of this song, 'Hotel California,' we started thinking that it would be very cinematic to do it sort of like the *Twilight Zone*. One line says there is a guy on the highway, the next line says there is a hotel in the distance, then there's a woman there, then he walks in—you know, it's all one shot just sort of strung together and you sort of draw your own conclusions from it. So we were sort of trying to expand our lyrical horizons and just try to take on something in the realm of the bizarre."

House

The house is typically seen as a projection or emanation of the person occupying it. The rooms of the house are thought to correspond to the various parts of a person's psyche—with the basement being the unconscious, the attic representing memories, and so on. A house can be a safe place, or it can be a place of discord, fear, and even horror. A house in which a murder has taken place often cannot be sold, or sometimes it sells for much less than its market value. People fear houses where bad things have happened. A nightmare in which the dreamer is in a foreboding or threatening house may indicate domestic or relational problems, or more likely it may be an indication of how the dreamer sees himself in general.

Hunted

Humans are at the top of the food chain, but we are still vulnerable to attack by wild animals, and even predators from our own species. A nightmare about being chased and hunted needs to be interpreted within the context of the emotions evoked in the dreamer. An exciting yet frightening hunt scene (see William Golding's book *Lord of the Flies* for a disturbing rendition of this) may indicate that there is some primal competition or territorial behavior occurring in the life of the dreamer—perhaps in the workplace, but also possibly in a rivalry with an acquaintance. Or it might even be a competition for a love interest with another suitor. Alternately, the sheer terror of being hunted in a dream may indicate that the dreamer is experiencing feelings of high anxiety and helplessness in his or her waking life. Victims of trauma often have nightmares in which they are being hunted, chased, or attacked.

Hypnagogic Hallucination

Hypnagogic hallucinations are dreamlike images and sounds that may occur just as a person is falling asleep or waking up. The hallucinations can be nightmarish and frightening. In the semiconscious state between sleep and waking, a dream may begin, at which point the dreamer wakes enough to open their eyes and recognize their surroundings (for example, the bedroom), but the image from the dream is now somehow translated to those surroundings. This can be particularly frightening if the dreamer is in the midst of a nightmare and now sees the scary image from the dream in the waking world. The image typically fades in a matter of a few seconds.

(See also *Hypnopopic Hallucination*)

Hypnopopic Hallucination

A hypnopopic hallucination is identical to a hypnagogic hallucination except that it only occurs after a deep sleep. Both hypnopopic and hypnagogic hallucinations are associated with the phenomenon known as Old Hag Syndrome.

(See also *Old Hag Syndrome*)

Ice

An icy landscape is a bleak and austere image. The accompanying cold saps us of strength, and violent shivers can make our muscles and very bones ache. A nightmare in an icy landscape bodes of isolation and longing for love. Blocks of ice represent issues of the heart that need to be dealt with. For the ice to melt, communication is key.

Walking across a frozen body of water may mean that you are cut off from an emotional connection, while walking on thin ice may mean you are feeling more fearful the closer you get to a resolution. At the end of Mary Shelley's *Frankenstein*, the monster is last seen walking across a frozen, desolate landscape, indicating that he has been cut off from humanity and all possibility of redemption.

Ice pick

The ice pick is a tool used to chip away chunks of ice from a block—a way to break up larger chunks into more manageable ones. The solid handle and sharp point also make the ice pick a deadly weapon. The ice pick was the featured murder weapon in the 1992 sexually charged thriller *Basic Instinct*, starring Sharon Stone. The film opens with a sex scene featuring an attractive woman straddling a man beneath her. The woman ties the man's hands to the bed frame and then stabs him repeatedly with the ice pick, murdering him. Perhaps the most interesting aspect of this scene is that the murderess appropriates a traditional symbol of male sexuality and aggression, the ice pick, and uses it to express her own, intensely female, rage.

Ice picks don't cut, they stab. Unless it's very well placed, one stab with an ice pick isn't enough to kill another person, so the multiple wounds of this crime usually indicate a crime of passion. To have a nightmare involving an ice pick means you may be feeling some male aggression in your life that is likely sexual in nature.

I

Illness

When you experience a dream of ill health, pay particular attention to the location in your body that the dream emphasizes. There have been cases in which repeated dreams of illness or disease have presaged an actual sickness. If this nightmare is about someone else, do the best you can to determine if the ill person is someone you know, or if the sick person is merely a projection of yourself.

Imagery Rehearsal Therapy

This is a cognitive-behavioral treatment for sufferers of post-traumatic stress disorder–related nightmares that does not involve the use of medications. While patients are awake, they are helped to re-narrate the endings of their nightmares so that the ending is no longer upsetting. The client is then instructed to rehearse the new, nonthreatening images associated with the changed dream. Imagery rehearsal therapy also typically involves other components designed to help clients with the ancillary problems associated with nightmares, such as insomnia. For example, clients are taught basic strategies that may help them to improve the quality of their sleep, such as refraining from caffeine during the afternoon, having a consistent bedtime ritual, or refraining from watching TV in bed.

(See also *Post-Traumatic Stress Disorder*)

Immobility

In some nightmares we want to run, but can't. Something horrible and menacing may be chasing us, but somehow we are rooted to the ground, unable to move. There may be a physiological reason why one may feel "frozen" in a dream: Each night as sleepers go into the roughly 90-minute cycle of REM sleep, the body becomes paralyzed. During REM sleep, the brain is highly active, and if we weren't paralyzed, we could hurt others or ourselves by thrashing around during a particularly active dream. If the mind becomes even partially conscious of the paralysis during the dream, the feeling may translate readily into the nightmare and affect the imagery. This feeling of paralysis is also associated with Old Hag Syndrome.

Immobility within the dream may demonstrate an unwillingness or inability to concede a point, admit defeat, or confess a wrong. It may also indicate a feeling of helplessness or vulnerability in waking life, a feeling common to almost all nightmares

Incubi and Succubae

> [M]en may at times be begotten by means of Incubi and Succubae, [and] it is contrary to the words of the saints and even to the tradition of Holy Scripture to maintain the opposite opinion. (from *Malleus Maleficarum*)

The idea of spirit beings or demons that take the form of people in order to have sex with human beings is an ancient one. Incubi were sometimes referred to as *demon lovers*, while some writers asserted that the succubae were one and the same with the wood nymphs of European folklore. In Western demonological lore, speculation about such ideas was initially prompted by two short verses in chapter six of Genesis:

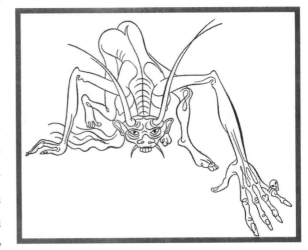

> **Genesis 6:2** "[T]he sons of God saw that the daughters of men were fair; and they took to wife such of them as they chose."

> **Genesis 6:4** "The Nephilim were on the earth in those days, and also afterward, when the sons of God came in to the daughters of men, and they bore children to them. These were the mighty men that were of old, the men of renown."

In these rather strange verses, the expression "sons of God" was taken to indicate angels, and while scripture does not seem to condemn the actions of these "Nephilim," the traditional interpretation of these passages is that these sons of God are *fallen* angels. This history of biblical interpretation legitimized and promulgated the notion of incubi and succubae. St. Augustine took up the theme of demonic, sexual beings when he wrote:

> It is a widespread opinion, confirmed by direct or indirect testimony of trustworthy persons, that the Sylvans and Fauns, commonly called Incubi, have often tormented women, solicited and obtained intercourse with them.

Such demons were thought to attack/seduce human beings most often at night, thus conveniently explaining why "virtuous" monks, nuns, and priests have erotic dreams. Although sterile themselves, the incubi (demons in male form) could supposedly impregnate women with seed taken by succubae (demons in female form) from men—a belief that was sometimes used to explain pregnancies resulting from clandestine love affairs. This type of explanation not only absolved women from charges of licentiousness, but, because the sperm was taken from men, it also saved the child from being executed as an offspring of a demon. The authors of the influential *Malleus Maleficarum*, or *The Witch Hammer* (1486), were seemingly obsessed with explaining this process, and devoted several sections to it (quoted material from this and following sections can be found at *www.maleusmaleficarum.org*):

> Devils do indeed collect human semen, by means of which they are able to produce bodily effects; but [t]his cannot be done without some local movement, therefore demons can transfer the semen which they have collected and inject it into the bodies of others.

It was thought that some demons would collect the semen from living men by assuming the form of succubae, after which they would transform themselves into incubi and inject the semen into a woman. In other cases, the reverse was thought to occur. Hienrich Kramer and James Sprenger, the authors of *Malleus*

Maleficarum, speculated that this division of labor may have arisen from the assignment of demons to specific people—apparently the diabolical equivalent of guardian angels:

> Perhaps one devil allotted to a woman, should receive semen from another devil, allotted to a man, that in this way each of them should be commissioned by the prince of devils to work some witchcraft; since to each one is allotted his own angel, even from among the evil ones....

However, the two authors speculated that this pairing of efforts arises out of necessity, from the "filthiness of the deed, which one devil would abhor to commit," implying that certain demons would object to the "gender bending" role in the semen-transfer process.

One would ask why demons are so intent on promoting human reproduction. Kramer and Sprenger provide a number of different reasons:

> The reason that devils turn themselves into Incubi or Succubae is not for the cause of pleasure, since a spirit has not flesh and blood; but chiefly it is with this intention, that through the vice of luxury they may work a twofold harm against men, that is, in body and in soul, that so men may be more given to all vices. And there is no doubt that they know under which stars the semen is most vigorous, and that men so conceived will be always perverted by witchcraft.

In other words, copulating with demons would corrupt people to the point that they would eventually give themselves up to Satan. So the demonic "work" had the goal of furthering the diabolical plan to corrupt and ensnare every human being.

There were, however, other medieval traditions that asserted that demons and humans could copulate and produce children. For instance, it was rumored that Merlin the magician was the offspring of such a union. This notion of semi-demonic children was used to explain such phenomena as deformed babies.

Mortals who willingly responded to the seductive attentions of these beings apparently risked damnation. A papal bull issued by Pope Innocent in 1484 asserted that: "Many persons of both sexes, forgetful of their own salvation, have abused incubi and succubae." Some of the church fathers, such as St. Anthony, asserted that demons in the form of seductive naked women would try to lure him away from his devotions. These experiences were later taken as evidence for the real existence of succubae.

In the 17th century, Franciscan author Ludovico Sinistrari suggested that incubi were not demons, but rather higher beings found somewhere in the hierarchy between men and angels, and who honored humankind with their attentions. Because exorcism was thought to have no effect on these beings, Sinistrari used this to support his theory that they were separate and distinct from the evil fiends. In accordance with the prevailing views of the church, Sinistrari maintained that "relations" with these beings could be sinful if people believed they were actually with a demon. Thus, he suggested that the sin was rooted not so much in the act itself, but rather in the belief that a sin had in fact been committed.

India

Throughout history, India has been host to the birth of many of the world's most ancient religions, including Hinduism, Buddhism, Jainism, and Sikhism. The people of ancient India attributed a deep significance and importance to their dreams and visions. Like many other ancient and traditional societies, the ancient Indians felt that dreams were a communication from the divine. They also felt that life *was* a dream, but a dream filled with certain suffering, and one from which there was little chance of waking.

In fact, dreams have come to symbolize the unreality of the world. Mainstream Hindu religious thought, for example, that the endless cycle of reincarnation means that each soul is trapped in the sufferings of this world, with death offering no immediate reprieve or release. In fact, in most of the religious traditions of South Asia, the ultimate goal of the spiritual life *is* release or liberation from the cycle of death and rebirth, and the knowledge or enlightenment that leads to this liberation is often compared metaphorically to the process of awakening from a dream. In the philosophical tradition of Advaita Vedanta, in particular, this metaphor is embraced to stress the unreal and dreamlike quality of the world as we experience it in our normal states of consciousness. (The word *maya* refers to the actual doctrine of the unreality of this world.)

Much of this doctrine of unreality is explicated in the Vedas. Written around 1500 to 1000 B.C.E., the Vedas are Hinduism's most sacred books, containing much information pertaining to dreams and dream interpretation. For example, the Atharva Veda discusses dream symbols that are thought to indicate good or bad omens. So, according to this text, riding an elephant in a dream signifies that the dreamer will experience good luck, whereas riding a donkey presages bad luck on the horizon. Similar texts also discuss rites to thwart the negative omens of bad dreams, such as praying to the goddess Usas (who chases away evil dreams), chanting hymns, performing purification rituals, or a combination of all three.

The division of all dreams into either auspicious or inauspicious dreams has ancient roots, which makes it an important part of connecting dream interpretation to ancient ways. Within these two categories, violent images in dreams can be either good or bad, depending on the response that is evoked in the dreamer. Aggression and passivity especially seem to have a great bearing on interpretation. For example, if the dreamer is an active participant in the violent act itself, even if he or she is injured as a result, it is seen as an auspicious dream. However, if the dreamer is a passive recipient of injury in the dream, then the dream is regarded as negative.

Human nature is also taken into consideration as a factor in dreams and their interpretation. In the Atharva Veda, for example, human beings are said to have one of three temperaments: bilious, phlegmatic, or sanguine (a fourth is usually cited: melancholy). People with a bilious temperament are said to dream of arid deserts and burning objects, phlegmatics are said to dream of the burgeoning life and beauty of nature, and sanguines are said to dream of racing clouds and forest creatures running in terror. As we now are starting to understand how our dominant emotional states play a part in dream imagery, this may not be far off from the truth; although, of course, the imagery would be likely to change in a modern dreamscape.

The ancient Indian texts were fairly sophisticated in that they also endeavored to explain the *why* of dreaming. Like many traditional tribal societies, the Hindus regarded dreams as the result of the experiences of the itinerant soul. In the Hindu view, the soul or spirit that is the basis for dream consciousness can detach itself from the physical body and wander. In the early Indian Buddhist work *Questions of King Milinda*, it is said that a person who dreams is either under the influence of a deity, overly affected or controlled by their waking experiences, or under the sway of a prophecy. And according to some Indian medical texts, dreams are merely the dreamer's way of grappling with past-life experiences, while others are simply thought of as wish fulfillments. In contrast, the classical schools of Indian philosophy propose two different reasons for dreams and dreaming. The *presentative theory* explains dream cognition as the result of a resting, withdrawn mind, combined with a temporarily defunct body and senses. The *representative theory* holds that dream consciousness is merely a counterfeit memory. In both of these positions, there is the view that the mind functions as a kind of "sixth sense," whose sole object and purpose is to dream.

Infidelity

For people in committed relationships, experiencing infidelity can be their darkest, most painful hour. The person you've come to depend on and trust unconditionally has violated that trust and broken the bond you once shared. An infidelity nightmare usually occurs when one is feeling vulnerable in a relationship. The dreamer may explore worst-case scenarios in the dreamworld—scenarios that involve the emotions, heartache, and anger that the actual event would cause. This may also be a "warning dream" that indicates a need to address relationship issues before the nightmare becomes a reality.

Ingessana

The Ingessana peoples in the Republic of the Sudan take their dreams with great seriousness. According to the Ingessana, dreams may convey messages from parts of the dreamer's cosmological makeup, and certain significant dreams are seen as the result of the activities of supernatural beings.

In general, dreams and nightmares are seen as the manifestations of invisible entities, such as ghosts, ancestors, and gods, who make demands and issue warnings and instructions. The messages in dreams may concern the material well-being of the members of a household, or it may convey the entity's intentions and plans regarding the community or neighboring territories. Dreams also bridge the gap between the material and the spiritual world, and function as a means of restoration of relationship between the various entities and human beings. In this, the entities usually demand the observance of certain rituals and ceremonies that are designed to mediate between the spiritual and the natural realm. In some cases, the dream may promote the restoration of the souls of children.

Dream interpretation and divination follows a path typical to most tribal societies. Different dreamers are thought to be endowed with varying capacities and degrees of "sight." Doctor-diviners, and those who are believed to have the "second sight," are able to see things during waking hours that most people can only see during dreams, such as ghosts. These people are also endowed with a prodigious dreaming ability, and can see things in their sleep that ordinary dreamers cannot. Tribe members typically consult the doctor-diviners in order to find meaning in the more obscure elements of their dreams. The doctor-diviner's particular abilities of sight enable him to state with authority the meaning and significance of a dream. Dreams are thought to have a great power to affect the lives of people in the community, for good or bad. For example, dreams involving the *nengk*, the ghastly creatures thought to bring illness and death, are the most feared and perhaps socially significant dreams among the Ingessana.

Initiation

Initiation is a rite of passage, formal or informal, in which an individual goes through a transformative process that significantly alters his or her cultural, social, or religious status. In this rite or rites, revered and often privileged social or religious knowledge is often imparted to the initiate, and is a significant part of the initiation process.

In religious initiations, in particular, dreams frequently play a central role in the acquisition of this knowledge. Shamans, the "priests" of traditional hunter-gatherer societies, commonly begin their vocation when they are "called" in an initiatory dream. Very often, these dreams of calling involve nightmarish images, in which the initiate is dismembered and/or killed. Such dreams are thought to symbolize the transformative process, in which the initiate "dies" to his old life and takes up his new role in society as shaman. In the Islamic Sufi tradition, many Sufi mystics began their spiritual journeys after the appearance of spiritual guides in their dreams. In the tribes of the American Diegueno Indians, the training of religious healers involves a series of initiatory dreams, with the final dream revealing the medicine name of the would-be healer. Variations of this theme are found in the initiation rites of many Native American tribes, as well as in the Aboriginal tribes of Australia.

Insects

Insects are the creeping, slithering, scuttling, chattering things that most of us loathe to look at, let alone touch. Insect imagery in a nightmare may just be an indication of a phobic response to bugs, or it may be an indication that something in your life is "bugging" you. Unwanted "friends" and relatives may be functioning as parasites in your life. It may be time to call the exterminator and get rid of these pests.

(See also *Ants*)

Insomnia

Extremely frightening nightmares may cause some people to fear sleep and even avoid it altogether. The horrific imagery that may be waiting for them on the other side prevents the sleeper from getting the deep, uninterrupted sleep he or she so desperately needs. The disorder includes the obvious symptom of being unable to fall asleep, as well as the symptoms of waking up frequently, waking up too early without being able to fall back asleep, and sleeping without feeling refreshed. Untreated insomnia can lead to entrenched sleep deprivation—a state of severe exhaustion that can affect motor coordination; cause illness and hallucinations; and, if a person goes long enough without sleep, death.

Iroquois

According to the European Christian missionaries who first encountered them, the Iroquois of North America had "a faith in dreams that surpass[ed] all belief." This Native American tribe put great stock in their dreams: they looked at their dreams as divine ordinances and irrevocable decrees that should be heeded and obeyed without delay. Dreams had an oracular function that served as a means to predict future events and warn of impending misfortune. Dreams were also consulted in times of sickness in order to procure a cure.

Not all Iroquois dreams were held in high esteem. A dreamer's station in life played a large part in whether or not his dream would be regarded with interest or heeded as a message. "Vain" dreamers and poor people were not regarded as very significant or accurate dreamers, whereas the dreaming abilities of a person in fairly good social standing, who had been proven as an accurate predictive dreamer in the past, would be regarded with awe and respect. And even gifted dreamers recognized that some dreams were false and some were true. True dreams were regarded as quite rare.

Jacob

Jacob is considered the father of the chosen people, and his sons represent the heads of the 12 tribes of the children of Israel. The biblical Jacob was a prodigious dreamer. At the time of his first dream, Jacob was on his way to Haran to take a wife from among the daughters of his uncle Laban:

> When he had reached a certain place he passed the night there, since the sun had set. Taking one of the stones to be found at that place, he made it his pillow and lay down where he was. He had a dream: a ladder was there, standing on the ground with its top reaching to heaven; and there were angels of God going up it and coming down. And Yahweh was there, standing over him, saying, "I am Yahweh, the God of Abraham your father, and the God of Isaac. I will give to you and your descendants the land on which you are lying. Your descendants shall be like the specks of dust on the ground; you shall spread to the west and the east, to the north and the south, and all the tribes of the earth shall bless themselves by you and your descendants. Be sure that I am with you; I will keep you safe wherever you go, and bring you back to this land, for I will not desert you before I have done all that I have promised you." Then Jacob awoke from his sleep and said, "Truly, Yahweh is in this place and I never knew it!" And he was afraid, and said, "How awesome is this place!"
> (Genesis 28:11–17).

Despite the seemingly benign and comforting nature of this dream, Jacob wakes in a state of real fear, which indicates that it was a nightmare, or at least had a nightmarish aspect. The purpose of the dream is to confirm God's covenant with Abraham directly to Jacob, and to assure Jacob that, although he is in distress, he is yet the object of God's love and care.

The manifestation of God in his dream (or nightmare) completely alters Jacob's view of his own purpose and destiny. For Jacob, this is no mere dream, but a profound, life-changing spiritual experience.

The Bible records several other occasions in which God manifests to Jacob in a dream. Jacob has another dream 14 years after the ladder dream, in which he

realizes that he is destined to return to the land of his birth. There is also the famous dream of Peniel, in which God appeared to Jacob in the form of an angel, whom Jacob wrestled until daybreak. Jacob prevailed (or at least the angel allowed him to prevail), and he would not let the angel go until he had received a blessing. The angel blessed him, and also changed his name from Jacob to Israel. Jacob called the place Peniel, or "face of God," saying, "For I have seen God face to face, and my life is spared and not snatched away" (Genesis 32:30). Once again, although the result of the dream is positive, the alarming presence of the angel and the wrestling indicates a nightmarish aspect. Even so, Jacob receives a new identity and status, as the one who bequeathed his people with a name: Israel.

Jacob's Ladder

This 1990 movie stars Tim Robbins as Jacob Singer, an American soldier in the Mekong Delta during the Vietnam War. At the onset of the narrative, Jacob's unit is ambushed and the soldiers try to take cover. But something is seriously wrong; the battalion begins to exhibit strange and violent behavior for no apparent reason. Jacob tries to escape, only to be stabbed with a bayoneted rifle by an unseen enemy.

The narrative shifts between Vietnam, Jacob's memories of his son Gabriel and former wife, Sarah, and his present relationship with his girlfriend, Jezebel

(Elizabeth Pena), in New York. During this time, Jacob exhibits classic signs of paranoia, and faces several apparent threats to his life.

As his hallucinatory experiences—dreams? nightmares? paranoid delusions?—become more and more bizarre and frightening, Jacob eventually learns about secret chemical experiments performed on U.S. soldiers in Vietnam. A project working to create a drug (code name "ladder") to increase aggression in soldiers was tested on a group of Vietcong POWs and, later, on Jacob's unit. However, instead of targeting the enemy, Jacob's battalion turned on and viciously attacked one another.

The most frightening aspect about Jacob Singer's nightmare is that he isn't dreaming: Jacob never actually made it out of Vietnam. The entire series of experiences turns out to have been a dying hallucination on the operating table. Regardless, Jacob's experiences appear to be a form of cleansing or catharsis, in which he releases himself from his earthly attachments and finally joins his dead son, Gabriel, in the afterlife. The final scene of the movie shows him ascending a staircase—his final, heavenly ladder, in reference to the biblical story—toward a bright light. Jacob's friend and chiropractor Louis (played by Danny Aiello) states the theme of the film, namely that hell is really a kind of self-inflicted purgatory, and those who are ready to let go of their lives do not find the experience of death "hellish" at all.

At the end of the film, a message states that there were real allegations that the U.S. Army experimented with a hallucinogenic drug called BZ during the Vietnam War—allegations that the Pentagon later denied.

Jaw

A yawning maw is often seen as the symbol of the gates to the underworld. Like holes, doors, pits, and caves, jaws or mouths can represent a route to the unconscious.

Jaws

In 1975, Steven Spielberg directed the film version of Peter Benchley's classic horror story *Jaws*. The movie tapped into the primal fear humans have of being attacked and eaten alive. But Spielberg's monster is real, as sharks do in fact attack and eat people on occasion (though one is much more likely to win the lottery than be eaten by a shark). The story recounts the killing sprees of a great white shark—a shark with a mindless, soulless motive only to feed on humans. There is no explanation for why the shark attacks, only that it is inexorable, and seemingly intelligent and cunning. *Jaws* was such an effective horror movie that many people, decades after seeing the movie, still don't like venturing out beyond the most shallow ocean water.

Jaws has grown into movie monster icon status, and the great white has swam his way into the nightmares of young and old alike. Nightmares of shark attacks, like other animal attacks, may represent internalized fears of the animal itself, or it may indicate a more general feeling of anxiety and vulnerability in waking life. The dreamer may feel out his depth in "swimming with the sharks," perhaps in his profession, and may feel that he is being targeted as the next "meal."

Job/Career

For some people, their 9-to-5 occupation is a living nightmare. During work, others make unreasonable demands of our time and talent; they overwhelm us with deadlines and tasks, with recognition and rewards few and far between. For most people, job-related nightmares may reflect ordinary performance anxiety. The dreamer may have an extremely stressful job, such as an air traffic controller, and the stress and anxiety invades their sleep in the form of horrific nightmares. In any case, the dreamer's career and job functions are weighing heavily on the conscious and subconscious. When job-related nightmares become too frequent, it may be a sign of burnout.

Johnson, Lyndon B.

This former president of the United States suffered from chronic childhood nightmares that carried through into his adult life. As a young child he often dreamt that he was sitting paralyzed in a chair as he faced an oncoming cattle stampede.

After becoming the vice president in 1961, the setting of his nightmares changed to the Executive Office Building, but the paralysis theme remained the same. He often dreamt that he was sitting at his desk, just finishing a pile of paperwork. But when he tried to get up, he would discover ankle straps binding him to the heavy chair in which he sat. Because he would be unable to move, he resigned himself to continuing to do more paperwork that was still on his desk.

After the 1968 Tet Offensive in Vietnam, the content of his nightmares altered yet again; however, the theme of paralysis or immobility remained the same. In these dreams, he would find himself lying in a bed in the Red Room, unable to move or even speak. Instead of his own body on the bed, he would see that it was actually the frail, paralyzed body of Woodrow Wilson. The trauma of these nightmares carried over into his waking life, to the extent that Johnson regularly looked at the pictures of Wilson that hung in the White House halls just to assure himself that, while Wilson was dead, he himself remained alive and vital.

Johnson found himself in a difficult predicament as the Vietnam Conflict continued and casualties mounted. On one hand he felt he could not withdraw the troops and still maintain his pride; but on the other hand he also knew that fierce opposition to the war was gaining momentum throughout the country. He knew that support for the social programs he was promoting would be jeopardized if he remained in office and kept the status quo. Once again, his nightmares reflected the fears and uncertainties of his waking life. He began to dream that he was being swept down a river, struggling to swim to the shore. No matter how hard he swam, he was never able to reach safety, and eventually he would be swimming in circles, exhausting all his energy. This nightmare, in which he was "between a rock and hard place," signified his impossible situation. He realized that the only proper and effective solution was to remove himself as an active participant. Shortly after having this nightmare, he announced his decision not to seek another term in office.

Judaism

Traditional Judaism contains extensive lore relating to dreams and their interpretation. Like other early civilizations, the Jews believed it was important to distinguish between dreams and nightmares—between good omens and bad ones.

The largest collection of ancient Judaist sacred writings is the Babylonian Talmud. It contains an abundance of dream references, rules concerning dream interpretation, and different prayers and rituals for avoiding evil dreams. One of the more common themes in the Talmud is the enigmatic nature of dreams in general. Apparently the ancient Jews placed great stock in the correct interpretation of dreams, regardless of how difficult or complex they seemed. To this end, the Jews emphasized the importance of a dream interpreter's ability to distinguish between meaningful, relevant dreams and worthless ones. Recognizing that religious heresy could easily arise from incorrect dream interpretations, several prophets warned against false dreams as well as false interpreters.

Rabbinic Judaism also laid considerable emphasis on the interpretation of dreams. According to this tradition, a dream that isn't interpreted is like an unread letter; without conscious, purposeful interpretation, the dream's meaning will eventually be lost. Not surprisingly, many important passages from the Torah relate to dreams found in the Scriptures.

Like the early Christians, the Jews believed that only God could be the source of divine revelations in dreams. This view was different from the common views of the time, such as the belief that dreams could come from ancestors or from a variety of gods and deities. Because Yahweh was God only to the Jewish nation, the Jews believed that he spoke clearly and directly to them and them alone, and this communication was usually accomplished through dreams. A dreamer could hear the voice of God in a dream or, as in the case of Solomon, see God himself. When an angelic messenger conveyed God's wishes, it was considered more difficult to decipher the exact meanings of the dream symbols involved. Jewish texts also recognized the difficulty involved in making the distinction between dreams and visions.

The Jewish tradition of dream interpretation also maintained that, as God spoke only to the Jews in dreams, only Jews could correctly interpret these dream messages. Regardless of this fact, non-Jewish gentiles were actually responsible for many of the dreams mentioned in the Hebrew Scriptures. The enigmatic messages sent to the Pharaoh of the Exodus and to King Nebuchadnezzar had to be interpreted by Joseph and Daniel, respectively. The correct interpretations earned the interpreters status and power, which was later used for the greater good of the Jewish people. Despite the various conceptions of dreams and dreaming within Judaism, the categories for dreams (prophetic, cautionary, and so on.) were generally the same as those in neighboring, non-Jewish cultures.

(See also *Talmud*)

Judge/Jury

Judges or juries can represent that part of the self that makes judgments (the subconscious), or an authority figure in the dreamer's life. A dreamer with guilt feelings may dream of being on display in a courtroom with "judge, jury, and executioner" looking on, ready to submit their verdict.

Judgment

Real or imagined wrongs, and the attendant feelings of guilt, may get "lodged" in a dreamer's unconscious, and are likely to generate guilt nightmares. These nightmares can often have themes of judgment or sentencing, such as dreams of punishment or social alienation. People who are very sensitive to the opinions of others, having what Dr. Ernest Hartmann would call "thin boundaries," may have dreams in which they are the subject of ridicule or condemnation by society or their peers.

Jumping

To jump from a tall building, bridge, or cliff in suicidal desperation in a nightmare shows the dreamer is eager to get out of a particular situation in his or her life. The discomfort has become so great that jumping into an unknown abyss is better than the status quo. The image indicates a need to examine the uncomfortable situation and plan a better way out.

Jung, Carl Gustav

"Personal opinions are more or less arbitrary judgments and may be all wrong; we are never sure of being right. Therefore we should seek the facts provided by dreams. Dreams are objective facts. They do not answer our expectations."

—C.G. Jung

Born July 26, 1875, in Kessewil, Switzerland, Carl Jung was a student and colleague of Sigmund Freud (see also *Freud, Sigmund*), and was committed to the study of personality and the unconscious mind. Dreamwork served as the cornerstone of Jung's practice of psychology and analysis, in which he also incorporated mythology, philosophy, religion, and even the occult. Jung knew that disparate religions and myths contain many symbols in common, and he saw these symbols as a kind of "inheritance" held in common from the collective history of the human race. He thought that these symbols, or archetypes, were common in all human beings no matter their location, nationality, religion, upbringing, or socioeconomic background. They were the key to communicating with the subconscious mind, as well as the means to tap into the "collective unconscious." Jung believed that if we could "unpack" the meaning of the symbols and narratives of various religions and mythologies, we could better understand the nature of the human psychology and its disorders.

"In sleep, fantasy takes the form of dreams. But in waking life, too, we continue to dream beneath the threshold of consciousness, especially when under the influence of repressed or other unconscious complexes."

—C.G. Jung

Jung felt these universal symbols or archetypes could help us understand dreams as well. Some of Jung's universal archetypes include mother, father, self, hero, shadow, and trickster, among many others (see also *Archetypes*).

Though both Freud and Jung agreed that dreams were an important analysis tool, they differed greatly in their beliefs as to why people dream. For Freud, a dream was simply wish fulfillment obfuscated, and served to preserve sleep by giving our unacceptable thoughts and desires an outlet as well as a disguise. Jung felt dreams were natural and purposeful communications from the unconscious meant to guide and inform consciousness. He felt the dreamer was always the person best suited to interpret the "language" of his dream. When treating patients, Jung asked his subjects to describe their dreams, then to do some free-association work on the images from the dream. Next, he looked for archetypes within the dream and the free associations of the patient. As part of the "collective unconscious," Jung felt the archetypes could be used to help further decode the dream's meaning. Jung's objective was to unite his patient's conscious and unconscious minds so they could freely communicate, thus helping to solve the patient's psychological problems, as well as improve his quality of life in general.

Jung was also an avid lucid dreamer himself (see also *Lucid Dreaming*), and at times even saw visions. In 1913, he dreamt of a flood that engulfed most of Europe. He saw thousands of people drowning in floodwaters that turned to blood, and subsequent dreams gave Jung visions of endless winters and rivers of blood. Jung actually doubted his own sanity because of these dreams, but when, on August 1 of 1913, World War I began, he realized the significance of his vision dreams.

> "The dream shows the inner truth and reality of the patient as it really is: not as I conjecture it to be, and not as he would like it to be, but *as it is.*"

—C.G. Jung

After the conclusion of World War I, Jung traveled extensively to study different socioeconomic and religious groups in order to gain more credence for his theory that much of world mythology and folklore represented manifestations of the collective unconscious. He based his theory in part on his discovery that the dreams and nightmares of his clients frequently contained images with which they were completely unfamiliar, but which seemed to reflect symbols that could be found in the mythological systems of other cultures. Jung contested that if he could discover the meaning of these images and symbols in the cultures from which they sprung, he could better understand the dreams and nightmares of his clients. The process of seeking such meanings through this cultural "excavation" is referred to as *amplification*.

> "Anyone who wishes to interpret a dream must himself be on approximately the same level as the dream, for nowhere can he see anything more than what he is himself."
>
> —C.G. Jung

After his wife died in 1955, Jung retreated from the public eye until his own death June 6, 1961, in Zurich, Switzerland.

Jungle

The jungle is a twisted landscape of vines, trees, and plants. It's a cacophony of bugs, birds, and other creatures, and can be as dark as night in the dense underbrush. Jungle nightmares tap into our primal, untamed side, and usually hint of sexual desires. The jungle itself is a dangerous place where one can easily be lost or eaten by a predator, which indicates some fear and confusion surrounding these desires.

Kidnapping

Being abducted is one of the most personally violating experiences one can have. A kidnapping victim is brought to an unknown location for a reason he or she may not understand. A nightmare about being kidnapped indicates a loss of control and security. A negative outside influence may be strongly forcing its way into your life and making you feel helpless. People who have experienced and survived real-life kidnappings and hostage situations often have recurring nightmares that replay the scenario, or some variation of it, again and again.

Killing

The act of killing in a dream is not necessarily negative. As we grow and change, it often feels as if we are "killing off" old parts of ourselves. A nightmare about being killed may represent feelings of fear or helplessness, while killing others may indicate latent hostility or rage. In interpreting this dream, there are several significant variables that will affect the meaning, such as how the killing is being done; the weapon or means used; the target; and, of course, the feelings engendered by the dream.

Knife

A knife is an important tool for survival, but it is also a weapon. Symbolic "knives" can cut to the quick and lay open one's innermost weaknesses and fears. Threatening knife imagery in a nightmare may indicate that the dreamer is feeling "stabbed in the back" through malicious gossip or betrayal. If the dreamer

K

is wielding the knife, it may signify anger or the desire to perpetrate violence. For Freud, a knife was a symbol of aggressive male sexuality.

(See also *Killing*)

Knocking

Mysterious, late-night knocks at your door can cause surges of adrenaline and fear to course through your body. In a nightmare, the knock itself may cause the dreamer's heart rate to race, and there is the implied dread of who (or what) might be behind the door. In this dream, an unknown aspect of your personality, probably your "shadow self" or unconscious, is trying to get your attention and gain admittance.

(See also *Doors*)

Knots

Ropes, strings, shoelaces, and wires tied in knots are the little problems of our lives. Being surrounded by knots is a sign that you are focused on too many of these minor problems and are losing sight of the larger picture. Knots may also represent trepidation about an upcoming event. The knot in a noose for

hanging may indicate guilt and an expectation of, or even a desire for, punishment and retribution.

Lamia

In Greek mythology, Hera turns Lamia (daughter of Lybie and Poseidon) into a monster, and then murders her children. Part of Lamia's curse is an  inability to close her eyes, so that the images of her dead children stay with her forever. With the body of a serpent and upper-body and head of a woman, Lamia is envious of other mothers, and tends to eat their children if she has the chance. The god Zeus provides her one solace: the gift of removing her own eyes to find respite from the horrible imagery of her dead children.

language

The ability to express ourselves through spoken word is arguably the most critically important aspect to human evolution and of the building of a complex society. To find yourself alienated—a "stranger in a strange land"— because of a language barrier can engender feelings of helplessness and anxiety. A nightmare in which you are in a foreign country, unable to speak or understand anything, may indicate that you are having difficulty communicating with another person or persons, and you should make an effort to "talk the same language" in order to solve the problem. You may also be experiencing general feelings of alienation—a sort of "reverse xenophobia"—and the language barrier in your dream is your unconscious's way of signaling this.

lawyers

To be on the receiving end of a lawyer's wrath is daunting. A lawyer is a person of some authority and power, who may be speaking "legalese," which sounds like one's native language yet is confounding and often completely incomprehensible. If you are truly embroiled in legal difficulties during your waking life, the fear of losing your freedom (as in a criminal case) or money (as with a civil suit) can cause extreme anxiety. A nightmare involving

L

lawyers may mean that you require some kind of intervention in a business or personal conflict. Or perhaps there is someone in your life who is constantly interrogating you, in lawyer-fashion. If *you* are a lawyer, there's a good chance you have had nightmares of being caught unprepared during a case: another classic example of an anxiety dream that plagues many people.

Leaks

Leaks can be minor, such as an occasional small drip coming in from the roof, or they can be devastating, such as the small leak that eventually levels a dam. A leak in a nightmare always begins as a small issue, with dire consequences if left unattended. The leak represents the small issues in life that can quickly spiral out of control into something huge and destructive. The message of this nightmare is to stop procrastinating and deal with the minor problems now before they loom large and intractable.

Leprosy

Though leprosy is almost unheard of in developed nations today, the image and stigma of the disease is etched into our collective consciousness. Symptoms in-

clude sores and skin lesions that do not heal, and muscles that weaken to the point of complete atrophy. Lepers have traditionally been the undesirables of society—the marginalized and rejected with no social or political agency. Today, other diseases such as AIDS have the stigma leprosy once had.

A nightmare about being afflicted with a physically incapacitating and deforming affliction such as leprosy seems to indicate a concern for cleanliness and health, or there may be real and debilitating self-esteem issues that need to be dealt with. To see others around you with visible signs of affliction may mean that the dreamer is uncomfortable in his or her environment and may be having a difficult time relating to, or empathizing with, others.

Light

Light represents goodness, knowledge, insight, and the presence of the divine. People who have near-death experiences often recall a beatific presence accompanied by a bright white light. Lights going out in a nightmare may signify everything from the end of a relationship to the death of hope. The ensuing darkness may represent evil, unhappiness, fear (especially of the unknown), or the shadow side of the dreamer. Carl Jung  would say that the darkness in any nightmare would have to be faced and investigated in order to bring true meaning and resolution to the dream.

Lightning

Lightning is an awesome and often deadly display of Mother Nature. Children are usually terrified of lightning and the accompanying thunderclaps during a storm. Many adults (wisely) fear this phenomenon as well. Lightning is pure electrical energy with a great potential for unpredictability and destruction. Fearsome lightning in a nightmare may not just be "atmosphere," it may in fact be a display of your own creativity dancing around you—powers that are yet to be tapped and are begging expression.

Lilith

The ancient texts of the Assyro-Babylonian civilizations make the first recorded reference to Lilith. She is described as a sexual demon that resembles the medieval succubus, yet possesses characteristics similar to those of modern vampires (see also *Incubi and Succubae* and *Vampire*). Lilith is also referenced in Hebrew texts as the princess of the race of succubae. The name "Lilith" may be derived from the Hebrew word *lulti* meaning "lasciviousness," and possibly also *lailah*, meaning "night." Commentators sometimes saw oblique references to Lilith in the Hebrew Scriptures, or Old Testament, as well. For example, according to Midrashic literature, the serpent that tempted Eve in the Garden of Eden was Satan's minion Lilith, and not Satan himself.

The texts of some rabbinical translators present the first human being as a hermaphrodite, with Lilith functioning as the female half. God separated the two halves into their discrete genders, but Lilith fled the garden when she learned that God expected her to "lay under" Adam. It was after this incident that the more accommodating and submissive Eve was created from Adam's rib. Today there is a Jewish feminist magazine entitled *Lilith*, as a gesture of identification with Lilith's refusal to be subservient to Adam.

The 1940's movie *Nightmare Alley* also borrows from the Lilith myth. The female lead character, aptly named Lilith, is a demonic "consulting psychologist" who preys upon the minds and psyches of her patients. She extracts damning information from their nightmares and then uses the private information she obtains to blackmail them.

Lincoln, Abraham

One of the most infamous precognitive dreams in history was that of President Abraham Lincoln in 1865. According to Ward Hill Lamon's 1911 book *Recollections of Abraham Lincoln* (University of Nebraska Press, reprint edition, 1994), the president predicted his own demise just a few days before he was assassinated in Ford's Theater on April 14, 1865. Lamon was Lincoln's personal friend and bodyguard, and compiled his book based on conversations, letters, and interviews during their association. Lamon describes Lincoln recounting his nightmare:

> About ten days ago, I retired very late. I had been up waiting for important dispatches from the front. I could not have been long in bed when I fell into a slumber, for I was weary. I soon began to

dream. There seemed to be death-like stillness about me. Then I heard subdued sobs, as if a number of people were weeping. I thought I left my bed and wandered downstairs. There the silence was broken by the same pitiful sobbing, but the mourners were invisible. I went from room to room; no living person was in sight, but the same mournful sounds of distress met me as I passed along. It was light in all the rooms; every object was familiar to me; but where were all the people who were grieving as if their hearts would break? I was puzzled and alarmed. What could be the meaning of all this? Determined to find the cause of a state of things so mysterious and so shocking, I kept on until I arrived at the East Room, which I entered[.] There I met with a sickening surprise. Before me was a catafalque, on which rested a corpse wrapped in funeral vestments. Around it were stationed soldiers who were acting as guards; and there was a throng of people, some gazing mournfully upon the corpse, whose face was covered, others weeping pitifully. "Who is dead in the White House?" I demanded of one of the soldiers "The President" was his answer; "he was killed by an assassin!" Then came a loud burst of grief from the crowd, which awoke me from my dream.

Dreams or nightmares such as Lincoln's seem to demonstrate a real and concrete connection between dreaming and precognition, and do much to further that notion in popular culture.

Lion

The lion is the "king of the jungle"—majestic, beautiful, powerful, and a vicious predators by nature. The presence of a lion is always intimidating because there is an implied knowledge that the beast can maim and kill at will, and without warning. To be stalked by a lion in a nightmare may symbolize a relationship in which you occupy a submissive or powerless position. It could also represent an unequal work dynamic, such as that in a supervisor/subordinate relationship.

Locked Out

For most people, a sense of belonging and inclusion is generally an important part of feeling content and whole as a human being. Like being abandoned or lost, being locked out of one's house or car could be an indication of a disconnect (purposeful or not) from family or other intimates. To be locked out of an office, school, or other building means you might be feeling like an outsider or interloper in your educational or professional milieu.

Lost

Children who have been lost in waking life will often suffer from recurring nightmares about the experience. More symbolically, a nightmare in which the dreamer loses his way may indicate confusion over calling, vocation, or general life direction. The dreamer may feel he is "going in circles," or perhaps he hasn't achieved the level of satisfaction he had hoped for.

Lucid Dreaming

Lucid dreaming occurs when there is a state of partial or complete awareness during the dream state. This often comes during the "twilight" periods between waking and sleeping, although people adept at this technique (it can be taught and learned) can achieve this at almost any point in the dream state. This awareness enables lucid dreamers to consciously alter or re-narrate the content of their dreams, so researchers have begun to explore the possibilities of utilizing lucid dreaming for the treatment of nightmares and for other therapeutic purposes.

The first known recorded reference to lucid dreaming is in Aristotle's *On Dreams*, where he writes that "often when one is asleep, there is something in consciousness which declares that what then presents itself is but a dream." Saint Augustine and Saint Thomas Aquinas have also mentioned something like lucid dreaming in their writings. *Dreams and How to Guide Them* (1867) by Marquis Hervey de Saint-Denis, a professor of Chinese at the Collège de France, was probably the first extended inquiry into this state. Sigmund Freud accepted the idea that a dream could be lucid, while other psychologists attributed the phenomenon to a partial awakening during the dream state. For the most part, the intangible nature of this unusual state of consciousness discouraged psychologists from giving serious attention to lucid dreaming. However, the psychologist Stephen LaBerge conducted some remarkable research on lucid dreaming in the 1980s. He himself had experienced lucid dreams since childhood and resolved to finally study the phenomenon scientifically during his psychology graduate program at Stanford University. The fact that his lucid dreams were so infrequent posed a problem to his inquiry, something he dealt with by a kind of autosuggestion, repeating the phrase "tonight I *will* have a lucid dream" to himself before going to sleep. He eventually developed his own technique of dream induction, referred to as mnemonic induction of lucid dreams (MILD), which eventually increased his lucid dream rate to more than 20 dreams per month.

In order to accurately measure the incidence and rate of lucid dreaming in a subject, LaBerge had to find a way for dreamers to communicate with researchers during their lucid dreams. Initially, he learned to control his eye movements (with the muscles that remain active during the REM stage) during sleep, and later devised a more elaborate system of Morse code (delivered with clenching movements of the hand) to communicate with non-sleeping observers.

Eventually, LaBerge was able to train dozens of subjects to dream lucidly and communicate with researchers while asleep. These subjects were then instructed to perform a variety of tasks in their dreams, from counting to flying, and to signal the experimenter when their tasks were complete. The results of these experiments were reported in LaBerge's popular 1985 book on the subject, *Lucid Dreaming* (Tarcher). The success of this work was instrumental in stimulating the nationwide formation of dream groups, and in popularizing the idea in the mass media. Thus the term *lucid dreaming* was brought to the average person's awareness.

The findings of lucid dream research have already been applied to therapy. One sleep therapist, for example, has taught clients experiencing recurrent nightmares to activate a buzzer during bad dreams. The client is subsequently awakened, and the dream is analyzed. However, the therapist only buzzes the sleeper in reply, instead of waking him—a prearranged signal for the client to take control and "re-narrate" the nightmare into a more pleasant experience.

Psychologist Patricia Garfield has used lucid dreams for healing and pain relief in a manner similar to creative visualization. For instance, someone suffering from pain in a particular area of the body might visualize themselves delivering healing light or energy to that area. In her book *The Healing Power of Dreams* (Fireside 1992), Garfield suggested the following steps when using lucid dreams as healing aids:

Before a Lucid Healing Dream:

1. Select your healing goal and put it into words. *Examples:* "Teach me to reduce or eliminate my pain," "help me heal," and "show me contentment."

2. Rehearse your healing goal, repeating it before sleep.

3. Visualize your healing goal being fulfilled.

During a Lucid Healing Dream:

1. Become lucid in your dream.

2. Perform your dream healing or allow it to take place.

3. Accept the wisdom of your dream.

Achieving lucidity in a nightmare can be very empowering because it allows the dreamer to safely confront the fearful and unacceptable aspects of his or her unconscious. By purposefully approaching the terrifying image in the dream, the dreamer can discover what it symbolizes and, thus, overcome the fear. This discovery and eventual embracing of previously suppressed aspects of the dreamer's personality enable him to become a fully integrated and whole self. Many people find it easier to confront the source of their fears while in a lucid dream because they are able to retain control of their surroundings, and this sense of control is gradually carried over into their waking lives.

Macbeth

Shakespeare plumbed the depths of the human unconscious with precision, and was well aware of the influence of waking emotions, such as fear and guilt, on dreams and nightmares. In Act 3, Scene 2 of William Shakespeare's 1605 play, Macbeth says to his wife (this and following quotations are from *www.literaturepage.com/read/shakespeare_macbeth.html*):

> Ere we will eat our meal in fear, and sleep
> In the affliction of these terrible dreams
> That shake us nightly: better be with the dead,
> Whom we, to gain our peace, have sent to peace,
> Than on the torture of the mind to lie
> In restless ecstasy.

As in many of his plays, Shakespeare uses dreams—especially prophetic dreams, omens, and nightmares—as a literary device to foreshadow coming events. Early in the play, Macbeth learns through the prophecy of three witches that he will become King of Scotland. Eager to fulfill this prophecy and realize his ambitions, Macbeth murders the current king, King Duncan, while Duncan is a guest at Macbeth's castle, after which Macbeth and Lady Macbeth scheme to retain their titles. Those with suspicions, or who pose an obstacle to their ambitions, Macbeth simply has killed. The guilt weighs heavily on both Macbeth and his wife, and it begins to adversely affect their sleep. In Act 5, Scene 1, a doctor and gentlewoman are discussing Lady Macbeth's sleeping patterns:

> Since his majesty went into the field, I have seen her
> rise from her bed, throw her nightgown upon her, unlock her
> closet, take forth paper, fold it, write upon it, read it,
> afterwards seal it, and again return to bed; yet all this
> while in a most fast sleep.

M

Lady Macbeth talks in her sleep and performs a curious, repetitive action with her hands, which the doctor and gentlewoman observe as she sleepwalks into their midst. The doctor notes that Lady Macbeth is rubbing her hands, to which the gentlewoman replies:

> It is an accustomed action with her, to seem thus washing her
> hands: I have known her continue in this a quarter of an hour.

Symbolically, Lady Macbeth is trying to clean her hands of the blood/guilt for those she and her husband have plotted to murder. Lady Macbeth's guilt and anxiety finds full expression in her dreamworld, generating fits of sleepwalking, talking in her sleep, and obsessively attempting to clean blood that isn't there.

Mack, John E.

Author of *Nightmares and Human Conflict* (Columbia University Press, 1989; first published in 1970), John Mack studied the childlike characteristics of our reactions to threats in our nightmares. He recognized the fact that nightmares usually consist of powerful forces assaulting the dreamer—forces people are incapable of managing successfully. This inability or sense of helplessness corresponds to the way in which people saw the world around them in childhood. In this, the villains of nightmares are less important than the feelings of terror and vulnerability they evoke. Mack wrote that no matter what the source of the threat in our nightmares—whether it be a movie monster, death ray, or other fantastical force—the experience, at least momentarily, transforms the dreamer into the mentality of a helpless child facing overwhelming forces.

When comparing the differences in the types of nightmares children and adults experience, Mack observed that nightmares occur as a response to prominent fears humans experience at various stages of their development. For example, during infancy, we fear strangers and being abandoned by our caregivers; during early childhood, we fear injury to our bodies; and in adulthood, our primary fear is of failure, inadequacy, and death.

Adult nightmares are similar to children's in that they express a sense of vulnerability (a notion that the psychiatrist Ernest Hartmann emphasizes as well). The types and sources of anxieties may change, but feelings of helplessness and insecurity affect people of all ages.

Macrobius

Ambrosias Macrobius Theodosius was an author and philosopher of the early fifth century C.E. His work *Commentary on the Dream of Scipio* is one of the most influential dream books of the Latin Middle Ages(there were more than 37 editions printed before 1700). When compared to his contemporaries, Macrobius is considered negative and superstitious. His book clearly found inspiration in the

Oneirocritia, the great dream book of Artemidorus, but it is far more comprehensive, covering five different classes of dreams and including material on apparitions and nightmares that Artemidorus did not cover explicitly.

Macrobius classified dreams according to a Platonic hierarchy. He regarded the top three classes as the most significant because they are inspired by divine sources. These classes included ghostly ap-

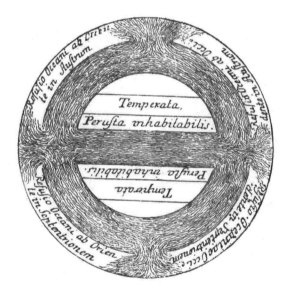

paritions (*phantasma*), enigmatic dreams (*somnium*), and oracular dreams (*oraculum*). Macrobius thought that nightmares (*insomnium*) and prophetic visions (*visio*) were inconsequential. He argued that the prophetic visions that appear in the twilight state between waking and sleeping are of no consequence because they are not actually dreams; therefore, they cannot be divinely inspired.

The *Commentary on the Dream of Scipio* covers three different causes behind nightmares. These include the malaises of the body, such as hunger or gluttony; malaises of the soul, such as love or loss; and difficulties relating to one's profession. Macrobius also included information about the incubi and succubae—in fact, this is the first reference to these demons in Christian literature. Although there are many stories about the incubi and succubae in early Jewish folklore, the fact that Macrobius made mention of them played a significant role in the development of the Christian conception of demons in later centuries.

(See also *Incubi and Succubae*)

Magic

In a nightmare, magic, or "black" magic, is rife with notions of evil, demons, oppression/possession, witchcraft, and sorcery. Scary dreams involving magic may indicate that the dreamer has real superstitions and fears of the supernatural. Magic can also involve "sleight of hand," so perhaps an issue in the dreamer's life may not be as it appears. Additionally, magic can represent a kind of creativity, in which the dreamer hopes to achieve something through "magical thinking."

Mask

As in the masks of ancient Greek drama, a mask represents a false self or *persona*, a way for someone to conceal who he is as well as invent who he is not. In a nightmare, a scary mask can represent a repressed fear. If you are wearing the mask, then you should examine who or what you may be hiding from. The symbol of a mask is also related to the notion of the "shadow self," the Jungian archetype that represents the darker, primal, unacceptable thoughts and urges. Depending on the emotional state of the dreamer, the mask may or may not be an accurate representation of this "shadow self."

Masochism

Masochism is the way in which sexual urges are gratified through degradation and pain. Some theorists contend that masochism is primarily a feminine attribute (something that the feminists naturally reject), but the reality is that both males and females can embrace this kind of sexual expression. Masochism in a dream doesn't necessarily mean that one is a masochist, but it may signify the way in which others are regarding you, an opinion you have internalized. This imagery may also speak to self-esteem issues. Perhaps you aren't convinced that you deserve to be treated decently by others, and so you have resigned yourself to living with, and maybe even enjoying, subpar treatment.

Maury, Alfred

The French scientist Alfred Maury published his seminal work, *Sleep and Dreams*, in 1861. He kept a journal of his dreams, paying extra attention to the circumstances he believed affected their content and intensity. Among the external factors he placed great importance on were his diet and atmospheric changes in the environment around him. He also paid extra attention to the hypnagogic hallucinations that he experienced in the moments before he drifted off to sleep; it was his belief that these were the nascent manifestations of dreams that would follow.

In later experiments, he served as the primary subject, while an assistant introduced various stimuli, both auditory and olfactory, to his senses after he entered into the REM state of sleep. The hope was that he would be able to report the effect of outside stimuli on the content of his dreams. On one occasion, his assistant tickled his lips and the inside of his nostrils with a feather, and Maury dreamt that the skin in those places was being ripped from his face by a mass of burning pitch. In another instance, a heated iron was held close to him, and Maury reported a dream in which robbers were putting his feet to fire in an effort to extract the location of some money.

The experiments also indicated that scents could factor into our dream content. When his assistant held a burning match close to his nose, Maury dreamt that the magazine of his ship blew up, and he dreamt of a perfume shop when exposed to the scent of a bottle of cologne.

The results of these tests lend validity to the effects of the environment on what we experience while in a sleeping state.

Maze

Mazes can represent the hide-and-seek we play with issues that need to be simplified or faced more directly. They can also signify confusion and a lack of direction, or feeling like a "rat in a maze." Walking through a maze can also be a meditative aid, or *mandala*, and a means to tap into the unconscious. Walking a maze in a dream may indicate the dreamer's quest for harmony and wholeness.

Medieval Period

St. Jerome's mistranslation of certain key biblical passages in the Vulgate, or first Latin translation of the Bible, was of particular importance to the medieval conception of dreams and dream interpretation. The lines "you shall not practice augury witchcraft" were changed to "you shall not practice augury nor observe dreams." These explicit condemnations, in combination with the admonitions of writers such as Macrobius, who warned against the attacks of demons in one's sleep, served to effectively condemn dreams as the theater for Satan's minions to play out their drama of tempting the souls of the faithful.

The medieval attitude toward dreams is perfectly expressed in the *De Magia*, a 16th-century work by Benedict Peterius, a Jesuit priest:

> [T]he devil is most always implicated in dreams, filling the minds of men with poisonous superstition and not only uselessly deluding but perniciously deceiving them.

The notion of incubi and succubae (the demons that take the form of men and women in order to seduce mortals in their sleep) clearly demonstrates the medieval suspicion and fear of dreams. These creatures were a convenient explanation for sexual dreams in a society in which any form of illicit sexual activity was viewed as evil and demonically inspired. By attributing erotic dream images to evil and seductive spirits, the otherwise chaste and celibate clergy, priests, and nuns could absolve themselves of responsibility and guilt for such dreams.

(See also *Bible* and *Macrobius*)

Medium

In January of 2005, NBC launched a new dramatic television series called *Medium*. The show is based on real-life psychic and author Allison DuBois, who has worked on many murder and missing persons cases for various law-enforcement agencies. At the center of the show's theme are the prophetic dream visions of dead people that Allison DuBois (played by Patricia Arquette) experiences. Allison's scientist husband, Joe (played by Jake Weber) begins to chronicle his wife's dreams and send them to various law-enforcement agencies, never expecting to hear back from anyone. To both Allison and Joe's surprise, Allison's dreams mirror actual cases, and her insights and visions help police around the country solve these crimes. On the Website of the real-life Allison DuBois, she says about *Medium*: "Every episode is not a biography of my life; it is simply based on my life experiences. It is an accurate portrayal of my life and the people who share it, with a little Hollywood magic thrown in." *Medium* is about a psychic's nightmares, which are real visions of true horrors that have already occurred. The dead contact DuBois for help in bringing justice to their killers.

Melatonin

Melatonin is an over-the-counter sleep aid and hormone supplement that is growing in popularity. The chemical melatonin is a natural hormone secreted in the human brain as it perceives nightfall coming, and is designed to help prepare us for our natural sleep cycle, or circadian rhythm. The supplement helps many people fall asleep easier without the narcotic side effects of prescription pills and over-the-counter sleep aids. One of the interesting, and sometimes distressing, side effects for many who take melatonin supplements is a noticeable increase in vividness of dream imagery and an increase in nightmares.

Metaphor

Metaphor is simply the noting of similarities. It is constantly used in everyday speech (usually unconsciously), in fantasies, and in dreams. Metaphor is not just a figure of speech or a rhetorical device, but a basic foundation to the way in which we perceive and categorize the world. Dreaming makes use of the more common metaphors used in speech, stories, myth, and art, and it also creates newer and more nuanced connections between these metaphors. Renowned psychiatrist Ernest Hartmann says that dreams are explanatory metaphors—designed to "contextualize" emotion and thus give meaning to the dream. For example, someone who has been traumatized will have dreams in which a tidal wave is breaking over them or a threatening figure is pursuing them. These images are the metaphors that explain the deeper and more complex emotional state and meaning behind the dream. The dream is not simple, object-to-object symbolism, but rather a more nuanced and stratified process that codes the dominant emotional state of the dreamer. Metaphors in dreams almost always have to do with the personal or interpersonal concerns of the dreamer.

Whether we view dreams as arenas in which to act out repressed desires, as coded and disguised communications from the unconscious to the conscious, or simply as reflections of our everyday concerns, one of the unique aspects of the language of dreams and nightmares is that it is often symbolic and indirect. Of course, the specific images that come up in a dream are affected by many factors, such as cultural and social influences. Depending on the other elements in the dream landscape, any one of several possible meanings may be indicated by the symbolic metaphors in a dream. Sometimes free association or simply thinking about the life circumstances of the dreamer will yield meaning, but sometimes the meaning will remain unclear. Yet, as Aristotle put it, "a good dream interpreter is one who notices similarities."

Military

To see people in military uniforms may simply reflect the real-life experiences and memories of someone who has been in the military. While military images (as opposed to actual combat) can represent every-

thing from authoritarianism to self-discipline. If the dreamer is in the Navy and on a ship, the dream may suggest navigating through emotional issues of divorce, or other personal loss.

Mirror

The mirror doesn't lie, and this is doubly true for a mirror in a dream. The dream mirror may reflect the inner depths of emotions, which can sometimes be unpleasant (as they are in nightmares). In a dream state, we're likely to look for the flaws as opposed to admiring what we see. If the mirror is clear, one might be gazing upon an aspect of one's true, whole self. A cracked or cloudy mirror reflects a distorted view, or a view of a disintegrated self.

Mohave

The Mohave, a Native American group of the desert Southwest, use dreams in order to interpret and give meaning to their culture, and not the other way around. For the Mohave, common omen dreams do not necessarily reflect something that will actually happen, but rather something that *could* happen, whereas the dreams of shamans and warriors are considered to have a power and agency all their own. In Mohave culture, two types of pathogenic, or contagious, dreams are thought to cause real illness. Someone experiencing a nightmare may be prone to illness because of the dangerous and potentially harmful adventures the itinerant soul may experience, such as the invasion of the psyche by a supernatural power, spirit, or witch, or when the soul visits the land of the dead. And there are nightmares that are so upsetting that the dreamer will react to them by falling ill.

Monster

Monsters created within individual imaginations are more frightening than anything Hollywood could invent, because each dreamer creates his or her monster from the elements and themes that scare them the most. Monsters in nightmares often represent repressed unpleasant emotions and fears, and are sometimes the manifestations of the darker "shadow self." Some ugly or frightening aspect of the dreamer's personality may be reflected in, or confronted during, an interaction with a monster. The monster may simply be the physical manifestation of all the unpleasant and unacceptable thoughts, desires, and urges that both society and the dreamer has rejected.

Morocco

Moroccans have a complex, ever-evolving tradition of dream interpretation, although they have not elaborated a particularly consistent dream theory, nor have they developed any dream-related rituals or ceremonies. The Moroccan theories of dream interpretation and dream classification reflect the various influences of daily experience, most notably folk Islam, classical Islam, popular and orthodox beliefs, and current attitudes and doctrines. These diverse and sometimes competing elements—everything from beliefs in the evil eye, to the Islamic ideal of the good man, to the *djinn* (the good and bad spirits that oversee daily social interactions)—make the Moroccan view of dreams a rich and dynamic one. Most dreams are interpreted as omens of the future—omens that also provide courses of action that should be taken by the dreamer.

Like many other traditional societies, Moroccans believe that dreams result from the far-flung wandering of the soul during sleep (whereas daydreams occur when the soul leaves the body but stays close by). The wandering soul, then, is able to witness real events that happen elsewhere in space and time. These dream-events are seen as somehow significant for the dreamer's future, most often in a symbolic way. Moroccans classify dreams as being either truthful, divinely inspired dreams, or deceitful dreams coming from the Devil and other supernatural sources. Truthful dreams are associated with safety, while deceitful dreams, shaped by the evil intentions of spirits and men, presage harm.

Moroccans commonly share their dreams and rely on external dream specialists in order to settle on a good and accepted interpretation. The feeling is that not all dreams can be trusted, any more than all people can be trusted. Divinely inspired dreams can always be trusted, although it is difficult to distinguish them from those that are sent by evil influences. In order to make this determination, Moroccans don't seem to put great stock in the content of the dream itself; rather, it is the condition of the dreamer himself—what we would call his "dominant emotional state"—that determines whether a dream is true or false.

So-called visitation dreams, in which saints or other spiritual beings appear, usually serve to resolve suppressed or hidden conflicts in the dreamer, usually by providing an objective point of reference, a "compass" that directs the resolution process.

Morpheus

Morpheus is the principal Greek god of dreams and sleep. His name is derived from the Greek word *morphe*, meaning "he who forms, shapes, and molds."

According to myth, Morpheus has the ability to mimic any human's form in dreams. Hypnos, the god of sleep, is his father; Pasithea is his mother; and Thanatos, the personification of death, is his uncle. The sons of Hypnos, the Oneiroi, are also rulers of dreams in their own right; they include Icelus, Phobetor, and Phantasos.

In the *Metamorphoses* by the Roman poet Ovid, Morpheus sleeps on an ebony bed in a dimly lit cave, surrounded by poppy flowers. According to Ovid, Morpheus concentrates on the human elements of dreams, while his brothers Phobetor and Phantasos are responsible for animals and inanimate objects, respectively.

According to myth, Morpheus sends images of humans in dreams or visions, and is responsible for shaping dreams, or giving shape to the beings that inhabit dreams. Icelus assists with those aspects of dreams that reflect reality, Phobetor makes fearsome dreams or nightmares (hence the word *phobia*), and Phantasos produces tricky and unreal dreams (hence the words *fantasy* and *phantasmagoria*). Together, these sons of sleep rule the realm of dreams. However, Morpheus is entrusted with special responsiblity for the dreams of kings and heroes, and for this reason he is often referred to as "Morpheus, the Greek god of dreams," in superiority to his brothers. Morpheus is also popularly called the Sandman. The drug morphine (once called *morphium*) derives its name from Morpheus because of its dream-inducing effects.

(See also *Sandman*)

Mouth

A mouth can represent gossip and the spreading of lies, or spoken words of goodness and truth. Mouths, like doors, represent a gateway or portal from one place to another; therefore, they may signify transition and change. Issues relating to sexuality and sexual urges also can be associated with the mouth.

Mummy

Mummification is the ancient process of preserving the recently deceased. In ancient Egypt, the mummification process was not only an art form, it was also part of their belief system. Only a properly mummified body could pass to the afterlife intact. It was also something only the wealthy and powerful could afford, as it could take up to two months to prepare one body. From circa 3000 B.C.E. to the earliest days of the Common Era, the Egyptians incorporated specific ceremonies and rituals for preserving bodies. All of the organs, with the exception of

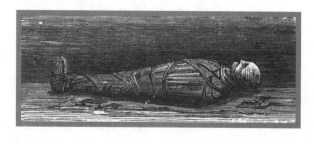

the heart, were carefully removed and placed in jars, and the skin was dried out over the course of weeks. The mummies were then wrapped in linen and placed into an intricate sarcophagus, if the deceased could afford one, or buried in a more frugal tomb. Inside the tomb, food, gold, and other personal belongings were placed with the body to accompany and serve the person in the afterlife. The ancient Egyptians did achieve a kind of immortality, because thousands of years later, we still know the names, and sometimes even the faces, of some of their nobles due to the sculptures, paintings, and, especially, the preserved bodies.

In nightmares, the mummy represents the dreamer's sense of mortality. The imagery may also be the personification of an idea or desire that should not be allowed to express itself.

Murder

Murder in a nightmare symbolizes aggression and repressed rage at the self or directed at others. If the dreamer is murdered, this can indicate everything from feelings of victimization and helplessness, to a major life transformation (in which the old self "dies"). Murderers and criminals in nightmares are often seen as representations of the unconscious, or "shadow self," of the dreamer.

Myclonic Jerks

Myclonic jerks are the sudden muscle spasms that have been observed in all mammals during the sleeping cycle. Sleep researchers have likened them to the reflexive actions we experience as hiccups. One hypothesis as to their cause is that the "jerk," or spasm, is part of an innate arousal mechanism acquired through evolution. The theory is that this mechanism allows the sleeper to awaken quickly in response to possible environmental threats, such as an attacker or a wild animal. Myclonic jerks are often concurrent with falling dreams, with the dreamer's muscles contracting and waking him just as he hits the ground.

Nail

A nail is a tool that holds or binds objects together, and it can indicate something that needs to be fixed or repaired. To "get nailed" in a dream means you got caught doing something, whereas "hitting the nail on the head" may indicate an accurate appraisal of the dream's symbolism or meaning.

Nakedness

Being naked in a dream suggests exposure of the inner self to others, being vulnerable to others, or feeling ashamed and afraid of being found out. Nakedness can also represent the desire for freedom or a lack of guile, and the rejection of the confinement of clothes can be a harking back to childhood and its lack of cares. Many people have experienced the dream of being naked and feeling ashamed in a public setting or in front of an audience. This can also indicate you're feeling unprepared for something. Nakedness and shame in dreams may also represent a time when the dreamer was taught that the body is something shameful and should be hidden.

Narcolepsy

Narcolepsy is a neurological disorder that causes people to involuntarily fall asleep due to their brain's inability to regulate sleeping and waking cycles. The dozing episodes may last from just a few seconds, to as long as an hour in more extreme episodes. Additionally, narcolepsy sufferers may experience vivid and sometimes unpleasant hallucinations as they either fall asleep or come out of sleep (see also *Hypnagogic Hallucinations* and *Hypnopopic Hallucinations*), which at times makes it difficult for them to differentiate between the dream world and the waking world. The cause of narcolepsy is unknown and there is currently no cure.

Native Americans

American Indian tribes vary in the meaning and importance they invest in sleep and dreaming. Dream theories are shaped by the various supernatural, religious, cultural, and mythological traditions of each tribe. In general, however, dreams are regarded as the most important experience in the individual's life and as one of the determining factors that will equip the individual to enter into the life of the tribe. In this, dreams have significance mostly for the individual, and only secondarily for the tribal community at large, and any dream's influence is judged as good or bad, favorable or unfavorable, pure or impure, partly as a result of its content and partly from its effects on the dreamer. For example, the Navajo, Kwakiutl, and Woodlands tribes usually interpret individual dreams within the context of their influence on the life of the individual. If the dream seems to indicate a violation of taboos, it will lead to purification and other rituals. If it indicates illness, it will lead to curing rituals.

The Yuma in the lower Colorado region make a clear distinction between the power-bestowing dream or dream vision, and the less significant dream of every-day life. For the Yuma, there is an inextricable link between reality and dream-ing. Dreams are considered the direct basis for, and emanation of, all religion, myth, tradition, and shamanic power, and are believed to have a deeper reality than waking. They believe that whatever happens in a dream has already hap-pened, or is about to happen, in waking life. While the Mohave also believe that dreams are the basis of all reality, good dreams are thought to indicate good luck, whereas bad dreams are thought to indicate bad luck. Also, they believe that shamans, or "medicine men," acquire their powers through dreams, dreams in which a tutelary spirit or ancestor visits the initiate, usually while he is sick or on the verge of death, and "calls" him to become a shaman (see also *Mohave*). According to the Kamia of Imperial Valley, dreams are best for young people, as an older dreamer might die because of his dreams. And, as in many traditional cultures, they believe that the knowledge of the destiny of human souls can be derived through dreams. For the Dakota, dreams are revelations from the spirit world, and prophetic dreams recount what the dreamer saw and knew in a former state of existence.

The Navajo of the Southwest believe that gods, dreams, and sickness are causally related. Dreams are often thought to be the cause of illness, and such dreams are referred to diagnosticians, who reveal the cause and prescribe a cure. Again, a dream is viewed as good or bad according to the effect of the dream, but certain dreams, such as death dreams, have fairly standardized interpretations. It is thought that good dreams come true once in a while, whereas bad dreams are always realized. In general, however, divine beings and the spirits of deceased people and animals are thought to be responsible for putting dreams, both good and bad, into people's heads.

Fasting has a close connection to the dreaming life of many Native American peoples. For example, the fasting of girls and the telling of their dreams to their parents is a tradition among the Menomini, the Central Algonkin, and among the Woodland Potawatomi, while among the Eastern Cree the fasting dream must never be repeated lest it give offense to the spirits. Fasting is also an important aspect of dreaming among the Kwakiutl Indians when they petition the help of the spirits. In response to these petitions, hunting dreams are always regarded as good dreams, while some dreams are thought to indicate auspicious conditions for fishing. Dreams of the dead are regarded as bad dreams and are thought to presage an epidemic illness in which many will die.

Due to the groundbreaking research of Ruth Benedict during the 1920s, the dreaming practices of the tribes of the central plains are probably the most well known of all the Native American tribes. She discovered that the Native Americans didn't make much distinction between visions and dreams, both of which they considered as signs of favor from the spiritual world. Dream reenactment provided an opportunity for the dreamer to demonstrate the particular power bestowed in the dream, and was necessary in order for the dream to be seen as sacred and, thus, accepted by the tribe.

In general, most Native American tribes generally thought that children were highly susceptible to the influences of evil spirits that were responsible for causing nightmares. In the Ottawa and the Ojibwa tribes, parents often encourage a child vision-seeker to keep dreaming until the dream is correct or good. The Chippewa were the first to use dream catchers to prevent the evil spirits from disturbing children during their sleep (see also *Dream Catchers*).

At the opposite end of the spectrum, certain tribes of the Southwest, such as the Navajos, held dreams in much lower esteem than their counterparts. The exact reason for this is unknown, although in the case of the Navajos it may have been an outgrowth of their complex healing rites, which did not normally allow for any innovation through dreams. Dreams typically played a part in the vocation of the dreamer, often determining what type of healer the dreamer was to become. The larger concerns of tradition, tribal knowledge, and a unity of culture were transmitted through the learning rites and songs of ceremonies, and not through dreaming practices.

Cultural anthropologist Dorothy Eggan collected Hopi dreams and studied them in an effort to discover how they affected the personal life of the dreamer. She found that dreams are not usually associated with any concrete religious practices, nor are they considered a prerequisite to participate in tribal ceremonies. The Hopis evaluate their dreams individually on a strictly good or bad basis; if necessary, they respond appropriately to counteract the effects of negative dreams. The Zunis evaluate their dreams in the same manner, and only share bad dreams on the communal level.

Natural Disasters

On October 21, 1966, a massive coal tip slid down the mountain and engulfed the Welsh mining village of Aberfan. This disaster killed 144 people, most of whom were schoolchildren. After the incident occurred, a national paper made an announcement asking for information pertaining to any precognitive experiences people may have had. The appeal resulted in 35 cases, 24 of which were reported to someone else before the disaster occurred or before the announcement appeared in the paper, and 25 cases specifically involved dreams. The most poignant of these was experienced by a young girl named Eryl Mai Jones. She tried to share her dreams with her mother on a regular basis, and her mother often dismissed them as pure fantasy. In this instance, however, she took the time to listen. Eryl Mai described the dream to her mother: "We go to school but there is no school there; something black has come down all over it," after which she asserted, "I'm not afraid to die, mommy. I'll be with Peter and Jane." Eryl Jones was among the 118 children buried alive in the tragedy.

Ian Stevenson conducted an investigation into the precognitive dreams concerning the sinking of the ocean liner *Titanic*. He collected information from 19 people who apparently had anticipated the sinking of the great ship, several of whom had received their visions in the form of dreams. One man, who was supposed to be on the ship when it sank, dreamt twice that he saw the ship floating, keel up, with people swimming all around it. These dreams were not enough to make him cancel his voyage, but "fate" intervened and he was obliged to cancel the trip for other personal reasons.

President Franklin Delano Roosevelt claimed to have experienced this type of precognitive natural disaster dream. On May 25, 1941, he dreamt that the

Japanese were bombing New York City while he was safe in his home in Hyde Park. The general opinion about this dream is that it indicated that the president knew, probably at some deep unconscious level, that the Japanese were capable of a direct assault on American soil, but that the country would be able to withstand the damage.

As it is with so many cases of "precognition," hindsight seemed to play a large part in the interpretation of this dream as prophetic. Such interpretations are usually retrospective by necessity, which naturally opens them to doubt and debate.

Nausea

Nausea indicates the body's rejection of something, whether it be food, a virus, poison, or some other factor. Feeling sick and ready to throw up in a dream may indicate you are actually ill and may need to wake up at any moment to sprint for the bathroom. To witness yourself or others purging in a dream may indicate a need to remove yourself from a sickening situation.

(See also *Vomit*)

Needle

In a nightmare, needles may indicate the dreamer is being "needled" by someone during waking hours. The pinching pain of a needle or multiple needles, while not deadly, may signify an annoyance in the dreamer's life. A threaded needle can indicate the reparation or closure of unfinished issues in your personal or business life.

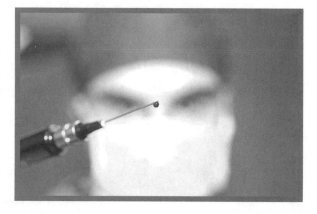

Neptune

Discovered in 1856, the planet Neptune is considered the planet of dreams. Neptune is the eighth planet from the sun, taking 165 Earth-years to complete one rotation around it. Named for the mythical ruler of the sea, Neptune is considered the planet of dreams because, like water, dreams distort and cloud images and meaning. Additionally, water represents the depths of the unconscious and our emotional selves in dream imagery—places that our dreams are said to take us.

Night

Dreaming about the inky darkness of night encroaching on us can indicate a lack of clarity, or it can symbolize more primal fears of the dark and all its attendant horrors. The dark is also symbolic of the repressed thoughts and urges that reside in the unconscious and that often frighten or discomfit us.

There may be a situation in the dreamer's life that needs clarity, or the dreamer may be doing "shadow work."

Night Terrors

Night terrors are the most dramatic of a set of phenomena referred to as *parasomnia*. They are similar to nightmares in many ways, but they are not nightmares in the technical sense. Sufferers of night terrors usually cannot recall what it was that awakened them, usually screaming in fear, from their sleep, although they will generally cite a sense of fear or oppression in a more general sense. If the dreamer remembers anything at all, it is usually only vague impressions, such as "I was being chased" or "Something was strangling me." More specific recall remains elusive. Night terrors occur during the third or fourth stages of the sleep cycle, usually within the first two hours after falling asleep. This is actually the non-REM stage of the sleep cycle, characterized by the existence of little or no

dream activity. Nightmares, however, occur exclusively during REM sleep, and it is this, along with a nightmare sufferer's ability to recall his or her dream, that differentiates nightmares from night terrors.

The exact cause of night terrors remains unknown. While they occur most often in young children, the phenomenon can be carried over into adulthood. It has been suggested that people who suffer from night terrors have some unique, unifying characteristics, such as high stress or arousal, an overall lack of sleep, or current abuse of drugs or alcohol, but this has not been proven conclusively. Studies of the biological responses of children and adults suffering from night terrors indicate that a nervous bodily reaction, in which heart and respiratory rates can double in a few seconds, occurs just before the dreamer awakens. The dreamer often experiences a lingering sense of disorientation for 10 to 20 minutes after awakening.

Night terrors do seem to have some biological basis. In 1899, the *British Medical Journal* published the results of a study of 30 people who suffered from night terrors. Seventeen of the 30 people studied experienced an early onset of heart disease. This seems to indicate some kind of correlation between the factors leading to heart disease and those predisposing people to night terrors. In the 1960s, a group of 23 children, all of whom suffered from night terrors, had their adenoids removed. The terrors stopped immediately for 22 of these children.

Studies of adults who suffer from this "arousal disorder" do not seem to share any predominate personality traits, but those intimately involved in the personal lives of some of those afflicted often describe them as being "tightly wound" or "type-A" individuals.

From *On Dreams*, here is Aristotle's take on night terrors:

> And indeed some very young persons, if it is dark, though looking with wide-open eyes, see multitudes of phantom figures moving before them, so that they often cover up their heads in terror.

Nightmare

The etymology of the word *nightmare* is a bit of an enigma. The word has its history in Old English as well as Indo-European roots. The *night* part of the word is obvious: the event mostly happens at night when people are sleeping. The word *night* is a Middle English word derived from the Old English *niht*, meaning the period between sundown and sunup, while *mare*, or *mære* in Old English, means a goblin or incubus. Another layer of meaning is added with the root word *mer*, meaning "to harm" or "to die." The word *nightmare* first appeared in language as early as 1290 C.E. Thus the etymology of the word *nightmare* has connotations of being harmed by demonic forces.

Nightmare Before Christmas, The

In 1993, Tim Burton released his Academy Award–nominated, stop-motion animated feature film, *Nightmare Before Christmas*. In the nightmarish world Burton creates within the movie, each of the major holidays has a land all its own, and once a year, during the appropriate holiday, that land has the opportunity to "do its thing" for the world. The movie's main character, Jack Skellington, is the pumpkin king of Halloween Town, where every day is filled with creeping and crawling ghouls and monsters that prepare and practice for the next Halloween—their one day to shine. But Jack is growing bored with the routine of scaring the pants off of folks every year, so he wanders into the woods and gets lost. When Jack stumbles upon Christmas Town, he becomes captivated by the bright and colorful lights, the pretty white snow, and the jolly man in the red suit ("Sandy Claws")—Jack wants his chance to run Christmas. The tale that follows is macabre, wacky, and touching—classic Tim Burton.

The exaggerated and dark scenery featured in *Nightmare Before Christmas* is as critical to the story as the characters are. Burton creates a land where every day is Halloween, and he draws on everything from folk tradition to horror in order to make his nightmare a reality.

Nightmare on Elm Street, A

Wes Craven is one of the acknowledged masters of modern horror films. In 1984, Craven introduced the world to the character of Freddy Krueger—a severely burned man wearing a brown hat, red-and-green-striped sweater, and a glove on his right hand, with long razors for fingers. The back-story of Freddy Krueger indicates that he was once a child murderer on Elm Street, who met his end at the hands of a lynch mob. But Freddy was bound to return. At the time of this writing there have been seven films in the *Nightmare on Elm Street* series, and an eighth film if you include *Freddy vs. Jason*—a 2003 movie release that pitted the popular *Elm Street* and *Friday the 13th* movie monsters in a face-off.

One of the biggest downfalls to traditional horror movies is that they are set in a specific location, such as a possessed house. Though these movies may offer a good scare, the audience members have to ask themselves at one point in the movie, *Why don't you just leave the house? A Nightmare on Elm Street* and Freddy Krueger are so effective because Freddy only attacks in his victims' nightmares. There is no place to hide, and you can't stay awake forever. His teenage victims first meet Freddy in a mild nightmare. But each dream becomes progressively more horrific, to the point that the kids are afraid to go to sleep. The teens of Elm Street quickly discover that if Freddy kills them in their dreams, they will also die in life. The only way to stop Freddy is to confront him, which is true for so many of our own nightmares.

Nuclear Explosion

A nuclear blast is an event that will destroy everything in its wake, and, once deployed, a nuclear bomb will start a war that no one will win. Like any explosion in a dream, the blast of an atom bomb in a nightmare probably represents the dreamer's extreme anger or rage. This is likely a big problem that threatens to do a lot of damage. However, because this is an act of war, the issue/frustration may be with something that is out of the dreamer's control.

(See also *Apocalypse*)

Numbness

Being unable to feel or move the body in a dream or nightmare indicates that the dreamer is in a state of REM (rapid eye movement) sleep, in which the body is temporarily paralyzed. Also, the blood supply to a limb may be cut off, resulting in the "pins and needles" and numbness that eventually wakes us and tells us to change position. As in amputation dreams, a numb body part may indicate a neglect, loss, or lack of faith in the talent or ability reflected by that limb. For example, a "has-been" jazz pianist may dream of numbness or immobility of the hands, whereas an accomplished but insecure ballet dancer may dream of numbness of the feet.

Obesity

The popular psychological interpretation of obesity is lack of self-esteem and over-indulgence. To dream of being obese signifies layers of protection that insulate the dreamer, a helplessness to wield power and authority, and a fear that rejection will be the only reward for one's efforts.

Ocean

Water, an ocean in particular, often signifies the deep wells of emotions and desires residing in the mysterious depth of the unconscious. If you're floating in the ocean in a small boat, lost and directionless, you may be feeling

isolated and bereft of resources. If the ocean waters are rough and you're feeling anxious, it may represent a fear of being out of control.

(See also *Sinking Ship*)

Ogre

An ogre in a dream may symbolize authority issues relating to business (insert reference to your boss here) or personal life. Alternatively, it may represent being an "ogre" to oneself, particularly through constant self-criticism.

Old Hag Syndrome

According to some estimates, Old Hag Syndrome is a frightening event that has occurred to as many as 40 percent of all people. In the most extreme examples, an Old Hag Syndrome "attack" involves a sleeper who, upon waking, immediately recognizes his surroundings but is unable to move. Some people report seeing a dark mass, sometimes a human-like figure, moving toward or over them and finally coming to rest on top of them. Panic, fear of a ghost, and fear of death all run through the person's mind—the heart races, the chest feels heavy, and breathing is labored. Within a few seconds, sometimes as long as a minute (though the seconds may seem like hours to the panicked "victim"), the dark cloud or figure dissipates and the dreamer once again regains his powers of mobility.

The scientific community's explanation for this event is that it is a kind of sleep paralysis (see also *Sleep Paralysis*), combined with a very vivid hypnagogic or hypnopopic hallucination (see also *Hypnagogic Hallucinations* and *Hypnopopic Hallucinations*). The folkloric, and perhaps more poetic, explanation is that this episode is caused by witchcraft—thus the name "Old Hag," who was coming to get you in your sleep.

In 1971, folklore researcher David Hufford collected accounts in Newfoundland of people who had suffered Old Hag episodes. Hufford documented his findings in his book, *The Terror That Comes in the Night* (University of Pennsylvania Press, 1982). Hufford eventually found that people all over North America have experienced some version of the Old Hag experience, even if they didn't name it as such. Apparently this phenomenon happens worldwide as well—for example, in Laos in southeast Asia, the Hmong people cite a phenomenon called *tsog tsuam*, which is essentially the same phenomena as Old Hag Syndrome. The Hmong believe that a monster from underground sometimes tries to suffocate them in their sleep. Ritual offerings to Hmong ancestors enable the spirits of the ancestors to keep the monster at bay. If a family becomes lazy or too casual in their offerings, the monster may get through and attack. In the mid- to late-1970s, when many Hmong were displaced after the Vietnam War, there were several cases of otherwise healthy men dying in their sleep for no known reason. The medical community dubbed the phenomena sudden unexplained nocturnal death syndrome (SUNDS). One theory suggests that the displaced Hmong, living in the strange environment of the city or some other place far from home, ceased making these offerings to their ancestors in an effort to blend in with their new cultural surroundings. The *tsog tsuam* may then have loomed unstoppable in their dreams, and the fear of the event was fatal to some.

In his book *Monsters* (Llewellyn Publications, 2002), John Michael Greer wrote of the experience: "There is another potential explanation for the Old Hag phenomenon, of course—one that neatly and efficiently accounts for the entire range of details reported by people who have experienced an attack by the Hag, or by her many equivalents in other cultures. This is the hypothesis that the Old Hag experience is, in fact, exactly what is seems to be: a visitation by a hostile spirit."

Ultimately, it is the victims who decide whether the experience is simply a synapse misfire in their brains or an actual spectral attack. Regardless of the cause, the phenomenon happens to millions of people, and it remains a terrifying experience. Medical professionals who study sleep paralysis and the hallucinations that occasionally accompany these events say that people who frequently experience the Old Hag phenomena might have a sleep disorder and should seek medical help.

Ononharoia

The Ononharoia was a midwinter ceremony and festival among the five nations of the Iroquois tribes, and it literally means "turning the brain upside down." The first Europeans to make contact with these tribes observed that every February, the Iroquois celebrated this Ononharoia, which involved dancing, curing illness, and interpreting dreams. Their dreams, in turn, usually concerned a feast, a song, a dance, or a game. The Iroquois view of the afterlife included the belief that every individual had many souls, each with a distinct function. The hidden desires of the soul could be revealed through these dreams or visions, or sometimes by a shaman who would stare into fire or water for some time and work himself into a frenzy. These soul desires would typically be a longing for an object, a ritual, or for some action outside of their social norms and mores. Often these rituals had sexual overtones, some of which were so shocking to the Europeans (and especially the Jesuit missionaries) that they were hesitant to mention them in their reports.

Operation

A medical procedure or surgery being per-formed on the dreamer may signify old issues being "cut out" or patched up. If the dreamer is doing the operating, then deep unconscious issues are being faced and excavated. There may also be nega-tive past experiences with medical opera-tions that are finding expression in nightmares.

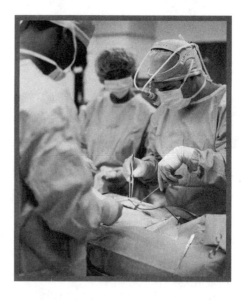

Orgy

A dream about an orgy suggests repressed desires, particularly desires for ex-pression of one's sexuality and passion. This can be a nightmare if the dreamer is afraid of his desires and/or feels guilty or dirty for having them.

Orphan

The orphan is a metaphor for the part of us that needs love, shelter, and all of the other creature comforts many of us take for granted. Dreaming about orphans or about being an orphan may represent childhood memories and fears of being abandoned. The dreamer may also be resisting inner urges to be childlike.

Orwell, George

Eric Arthur Blair (1903–1950), better known by his nom de plume, "George Orwell," was a British author who wrote satirical pieces about totalitarianism and the problems he saw with imperialistic governments with too much power. Orwell lived through both World Wars in Europe; consequently, it can be argued that most of his short life was surrounded by battles.

Orwell rose to critical acclaim during the second half of the 1940s with two novels. In 1945, Orwell penned *Animal Farm*, a satirical look at the Russian Revolution in the context of a farm. In the novel, the pigs on the farm lead a revolt against their human masters and establish a new regime, which ultimately becomes corruptible and fails. In 1949, Orwell wrote his masterpiece, *Nineteen Eighty-Four*.

Nineteen Eighty-Four is Orwell's nightmare vision of what the future will be like. In 1984, the world is divided into three countries: Oceania, Eurasia, and Eastasia. Totalitarian governments rule all three countries, and, at the very top, "Big Brother" watches everything. Big Brother censors the news, people's behaviors, and people's inner lives and thoughts. Even romantic relationships are forbidden. Posters proclaiming, "Big Brother Is Watching You," are everywhere, and omnipresent television screens that cannot be turned off are constantly "educating" the citizens. The novel's main character, Winston Smith, becomes revolted by his existence in a place where the government's "Ministry of Truth" tells its citizens, "War Is Peace, Freedom Is Slavery, and Ignorance Is Strength."

In the first chapter, Winston's emancipation begins as he discovers he can channel his anger at anyone he feels like, not just the people he is told to hate. Winston and the people around him are experiencing "Two Minutes of Hate"— a daily video program that encourages and teaches citizens to despise enemies of the state and adore Big Brother, who protects them. Around him, attractive men and women watch and jeer the enemy on the screen. Orwell acknowledges the horrific dreamlike state of the world he has created by having the imagery of the main character's "waking" moment be that of a nightmare:

> Suddenly, by the sort of violent effort with which one wrenches one's head away from the pillow in a nightmare, Winston succeeded in transferring his hatred from the face on the screen to the dark-haired girl behind him. Vivid, beautiful hallucinations flashed through his mind.

Orwell's nightmare is a land where no one thinks for themself, where people only do as they're told, hate who they are supposed to hate, and never question anything—a nightmare the protagonist cannot wake from, and a nightmare the reader hopes to never have.

Ouija Boards

Talking boards (or Ouija boards, which is the brandname they're more commonly known by today) were an invention of the Spiritualist movement that began in 1848 in Hydesville, New York. The Ouija board is a piece of wood or cardboard with the alphabet spelled out across it, along with words such as "yes," "no," and "goodbye," and the numerals zero through nine. The board users place their hands on a small, table-like device called a "planchette" that rests on the board. The users ask a question, and the planchette begins to move around the board, spelling out words, sentences, and sometimes entire messages. Whether those messages are from the spirit realm or the user's unconscious can be debated. But the device does seem to have the ability to spell out specific communications. Some occult-minded dreamers may witness the Ouija board spell out a message within their dreams. In this context, the message is usually taken at face value, though the dreamer should determine exactly whom or what that message is coming from before taking any action.

Thanks to movies such as *The Exorcist* (1973) and *Witchboard* (1987), the Ouija board has gained a dark reputation as a portal that can allow negative spirits into the bodies of unsuspecting users.

Overeating

To be caught in a grotesque binge is a sign of starvation for nourishment. The nourishment in the dream is represented by the food, but the real nourishment may be an emotional or physical need that isn't being met. The dream can also indicate issues with food, such as an eating disorder. If the object of the rage in the nightmare is the food, you might want to look at your own eating habits. People who are starving tend to have extremely vivid dreams about food.

Ovid

Ovid was a postclassical poet of the early Roman Empire. He was well known for his ability to meld the reality of the waking world with the dreamlike, and often nightmarish, elements in his prose and poetry. Scholars refer to Ovid as being

either the last of the poets of the golden age, or the first of the poets of the silver age. When he was banished to Tomis in 11 C.E., he penned a letter in which he described an agony that refused to leave him, even while asleep—the terrible, suppressed desires and impulses that found expression in his nightmares.

In his great work, *Metamorphoses*, he devotes a section to the description of the "Dream of Erysichthon." This nightmare recounts how Erysichthon was cursed to starve no matter what he eats, which causes him to devour the entire world and finally rend his own flesh.

Pain

Experiencing pain in one's dream may be a reflection of real pain that exists somewhere in the dreamer's body. Alternatively, the dreamer may consider someone or something to be a "pain." The suppression of painful memories may also be an issue.

Paper

In an office environment, paper plays a significant role in our working lives. Memos, manuscripts, proposals, news items, and reports all cross the corporate desk and land in the in-bin or other paper piles. Because of paper's heavy influence in our working lives, these stacks have also made it into our nightmares. To dream of falling paper indicates a feeling of being inundated at work—a sense that you're not able to keep up with the demands of your job. It may be time to either start working weekends or delegate.

Paralysis

Feeling "rooted to the spot" in a nightmare—powerless to escape or fend off harm—is a common theme. Being unable to move in a nightmare may indicate feelings of helplessness or lack of control during waking life. Alternatively, perhaps the dreamer needs to "freeze" and do nothing about some issue for a while.

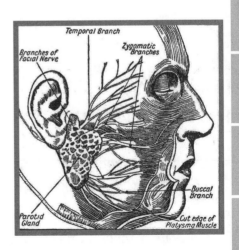

(See also *Numbness* and *Sleep Paralysis*)

Path

A quiet, spiritual walk down an unobstructed, open path signifies clarity of thought and peace of mind. A blocked, twisted, or dangerous path, however, may mean that the dreamer's life direction or choice of vocation needs to be reevaluated. In a nightmare, you may find yourself attacked or waylaid while walking down a path, which is another indication that you may be following a dangerous course.

Perlz, Fritz

Frederick S. "Fritz" Perlz (1883–1970) was the founder of the Gestalt school of psychotherapy. Perlz originally received his psychoanalytical training in the Freudian school in Germany before leaving the country when the Nazi party came to power in the 1930s. While in South Africa, he spent an extensive period studying the Gestalt approach to cognitive theory. His observations on the benefits of group therapy prompted him to develop an intensive method of treatment that was an amalgam of Freudian psychoanalysis, existentialism, and Gestalt psychology. *Gestalt* is the German word for "whole," "pattern," or "relationship." (See also *Gestalt*)

Perlz's method, based in part on the humanistic psychology movement initiated by Abraham Maslow and Carl Rogers, has become quite popular. It focuses primarily on promoting a healthy psychological state through the experience of creative or healthy thinking. Perlz implemented his approach in therapy groups he initiated during the mid-1960s at the Esalen Institute in California. It was his belief that dreams represented the rejected or neglected parts of the psyche—analyzing dreams and, thus, discovering the missing pieces of the psyche would enable the healing process to begin. As an outgrowth of his theory that all elements of a dream reflect some hidden aspect of the dreamer, Perlz maintained that one could receive "an existential message...of yourself, from yourself." This approach to dreaming was radically different from that used by Freud, but was closer in theory to the "subjective" technique developed and practiced by Jung.

In Perlz's group therapy dream workshops, the dreamer was given the opportunity to re-experience the dream (and thus achieve greater self-knowledge) while under the watchful guidance of a professional dream analyst. Perlz insisted that the dreamers describe their dreams in the present tense, similar to the convention of literary criticism, in which all works exist always in the present. He also gave dreamers the opportunity to assume the "role" of each element present in their dream. The role-playing techniques he pioneered involve the dreamer acting out dream scenarios. Perlz admitted that the process of role-playing was often difficult and trying, but he maintained his belief that, over time, the dreamer would be able to gain valuable self-knowledge and self-integration.

Pirates

Though pirates have long been romanticized in books, movies, and songs, the pirates of real life (either from centuries past or even in some parts of the world

today) were and are a real threat. Pirates are deceitful: they lure other ships in close and then strike without warning, leaving the victimized boat possibly without fuel, food, or crew, and thus available to be commandeered. To dream of pirates may mean that there are some outwardly friendly people in the dreamer's life who may have hostile ulterior motives. The dreamer may be feeling used or about to be used for the gain of others.

Pit

Pits are traditional symbols of hell, death, the afterworld, and the unconscious. A dream about being in a pit may indicate a feeling of hopelessness or despair. Pits can also symbolize "shadow work," in which the dreamer is discovering or tapping into the less-known, darker aspects of the psyche.

Plants

"Feed me!" the man-eating plant affectionately named Audrey II repeatedly cries in the 1960 musical film *Little Shop of Horrors*. The film was later remade into a stage musical, and then into another film in 1986. Audrey's insatiable appetite for blood was the theme of this wacky horror movie. But plants don't necessarily have to be man-eaters or even meat-eaters such as the Venus flytrap in order to invade our nightmares. Extensions of plants and vines may slither snakelike in our dreams, surrounding and smothering us.

Flowers and vines can grow at noticeable rates in only a day. To dream of plants that grow at an alarming and/or threatening rate indicate rapid changes happening in the dreamer's life that may be overwhelming. But these changes may result in emotional or spiritual growth in the end.

To dream of plants that turn into a monster such as Audrey II may mean you feel that your close family is placing too many demands on you to the point that you're losing yourself and being swallowed up.

Poison

Poison is something potentially deadly that enters the body covertly. Once inside, the body reacts, sometimes violently, in an effort to expel the foreign substance. Poison in a dream may represent an attempt to get rid of something within oneself. A violent rejection of a condition or a relationship may be causing the dreamer to suffer.

Police

Police officers are the authority figures that enforce the rules in life. Dreaming about police can indicate apprehension over failure to perform or to honor obligations and commitments. It can also be a warning to avoid reckless behavior.

Possession

Demonic possession has been blamed for everything from bad behavior in young children to full-blown madness. Traditionally, the appropriate "therapy" was some form of exorcism, intended to free the individual of the intruding, opressive entity.

In later times, some believed that real creativity depended on a state of possession or "divine insanity," which gave access to the subconscious in a liminal state. When a person is able to enter a liminal state, it potentially gives them free access to their creative faculties. These are usually highly charismatic people with thin barriers between their conscious and unconscious minds.

PTSD and a Little Girl's Screams

In March of 2000, 35-year-old Mark B. was serving in the medical branch of the Canadian Army, and was stationed in the war-torn country of Kosovo. He and his unit were helping with the post-war efforts in the region. Mark B. now lives in Barrie, Ontario. For some, nightmare imagery is simply a metaphor for other emotions, feelings, and objects within their lives. For those who suffer from post-traumatic stress disorder, nightmares are a reply to one of the most (if not *the* most) horrific events in the dreamer's life.

The Nightmare:

> *I am in a medical station in a war-torn country. I am worn out, tired, and hungry. The door flies open, and a little girl about 5 years old is carried in in the arms of her mother. She has second- and third-degree burns to her face and arms from an explosion. She is screaming in pain; her mother is in tears The trauma team is standing there looking at me for leadership, and all I can think about is my own daughter at home, and I am frozen, unable to move. I wake up in tears, with the sounds of the screams still going through my head.*
>
> *Nightmares that are symbolic I can live with, and get over them, but for any who have nightmares based on real events, you know how hard it is to shake them.*

Mark later described the actual event that led to this recurring nightmare. "The story that was given to us by the family is that the little girl was lighting the family stove, and there was an explosion," he said. "The stove was fueled with some type of gas, and apparently the gas had built up before the little girl could light the match. We were shocked to hear that a 5-year-old girl would be responsible for lighting the family stove; however, it was post-war, and their culture is different from ours. She received second- and third-degree burns to her face and hands.

"The family had received a humanitarian assistance package, and in the package was a tube of some type of cream that they couldn't read, as it was in English. They assumed it would soothe the burns, so they caked it onto the burnt areas thickly. It was a tube of toothpaste. Before we could even begin to treat the wounds, we had to clean the toothpaste out of them. You can imagine the screaming that accompanied it. We did administer some type of pain medication; however, it took awhile to take effect."

Soon after treating the girl, Mark had this same nightmare almost nightly. "In fact, whenever I closed my eyes, I would see her face," he said. "It got to the point where I would stay awake as long as I could until I was so exhausted I had no choice but to sleep. When it [the frequency of the nightmare] was at its worst, I was getting a couple of hours of restless sleep a night.

"When the incident first happened, I had a hard time dealing with it. However, I managed to push it aside and move on with my life. Three years later, there was a young soldier that I was training who received burns to his face from a flash fire—that incident triggered the PTSD."

Mark still has this nightmare, though not as often as he used to. He said he has the dream about once or twice per week now, and is even taking medication to help reduce the chances of nightmares. He has also learned to focus on the positive aspects of his life when he goes to bed. "This stops the images; however, the nightmare still comes back," he said. "According to my doctor, I may have this for the rest of my life. I just need to learn how to cope with it."

He doesn't know if the little girl from Kosovo actually survived, but he likes to think she did. After Mark and his team treated her, the girl was transferred to the local University Hospital, but, because of the war, the hospital was limited in equipment and trained personnel, so Mark fears her chance of infection was high.

Mark asked that we not use his real name when publishing his nightmare and details of his experience because of the stigma that PTSD carries in the military. When asked more about the stigma, he said, "The stigma that comes with PTSD is one of weakness. The problem is that it is a real injury; however, you can't see it—it's an injury of the brain. If somebody loses an arm or a leg, people understand—you can see the injury. But people don't understand what they can't see. Military personnel are trained to be tough—you have to be in order to do the job you do. They are also taught to work as a team. When one member of a team goes down, the rest of the team has to work harder to cover for him. When you can't do your job as part of the team, you are isolated. The 'team' can't wait for you to get better; they still have to do the same job.

One of the worst responses I have heard is somebody saying, 'I was there and saw what he saw, and I don't have any problems.' As I said, it is an unseen wound, and, until you are actually suffering from it, you don't understand. For somebody who hasn't had it, he wonders why the person can't just shake it off, push it aside, and carry on with life. Our military has come a long way. We have social workers, psychiatrists, and mental health nurses who deal with this. We also have a peer network where you can call and talk to somebody else who is dealing with the same injury—somebody who understands."

The Analysis:

There isn't much to analyze with a PTSD dream. The nightmare imagery is a literal representation of a real-life event, and usually indicates an issue with which that person must deal. The person who suffered through the traumatic event must learn to cope with the events that transpired.

The good news about Mark is that he is getting help. He said, "I am seeing a psychiatrist and a social worker who have helped me rebuild my coping skills. My coworkers and superiors have also been extremely patient and understanding with me, trying to help me. This is probably because I work with medical people, and they know and understand what this is all about. I have come a long way, but I have a long way to go still."

■   ■   ■

Post-Traumatic Stress Disorder (PTSD)

When we have a nightmare, we can wake up and tell ourselves, "It was only a dream." We believe it, and start to calm down. We instill this idea in our children when they awake from frightening dreams. But what if your nightmare is a replay of an actual and gruesome event in your life? It's not just a dream in this case; it's torture being forced to relive your worst moments over again.

Post-traumatic stress disorder is associated with a set of characteristic symptoms, including nightmares and flashbacks to the traumatic event or events, signs of "psychic numbing," a sense of general detachment, and reduced emotional responsiveness. PTSD sufferers avoid situations or feelings that they associate with the precipitating trauma or traumas.

Repetitive nightmares depicting the traumatic event as it occurred, with very little variance of the details, is the earliest sign of PTSD. For example, someone who was in or near the Twin Towers on September 11, 2001, might experience frightening replays of the experience in dreams involving terrorists, airplane crashes, collapsing buildings, fires, people jumping from buildings, and so on. A rape survivor might experience disturbing dreams about the rape itself or some aspect of the experience that was particularly frightening. These dreams can be also accompanied by "survivor guilt," in which the dreamer takes the place of those who were killed.

After awhile the situation may become chronic, and the dream process becomes "stuck," with no progress or useful connections made between dream content and the healing process. Because of the extremely painful nature of these dreams, the dreamer may "wall off" the part of himself that feels, and any attempt at engagement—let alone treatment—is often resisted. It is more common for survivors to compartmentalize the traumatic event rather than deal with it. The protective boundaries that make it possible for the survivor to continue on make it difficult, if not impossible, to have relationships or deal with any emotions in general.

Alcohol abuse is a common means of numbing the pain associated with this disorder. This may decrease the severity and the number of frightening nightmares commonly experienced in PTSD, but may also promote the cycle of avoidance.

When Dreams Come True

In 1995, Cathy J. was a 32-year-old mom living in Naugatuck, Connecticut. She had been dating the same man since 1989. During the summer of 1995, Cathy started having a recurring nightmare.

The Nightmare:

> *I kept having this dream that my boyfriend was cheating on me. Little by little, the dreams got more clear, to the point where I could actually see the other woman in my dreams,*

as well as where she lived and so on. One time, I even witnessed myself in a dream going out to find my boyfriend and this woman together: in the dream, I saw myself in my car on the highway hitting the cement divider in the middle of the road.

About six months later, I had to act on this dream. I left for work early, and would you believe that I hit black ice on the road, which spun my car out of control? I hit the barrier five times as I kept spinning around and around. My car was totaled, and I ended up having to have an operation on my shoulder. I also suffered a number of bruises all over my body. The entire accident was just like in my dream!

Once I recovered from this, I continued to have the dream of my boyfriend and this woman—it was so real. I even recognized where she was and the places they went together— I pictured them in his car together, going to bars, seeing movies, and things like that. It was so real it felt like I was actually there. I was almost thinking it was astral projection and it was myself looking down at them. During one of the more vivid dreams, I saw her and him together in her apartment. I actually saw her address number and street— even what floor she lived on in the apartment building. In the dream, I saw them looking out the window together.

One night I got a babysitter and went to this place that I saw in my dreams and found my boyfriend there with the girl from my dream—it was a woman I worked with. I was so angry I took his car, and let's just say he had to sell it because I messed it up that bad.

Cathy claimed she didn't suspect her boyfriend was cheating on her during the time she continued to have the dreams. She said, at the time, her boyfriend was taking care of her and her kids.

The Analysis:

Cathy believes her dream was a premonition of something she wasn't conscious of. Clearly the dream requires no interpretation, as it was a literal foretelling of events that came to pass. Cathy experienced the car accident and later found out her boyfriend was in fact seeing this other woman. The dream did allow her to resolve her issue in a definitive way. How she was able to see who the actual woman was remains a mystery.

■　　■　　■

Precognitive Dreams

Precognitive dreams are a special case of extra-sensory perception. In a precognitive dream, the dreamer experiences an event, in whole or in part, before it occurs. Some experiences of déjà-vu (the uncanny sense of familiarity with an unknown place, as if one has been there before) may arise from the same source as precognitive dreams.

In response to a general appeal to the public through various forms of media, Dr. Louisa Rhine was able to compile accounts of more than 7,000 paranormal dreams. In 433 of these dreams, a negative outcome could have been avoided if the dreamer had taken the appropriate steps, but only 30 percent of the dreamers had actually heeded their dreams. In 50 percent of the dreams, the theme of death occurred most often, along with accidents and injuries, respectively. The precognitive dreams were usually particularly vivid and intense, with a tenacious emotional quality that often remained with the dreamer even after he wakened. They also depicted the people or events involved with an amazing accuracy, an accuracy not normally present in regular dreams.

David Ryback, a clinical psychologist in Atlanta, Georgia, administered a questionnaire to undergraduates, asking them to provide written accounts of dreams that they felt predicted the future. "Paranormal" dreams were experienced by 67 percent of the questioned students, and several of the dreams contained details about events that actually were realized. Ryback attempted to verify the content of these dreams by interviewing the dreamer and then contacting others who could corroborate the fulfillment of the dream. Through his studies, he was able to establish that roughly 8 percent of the dreams he studied could be considered truly paranormal; this research is reviewed in depth in his book *Dreams That Come True* (HarperCollins, 1989).

Premonition of a Sick Child

Linda P. is a 66-year-old registered nurse living in Hibbing, Minnesota. She's been a nurse her entire adult life, so it is not surprising that she has had a dream or two that involves medical issues. But she had one medical dream that was so vivid, she hasn't forgotten the details of it almost 40 years after the nightmare. Linda had this dream during the mid-1960s.

The Nightmare:

> My son, Brian, was 16 months old at the time— he was a toddler. You know how sometimes you have a dream because something bad happens during the day that brings it on? Well, I had a really pleasant day that day. Nothing was wrong at all. During that night, I had a dream about a small child about Brian's age, but his face was blank—the boy had no eyes, mouth, nose, or anything. This boy was lying on a small bed, on white sheets, and everything in the room was plain and white. But in the corner of the room was a huge, oversize outdoor thermometer that went from the floor to the ceiling. I could see that the red line on it went to 105 degrees, and in my mind I knew this child was dying. I woke up and it was so real to me that I had to go check on Brian. I went into his room, but he was fine.
>
> It bothered me so much that I called my cousin, Mary Ann, who has a son named Tony about the same age as my Brian. I figured if it wasn't Brian, then it must have been someone else close to me. I said to Mary Ann, "I know this sounds crazy..." and I told her about the dream. I told her if Tony gets the slightest fever to call the doctor right away.
>
> All through the following day, I kept checking on Brian. In the middle of the afternoon, I went into the living room and found him lying in the middle of the floor. I felt his head and he was burning up. I rushed him to the hospital and found he had a fever of 105. The doctors ran some tests and determined he had a wild strain of scarlet fever. They said he probably wouldn't live through the night because his body wasn't responding to the penicillin and his fever wasn't going down. Finally they gave Brian other drugs and the fever started to come down. He was in the hospital for a week after that—his toenails and fingernails fell out, all of his hair fell out, and he had to learn to walk again after he came home.

When asked if Linda thought she would have reacted to Brian's fever the way she did had she not had the dream, she said, "I wouldn't have been checking on him as often as I did. I checked him many times during that day and I might have kept him at home and figured it was just a high fever had I not had the dream. I remember waking up after that dream, and I just knew in my mind that this was something that was actually going to happen. I'll never forget that dream as long as I live."

The Analysis:

> Clearly, this nightmare has affected Linda to the point where she can still recall the details decades later. The events of the following day proved to her that her dream was actually a premonition. Carl Jung would likely agree. Fortunately, her health guard was at its highest, and she didn't hesitate to get her son medical attention as soon as she discovered he was sick.

■   ■   ■

Pregnancy

The elevated levels of stress—both good and bad stress—that pregnant women experience may be responsible for a greater incidence of nightmares and anxiety dreams. Patricia Maybruck conducted a survey on the dreams of pregnant women, in which she collected 1,048 dreams. She found that 70 percent of these dreams were unpleasant, and of the original 70 percent of unpleasant dreams, 40 percent of those were actual nightmares. She found no direct correlation between the rate of occurrence of nightmares and the duration of labor in each woman. However, she did discover a correlation between labor duration and the way in which some of the women tended to assertively confront their fears in the nightmares. Of the women who experienced a relatively short labor of less than 10 hours, 94 percent were assertive in at least one nightmare. And 70 percent of the women who had long labors (more than 10 hours) were victimized in their nightmares.

Folklore and "old wives' tales" invest a precognitive aspect in pregnancy dreams and nightmares. Reality *seems* to bear this out: there have been numerous accounts of women who have reportedly dreamt of being pregnant to discover later that they actually were. Most of these reports have the benefit of hindsight, and as such they cannot be used for scientific or systematic investigation. These claims are suspect because they were not typically reported until after the foretold event took place.

Architecture seems to be a common symbol or theme in pregnancy dreams, as structures, buildings, or rooms may represent the body or womb of the pregnant woman. In the first trimester, pregnant women tend to dream of small animals— probably because these animals remind the woman of the fetus. Dreams of being unattractive or undesirable, and dreams of unresolved parenting issues and fears of inadequacy, are most frequent in the second trimester. The appearance of actual babies does not become regular until the woman enters the third trimester. Threatening dreams of robbers, intruders, fires, earthquakes, and the like also become more frequent in the third trimester. These may reflect the woman's fears concerning complications during labor, as well as the daunting task of parenting that follows. Themes of water and waterways are common as well, perhaps symbolic of amniotic fluid and birth canals, and themes of growing plants and gardens are common throughout the entire length of the pregnancy.

In general, pregnant women remember more of their dreams than other groups that have been studied. The extreme hormonal changes, irregular sleep patterns, and attendant anxieties and emotions may all be responsible for this. Pregnancy dreams are also often described as abnormally vivid.

Expectant fathers also experience pregnancy nightmares, although emotional stress is probably the sole cause. These nightmares often reflect the concerns that face an expectant father (for example, "Will I be displaced in the mother's affections?") specifically concerns about being able to emotionally and financially support his growing family, as well as about the health of both the mother and the child.

Prison

A prison may indicate that some part of the dreamer's personality or creativity is being stifled and needs to be released to allow for self-expression. Alternatively, the dreamer may need to "put a lock on" certain actions and behavior.

Public Humiliation

Public humiliation dreams range from the subtle to not-so-subtle, from walking around with one's fly open, to standing naked in the front of St. John's Cathedral during Easter Sunday service with the Pope presiding. The underlying message of humiliation nightmares is a concern of being ill-prepared, or somehow unacceptable or incompetent. To dream of being in a business meeting and not having your presentation ready, or standing to deliver a toast with nothing to say, all tap into natural fears concerning readiness or ability. By experiencing embarrassment or humiliation in dreams, the dreamer may be inspired to take extra care with any preparations for exams, presentations, interviews, and the like. Paradoxically, high achievers often have such dreams, perhaps because they invest much more importance in their performances than most people. Their identities are tied to their accomplishments; therefore, failure means they have much more to lose.

Public Speaking

For many people, there is no greater fear than speaking in public. To be in the spotlight with an audience listening to and scrutinizing every word is more than some people can bear. A nightmare about public speaking indicates a fear of being judged and found wanting. The "audience" may be your peers, bosses, or parents. In most cases involving public speaking dreams, the fear comes from lack of preparation. When you "know your stuff," there's often less to fear. (See also *Public Humiliation* and *Examinations*)

Punishment

Punishment in a dream usually reflects internalized guilt or shame over real or imagined transgressions. Even if the punishment is being inflicted upon someone else, say, a criminal, it may represent an aspect of the dreamer's psyche—most likely the "shadow self"—that the dreamer is uncomfortable with or ashamed of, and which needs controlling or sublimating.

Quake

Tumultuous movements or quaking in a dream may indicate inner turmoil and upset in the dreamer's life that needs to be addressed. The dreamer may be repressing anxiety and need to change some conditions in order to alleviate it. Such movements in a dream may also be a part of "shaking bed syndrome," in which the dreamer becomes convinced that his bed is shaking or undulating.

(See also *Earthquake*)

Quarrel

Fighting in a dream often suggests an inner conflict in the dreamer's psyche, perhaps over ideals and values. Alternatively, you may feel burdened or oppressed by a person in authority over you and wish to be able to voice your opinion.

Quiché

The Quiché Maya are located in 26 different communities across Guatemala in South America. For these people, ancestors hold a place of great importance: they are thought to visit the living in dreams—an experience that is most often described as positive. This experience is seen as positive even if the ancestor demands appeasement in the form of religious rituals or initiation into a religious group.

Human beings, or *winak*, are distinguished from other beings and creatures by their ability to speak articulately.

The concept of the soul, and the connection between death and dreaming, is an important aspect of the Quiché theory of dreaming. Depending on

their day of birth on the Mayan calendar, each person is said to possess one of 20 faces or destines, also called *life-souls*. The primary life-soul arrives at the moment of birth and takes up residence in the heart; if it leaves the body for any reason and for any length of time, the physical body will die. But it is the *free-soul*, and not the life-soul, that wanders during sleep—a conception that makes dreaming a less-threatening and anxiety-inducing experience for the Quiché. The dreamer's free-soul is thought to leave the body during sleep and wander through the world, meeting the free-souls of other people, and even animals. Gods or ancestors may also approach the sleeping dreamer's body and awaken his or her soul, at which point the dreamer vies with the visitors until they give him or her an important message. Therefore, the dream experience is generally described as a nightly struggle between the dreamer's free-soul and the free-souls of the deities and ancestors, who have important messages or predictions to convey concerning the future of the Quiché people. For this reason, the Quiché insist that it is necessary to report dreams in order for them to be of any benefit to their society. Dream sharing is an important aspect of daily life—all dreams, good and bad, are open to scrutiny and interpretation. Interestingly, the Quiché emphasize a conscious, volitional aspect to dreams and dreaming, as their verb for dreaming is transitive.

Quicksand

Solid ground, or *terra firma*, is something most people take for granted. We don't expect the ground to swallow us alive like a hungry monster. To dream of falling into quicksand means you're experiencing a loss of stability or predictability in your life. You may be feeling insecure in a relationship or work scenario, and you're being consumed by the problem.

Rabies

Rabid animals are known to growl and snarl, foam at the mouth, and stumble around in a seemingly drunken state as the neurological virus works its way deeper into the animal's brain. In its advanced stages, rabies is a lethal disease that can be spread through the infected animal's bite. Most common in dogs, cats, raccoons, and other small mammals, the disease turns the animal into a dangerous and deformed killer. Stephen King's 1981 novel *Cujo* (Viking Penguin) captured the horror of rabies as the book's four-legged main character, a Saint Bernard named Cujo, catches the sickness from a bat's bite and goes on a rampage.

To dream of a rabid animal stalking you displays fear of an issue that is both dangerous and unpredictable. Some outside force (represented by the rabies) is driving an otherwise benign creature to behave in ways beyond its control. This may speak of a person in the dreamer's life who is dealing with an addiction of some kind.

Rape

A dream about rape may symbolize a violent assault on the dreamer's physical environment or a devastating blow to the person's financial security. To dream of raping another person speaks of a desire to dominate and control by any means necessary. A rape dream may actually signify that the dreamer is feeling *dis*empowered, and as horrific or disturbing as the imagery is, it is a way for the unconscious to reassert agency.

Rapid Eye Movement (REM) Sleep

Nightmares occur almost exclusively during rapid eye movement (REM) sleep. Although REM sleep occurs on and off throughout the night, REM sleep periods become longer and dreaming tends to become more intense in the second half of the night. As a result, nightmares are more likely to occur during this time.

Rat

Rats are often associated with the decaying conditions of poverty or contagious illness. Also, to betray someone is to "rat" on them. Dreams of rats might also indicate a need to take some time out from the "rat race."

Raven

Ravens are traditionally seen as the harbingers of bad news, evil, or death. This black bird may indicate that the dreamer is thinking about, or pre-occupied with, death and dying.

"Raven, The"

Long before Stephen King and Dean Koontz there was the godfather of the thriller-mystery genre: Edgar Allen Poe. In 1845, Poe published one of the most frightening poems ever written: "The Raven." The poem speaks of lost love, and brought Poe fame in the United States.

The poem begins as the main character is stirred from his sleep:

> Once upon a midnight dreary, while I pondered,
> weak and weary,
> Over many a quaint and curious volume of forgotten lore,
> While I nodded, nearly napping, suddenly there came a tapping,

As of someone gently rapping, rapping at my chamber door.
"'Tis some visitor," I muttered, "tapping at my chamber door;
Only this, and nothing more."

(*www.literaturepage.com/read/poe-the-raven-1.html*)

As the stanzas proceed, further horrors come to the narrator, who is lamenting for his lost love, Lenore. No one is at his chamber door, yet the knocking continues. His imagination runs wild as he looks down the hallway:

Deep into the darkness peering, long I stood there,
wondering, fearing
Doubting, dreaming dreams no mortals
ever dared to dream before;
But the silence was unbroken, and the stillness gave no token,
And the only word there spoken was the whispered word,
"Lenore!"
This I whispered, and an echo murmured back the word,
"Lenore!"
Merely this, and nothing more.

In life, Edgar Allan Poe was a drug and alcohol abuser who grappled with depression, and even madness. When the narrator speaks of the "dreams no mortals ever dared to dream before," it's easy to imagine that the imagery in Poe's own head was likely even more terrifying than that of his own work.

Recurring Nightmares

Recurring nightmares are nightmares that are the exact, or virtually exact, replays of the same scenario or scenarios. For example, if someone dreams of falling off a bridge, and this dream occurs once a week, or once or twice a month, with precisely the same content and imagery, it is a recurring nightmare. If this person experiences other falling dreams that don't involve the same imagery, the dreams are still classified as recurring dreams or nightmares. Thus the classification is determined by the emotional tone and context of the dream, rather than the details it contains.

Recurring nightmares usually indicate that the dreamer is dealing with some unresolved issues that are "stuck" in the unconscious and making themselves known in the dreams. The issue may not be clear, and the simple repetition in the dream will probably not make the issue any clearer to the dreamer. In any event, it is not abnormal or even unusual to experience recurring dreams or nightmares. Nightmares resulting from traumatic events are often recurrent. Although the dream landscape may seem to have no similarities to the event itself, it is important that the latent content be examined. Often, as is the case with post-traumatic stress disorder, nightmares will continue until the individual seeks treatment and is able to integrate the traumatic experience into his or her waking life.

Remote Viewing

Remote viewing (RV) involves using psychic ability to gather visual information about a "target." The "target" is typically a place or a specific point in time. For example, a remote viewer may be able to look in the backyard of a house that may be thousands of miles away and identify the activities happening in that yard. There are several organizations that offer training in this field. The United States government conducted espionage experiments using remote viewers throughout the second half of the 20th century (see also *STARGATE*). Remote viewing organizations claim that this ability does not happen in an altered state. Indeed, viewers appear to be completely awake and cogent during the practice. This is in contrast to astral projection, a phenomenon that supposedly offers an unconscious, out-of-body experience.

(See *Astral Projection*)

Repression

In the psychological context, repression refers to the psyche's repression of undesirable thoughts, feelings, or urges into the unconscious. Different schools of depth psychology propose that there are, in fact, a few different types of repression. In Freudian analysis, repression is typically the subjugation of unacceptable urges of a sexual or aggressive nature. An example of such an urge is the desire to kill one's father—a desire that Freud viewed as common among men. On the other hand, Carl Jung taught that there is a much larger and more diverse range of things that our minds repress, including, but certainly not limited to, both sexual and aggressive urges.

The thoughts and desires that are repressed by the psyche do not disappear, however. They commonly reemerge and find expression in dreams and nightmares. Freud's view (which he modified in his later years) was that all dreams and nightmares are simply wish fulfillment, allowing us to satisfy, by proxy, the fantasies and instinctual urges we have repressed. The urge for parricide, for example, may be acted out in a dream of slaying an oppressive ogre or tyrant. Jung suggested that dreams fulfill a kind of balancing function, so that the repressed aspects of the psyche can reemerge and enrich the limited self we project in our daytime personas. For Freud, Jung, and other depth psychologists, dreams reveal what the patient is repressing, and part of the task of psychotherapeutic dream interpretation is to use the dream to discover what this is.

Revelation, Book of

Arguably the most powerful and vivid dream vision in the Bible is found in the last book, Revelation. The only book of prophecy in the New Testament, it supposedly represents the written account of a series of visions experienced by the prophet John, on the Isle of Patmos. After John's brother James was slain by Herod Agrippa, John left Palestine and traveled to Asia Minor in order to do missionary work. Under the reign of the Roman emperor Domitian, John was banished to the desolate isle of Patmos, off the coast of present-day Turkey, in the Aegean Sea. According to the text, this is where John was given this apocalyptic vision of the future that comprises the Book of Revelation.

Like all apocalyptic messages, the revelation is given to John through mysterious signs and symbols in a series of visions, which an angel then explains the meanings of. Much of the content of the revelation foretells the terrible events that are to unfold when Jesus returns to Earth in the last days. When the first vision begins, John appears to be in a trance-like state. Specifically, the author says that he was "in the Spirit" when he heard a loud voice. While the meaning of

this expression is open to interpretation, it appears to imply that John was in some sort of an altered state of consciousness.

In the Judeo-Christian scriptures, angels regularly relay divine messages to human beings, both in dreams and in waking visions. These communications are usually direct and explicit rather than indirect and symbolic, with the exception of certain dream messages. Thus it is not inconceivable that John's vision could have occurred in a dream. Certainly, the images are dreamlike and, in many places, even nightmarish.

"Revolution 9"

At eight minutes and 15 seconds, "Revolution 9" is the longest Beatles song from any of their albums. The song appears on the Beatles's 1968 classic *White Album*, and is an incoherent fusion of sounds and words. The "song" (if one can really call it that) is more like modern art through sound. "Revolution 9" is based on nightmare imagery John Lennon experienced while in India during the Beatles's transcendental meditation period. Lennon tried to turn that imagery into sound.

The tracks behind the voices are tape loops, and the "Number 9" that is repeated many times throughout the song is the voice of a sound engineer. The mood of the song creates a nightmarish landscape, with sounds rising and falling, backward tapes of other Beatles songs, and even violent sound effects. "Revolution 9" is more the representation of a mood than it is a song. John Lennon, Yoko Ono, and George Harrison are credited as the lead "vocals" in the song.

Robbery

Experiencing a break-in or theft can be very violating. Being robbed of valuables or money in a dream or nightmare may indicate that the dreamer is experiencing an identity crisis or a loss in his life (for example, a divorce or serious illness). The dreamer may also be feeling an intrusive influence in his life, such as a meddlesome relative or overbearing coworker.

Roller Coaster

A roller coaster may be exhilarating at the amusement park, but, in a dream, it shows that you are experiencing frequent and uncontrollable ups and downs, perhaps caused by erratic behavior on your part or on the part of someone you know. If fear is the dominant emotion in the dream, you may be feeling a loss of control or agency in your life, such as the helplessness brought about by life-changing and stressful events, such as divorce, death, or moving.

Rope

Being bound by rope signifies a loss of freedom and control. To be bound by rope in a dream may indicate that you are unable to express your emotions, thoughts, or desires in a situation. A hangman's noose shows that this stifling is clearly detrimental and will bring about an end—to a relationship, friendship, or work alliance.

Running/Runaway

Running away or escaping something shows the "flight" aspect of the fight-or-flight response in effect. Trying to escape something threatening or frightening is a common scenario in many night-mares. The dreamer may be experienc-ing undue stress or anxiety in his life—stress that is making him want to flee—or it may indicate that the dreamer is feeling helpless or vulner-able in a situation that is threatening to completely overwhelm him.

Sacrifice

A dream of human sacrifice may indicate that the dreamer feels "martyred" because of the time and energy he has invested in, and sacrificed for, others. The dreamer may need to rethink his codependency in order to allow for more productive and rewarding life experiences.

Saint Jerome

Jerome was a fourth-century Christian commissioned to translate the Bible into Latin by Pope Damasus I. His translation, known later as the Vulgate, was the authoritative Catholic version of the Bible for the next 1,500 years.

Due to careless or erroneous translations of certain key passages, Jerome helped to propagate a negative attitude toward dreams throughout Western Christendom.

As a young man, Jerome collected an extensive personal library of pagan literary works, even though he felt they conflicted with his Christian faith. This conflict found expression in a dream in which he was brought before the Throne of Judgment and told that he was a follower of Cicero rather than Christ. After being subjected to the punishment of whipping, Jerome pledged that he would never read such "worldly" books again. It is said that when he awakened, his back bore the marks of the lash, and he maintained that this was the proof of his nightmare's divine origin. Jerome's dream of divine judgment and punishment became the most famous dream recorded in Christian literature. (He later dreamed about his own death, as well as about having the supernatural power to fly.)

Even thought he obviously placed great stock in a dream's ability to convey divine messages, Jerome's errors in translation made the Bible appear to *discourage* attending to one's dreams. He mistranslated the Hebrew word for witchcraft, *anan*, as "observing dreams" (in Latin, *observo somnia*). *Anan* appears 10 times in the Hebrew Scriptures (the Old Testament), but he translates it as "observing dreams" only three times, in such statements as, "you shall not practice augury nor observe dreams," which more accurately reads, "you shall not practice augury or witchcraft." These small but crucial changes significantly altered the course of how dreams were viewed in Christendom for centuries.

Saint-Denys, Hervey de

The Frenchman Hervey de Saint-Denys (1822–1892) was a professor of ethnography, specializing in Chinese and Tartar-Manchu. His book, *Les Rêves et les Moyens de les Diriger*, was originally published in French in 1867. The English translation, *Dreams and How to Guide Them*, was not published until 1982 (Duckworth Publishing). Saint-Denys gained recognition as one of the founders of the technique known as lucid dreaming.

Saint-Denys first started to record his dreams at the age of 13. His dream journals are extensive, numbering 22 in total. In the journals, he reported 1,946 nights in which he recalled his dreams, and even included pictures of images he remembered from his nocturnal experiences. From his experience with lucid dreaming, he developed a series of mental exercises to increase his ability to achieve lucidity. Within the first six months of practicing these exercises, he was achieving lucidity two out of five nights on average, which increased to an average of three out of four nights of lucidity after a year. From these results he inferred that anyone seriously interested in lucid dreaming could achieve the same results with his exercises.

By applying this approach to nightmares, it is possible to change the imagery, and often even re-narrate an entire dream, thereby making it less frightening. When the dreamer develops the ability to control the dreaming process, the bizarre, unpleasant, and often frightening qualities can be replaced with more enjoyable images and scenarios. When dreamers are able to confront their fears and demonstrate power over nightmares, they decrease and sometimes stop altogether.

(See also *Lucid Dreaming*)

Sambia

The Sambia are a hunting and agrarian people living in the Eastern Highlands Province of Papua New Guinea. Many aspects of Sambia social interaction are characterized by a kind of watchfulness or suspiciousness—even paranoia—that they find necessary in order to anticipate hostile attacks from other tribes. This type of social paranoia inhabits and contextualizes dream experiences, as well as regulates their sharing and interpretation. In this, dreams are thought to convey explicit instructions to be followed in tribal rituals in order to head off these impending attacks. In general, the Sambia most often dream of feeling cheated or disgusted, being chased by malevolent people, being threatened with drowning, or seeing a raging fire.

As in many primitive cultures, dreams are thought to be the instances in which the soul and mind leave the body and visit various places. In this, the soul is seen as separate and distinct from the body, and the dreamer is not held responsible for the actions of his itinerant soul during sleep. The dreamworld is conceived of as a kind of parallel universe, in which dreams provide narratives of, and commentary on, actual events. The Sambia regard *all* dream images as having a supernatural origin because they communicate with the soul only and not with the body.

Dreams are most typically shared in the residence where a person sleeps, or in a healing ceremony in which *shamans* (the priests or mediators between the secular and the spiritual worlds) perform dream rituals. Dreams are also shared by elders and shamans in initiation rituals, in which dream interpretations and ritual secrets are taught. Dream sharing can be a public or private event, and can involve storytelling sessions; gossip and rumor exchanges; and stories told while on hunting, trading, or gardening trips.

As in any culture, factors such as age, gender, and social/ritual standing all affect the content of dreams and the way in which they are regarded. Men share their dreams more commonly and more readily than women do, and the elders share more than younger tribe members (an exception to this is children's nightmares, which are often considered threatening or foreboding enough to be shared). Only significant dreams are shared, and accounts of these dreams often become very stylized and self-conscious, occasionally becoming an important part of the tribe's shared cultural discourse and knowledge.

After a dream is shared, interpretation may reveal bad omens about future events. If a past dream is revisited, reinterpretation and hindsight sometimes indicate that it was in fact predictive. Dream interpretation is often almost a therapeutic venture, as the Sambia generally seek dream interpretation when they are beginning new or risky ventures, or when they are feeling troubled or anxious about their dreams in general.

Sandman

"A candy-colored clown they call the sandman / Tiptoes to my room every night / Just to sprinkle stardust and to whisper / Go to sleep, everything is all right," reads the first line of Roy Orbison's 1963 hit "In Dreams." Orbison wasn't the first or the last to incorporate the Sandman of folklore into a popular song. In 1954, The Chordettes had a number one hit with their song, "Mr. Sandman," its pop lyrics imploring the Sandman for an idealized image of love: "Mr. Sandman / bring me a dream / Make him the cutest that I've ever seen / Give him two lips like roses and clover / Then tell him that his lonesome nights are over." And Metallica's 1991 hit "Enter Sandman" was yet another song incorporating the dream-bringer (see also *"Enter Sandman"*).

The Sandman is the caretaker of the dreamworld of folkore, but he wasn't always portrayed as a sympathetic figure. In 1817, Ernst T.A. Hoffmann wrote the short story "The Sand-Man." In the story, an elderly woman who is an attendant of one of the younger children, describes the "Sand-man" to the oldest brother:

> He is a wicked man who comes to little children when they refuse to go to bed and throws handfuls of sand in their eyes till they bleed and pop out of their heads. Then he throws the eyes into a sack and takes them to the half-moon as food for his children, who sit in the nest and have crooked beaks like owls with which they pick up the eyes of human children who have been naughty.

(*Tales of E. T. A. Hoffman*, University of Chicago Press, 1969)

There was a tradition, especially in the Germanic region of Europe, to use children's "bedtime stories" as a way to frighten children into behaving better.

Over generations, the Sandman evolved into a clown-like figure that brought sleep to children by sprinkling dust over them in bed. Children were told the "grit" in the corners of their eyes in the morning was actually a little leftover sand from the Sandman.

Satan

Dreaming of Satan or some other demonic figure may symbolize evil, darkness, sin, oppression, sexuality, chaos, pride, ambition, or even creativity. The meaning of this figure in dreams can be highly stratified and nuanced, and variables such as the dreamer's religion and psychology should be taken into account before settling on an interpretation. Traditionally, dreams about a demon or angel indicate that the dreamer is actually being visited by that figure. In modern interpretation, however, the figure of Satan would likely be identified with the dreamer's unconscious or "shadow self."

(See also *Bible*, *Demons*, and *Evil*)

Saws

Saws are useful tools in construction, but they can often be dangerous. On occasion, saws have been utilized as mass-murder weapons (as in the 1974 film *Texas Chainsaw Massacre*). A nightmare involving the image of a homicidal, chainsaw-wielding maniac bent on murder may be an indication that you may be getting careless or

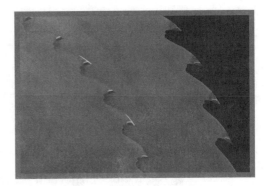

sloppy in your work. The potential for real injury warns of repercussions that may come from a lack of attention to detail. If someone else is carrying the saw in a threatening manner, the imagery may symbolize someone whose competitive nature may be turning hostile.

Schizophrenia

People with schizophrenia (literally meaning "split mind") often report hallucinations, and may express clearly delusional beliefs. Many otherwise healthy people who complain of recurring nightmares exhibit schizotypal personalities—that is, they show a tendency or predisposition for schizophrenia, or perhaps even have a "mild" case of it. Conversely, individuals who have been diagnosed as schizophrenics tend to report nightmares, especially during the onset of psychosis and before they start taking medication.

Scratching

The sound of scratching can be maddening when the source of the sound is completely unknown. This unknown can engender real fear: Is there an animal or some other type of vermin present? Or is the scratching from a larger, much scarier source? Like dreams of dripping or biting bugs, dreams involving scratching noises are usually trying to get the dreamer's attention while the issue is still small.

A dream in which the dreamer is literally being scratched signifies anxiety. The irritating sensation needs to be dealt with before the scratches turn to full-blown wounds.

Senoi

The Senoi are an Indonesian people related to the Highlanders of Indochina and Burma. They were all but wiped out during World War II by the Japanese. Today, the remnants live in the mountainous central area of mainland Malaysia. The Senoi are well known for their dream theory, as well as their dream control techniques.

According to the Senoi, the soul is divided into two distinct categories, one localized behind the center of the forehead (the *ruwaay*), and the other focused in the pupil of the eye. Dream experiences are simply the souls leaving the body when a person is asleep or in a trance, and the experiences these souls have when they encounter the souls of animals, trees, waterfalls, people, or supernatural beings. The *ruwaay* is considered the more important of the two souls when it comes to dreaming, and it is sometimes referred to as the dream-soul.

In Senoi culture, dreams are a popular topic of conversation in everyday life. Dreams are invested with great importance because they can inform and make predictions about natural events such as weather. Dreams are also considered the fundamental means of communication with the supernatural world, and because of this they play a significant role in healing ceremonies. The Senoi make a distinction between insignificant dreams and important dreams, but claim that everything in a dream has a larger purpose beyond the dreamer's understanding. They are taught how to attain dream lucidity and dream control in order to be able to understand this larger purpose and deal directly with the unconscious conflicts (although they don't name them as such) that could adversely affect their waking lives.

Dream interpretation is a major aspect of the education of children, and represents a common means of knowledge for many Senoi adults as well. According to the Senoi, children can and should make decisions during the night as well as during the day, by assuming a responsible attitude toward all psychic and supernatural forces. Children's minds in particular are considered powerful, rational, and adaptable. In dream interpretation, the child is invested with a power that can be controlled and directed. Fear is considered an obstruction to the free play of creative activity from which dreams arise.

Sewer

Sewers may signify the "rotting" remains of old circumstances or relationships. Waste also fertilizes and thus can signify regeneration as well.

Sexual Nightmares

As human beings, we all long to be unified with, and completely accepted by, our complementary opposites; the desire to be part of a complete "whole" makes sexual dreams a universal experience. The meaning of such dreams is thus not always necessarily erotic in nature (although eroticism is certainly a part of it), but instead represent a person's desire for completion. The archetypical male represents independence, assertiveness, aggressiveness, and possibly destructiveness, so to dream of sexual intercourse with a male figure, regardless of the dreamer's gender, will often signify the need to assimilate these opposite but complementary characteristics. In contrast, the archetypical female represents gestation, nurturing, and mutuality; if the dreamer needs these qualities in his or her life, it would not be uncommon to dream of sexual intercourse with a female figure.

While sex in dreams is a widespread occurrence, sexual nightmares are much less so. People who suffer from recurring nightmares in which the imagery changes but the general theme remains the same report a marked absence of sexual images in their dreams. This might reflect the fact that our society's views on sex have changed drastically over the past few generations. People no longer feel the need to hide their sexual desires, as was the case in the past, so sexual dreams do not carry the anxiety, guilt, and shame they once did.

Sexually Transmitted Diseases

In the era of HIV and AIDS, herpes, and gonorrhea, sexually transmitted diseases (STDs) are on the minds of most sexually active people, as contracting an STD can potentially mean a death sentence. A nightmare involving a sexual encounter that leads to an STD indicates sexual health and promiscuity are on the mind of the dreamer. This nightmare may also indicate doubts of the faithfulness of an intimate partner.

Shadow

A shadow is an archetype that represents the hidden and often "dark" aspects of the self. The dreamer may not accept these parts of his personality, in which case they are projected on other figures in the dream. The "shadow self" may manifest itself in dreams or frightening nightmares as a criminal, rapist, or even a demonic figure of some kind.

(See also *Jung, Carl* and *Archetypes*)

Shakespeare, William

In English Renaissance literature, dreams were an oft-used device to enable communication between humans and the divine, and provide the most intelligible form of supernatural warnings, premonitions, and omens. Elizabethan playwrights often used dreams as a literary device to foreshadow events and provide other information without losing the element of mystery. The idea of prophetic dreams found its origin in classical Greek philosophy, Roman literature, and English folklore, while the "dream vision" comes from medieval tradition.

In plays, dreams (along with monologues, soliloquies, and asides) convey the inner life of a character, displaying his or her memories, emotions, and imagination for the whole audience to see. They often employ vivid visualizations of archetypical characters, which help direct the audience to the moral ends that the story is meant to achieve.

SHAKESPEARE

Shakespeare frequently uses dreams as premonitions of death in his plays. For example, the first scene of the play *Richard III* details the dream of Clarence, which foretells an assassination. The omen or prediction is effected by the typical symbols of death, such as the crossing of the sea, the unsteady deck, and the stumbling and drowning. In the last scene of the play, King Richard and his rival Richmond experience parallel dreams on the eve of the last battle in Bosworth, and the ghosts of the murder victims of the play— Edward, Henry VI, Clarence, Rivers, Grey, Vaughn, and Hastings— make appearances throughout these dreams, in hopes of making Richard yield to remorse, while encouraging his rival to fight and conquer.

Similarly, in *Henry VI*, the Cardinal of Winchester predicts the death of the Duke of Gloucester in a dream, while, in *Romeo and Juliet*, Romeo dreams that Juliet finds him dead. In the same play, Balthazar dreams, in turn, of Romeo committing murder. *Julius Caesar* also makes use of dreams as a vital tool in plot development when Calpurnia's dream foreshadows Caesar's death. The dream of Cinna the poet and the misinterpreted advice of the arguers are key to the final tragedy. The interesting thing about these dreams is their ambiguity—an ambiguity that enables the characters to project their thoughts, desires, and weaknesses (hubris), which then enables the audience to better understand them. Shakespearean dreams usually serve to divide people into two categories: those who attempt to control their dreams and therefore their destinies, and those who are controlled by them.

Both *The Winter's Tale* and *The Tempest* are concerned with humans trying to comprehend the complex role of irrational dreams in waking life, while *A Midsummer Night's Dream* deals almost exclusively with dreaming by reversing the categories of reality and illusion, sleeping and waking, and reason and imagination. The central theme is that a dream is truer and more reliable than the reality of the waking world. By regarding facts as if they were dreams and dreams as if they were facts, Shakespeare shows how blurred these boundaries really are.

(See also *Macbeth*)

Shamanism

The word *shaman* comes from the Tungusic term *saman*, or religious specialist or expert. The term was originally coined by early generations of scholars who were studying societies in Siberia and central Asia, and it was later extended to similar religious systems found elsewhere in the world. Depending on how the available archaeological evidence is interpreted, shamanism is probably many thousands of years old.

Shamanism has sometimes been described as a "technique of ecstasy," alluding to the shaman's ability to enter altered states of consciousness,

including dream states, at will. Although the terms *shaman* and *shamanism* have come to be used quite loosely and metaphorically, in the disciplines of anthropology and comparative religion, shamanism refers to a very specific set of ideas and practices that can be found in various world cultures. A shaman is a healer, a guide for the souls of the dead to their home in the afterlife, and the general mediator between the surrounding community and the spirit world— particularly animal spirits and the spirits of the forces of nature.

In smaller agrarian and hunter-gatherer societies, shamans perform the functions of the doctors, priests, and therapists of contemporary Western societies. The religious specialists or "medicine men" of traditional Native American Indian societies are examples of shamans. True shamans are found more often in hunting societies than in pastoral or farming societies, although one can find shamanic practices in non-hunting cultures as well. Shamanism in the strictest sense doesn't exist in Africa, although there are religious authorities that occupy a similar position in traditional African societies.

A person may become a shaman through inheritance or through a calling from spiritual forces. This supernatural selection frequently involves a serious illness that brings the chosen person close to death, which also symbolizes the "death" of the individual's former life. This death theme is emphasized in certain traditions, where the chosen person experiences a nightmare in which they are killed or dismembered and then reborn or regenerated. Sometimes the shaman initiate learns how to enter altered states during dreams, in which he meets the tutelary spirit assigned to him when he reaches the full status of shaman. After recovering from his illness, a shaman initiate will then complete training, usually under the guidance of an experienced shaman.

The ability to enter an altered state is so important to the craft and art of shamanism that scholars have identified it as *the* defining characteristic. These altered states can be brought on by a variety of techniques, from drumming and chanting, to fasting and sweat baths. Shamans also sometimes make use of hallucinogenic drugs. Once in an altered state, shamans can see or sense realms that are normally invisible, and they are able to serve as medium, priest, or mediator between the community and the beings that inhabit these realms.

Sharks

Sharks are the hunters of the sea—the killing machines that we all fear when we swim in the ocean. A nightmare about a shark may indicate a real fear of the animal, or it may represent a fear of the unconscious, or "shadow," aspect of the self.

(See also *Jaws*)

Shelley, Percy Bysse

In his poem "Mutability," Percy Bysse Shelley (1792–1822) offers one quotable and relevant line on the topic of nightmares: "A dream has power to poison sleep."

Sheol

A Hebrew word for the abode of the dead; also literally meaning "unseen."

(See also *Hell* and *Underworld*)

Shot

Guns are a symbol of aggression and power, usually male power (Freud saw them as phallic symbols). When bullets start flying, the fight-or-flight response kicks in. The searing sting of a bullet in a nightmare may indicate the presence of an aggressor in the dreamer's life, or it may be indicative of more generalized feelings of anxiety or fear. To dream of being shot but continuing to run and/or fight anyway, shows a determination to overcome adversity and/or hostility, though not without paying some kind of professional or personal price. Veterans who have seen combat in waking life often have traumatic nightmares in which they are being shot at or attacked.

(See also *Gun*)

Shrinking

To find yourself shrinking in a dream to tininess, with the world around you growing to inconceivable proportions, indicates feelings of insignificance or abandonment. You may be feeling slighted or neglected in a formerly close relationship, which leaves you feeling alone in the nightmarish landscape of an overwhelming and threatening world. This dream may also represent the internalized fears of childhood, harking back to that feeling that everyone and everything is large, threatening, and powerful.

Sinking Ship

A sinking ship in a vast ocean is an image straight out of the worst of nightmares. A sinking ship requires a terrible choice: to stay on board means certain death, but to jump into the ocean without a lifeboat to swim to shore or rescue means only the slightest chance for survival. Sinking ships in dreams are significant, but to understand the meaning, one has to also understand the water imagery as well. The ship is the means of transport across the deep, mysterious, and often danger-ous waters—waters that can symbolize death and the underworld. Psychologi-cally speaking, deep, dark water can signify the unconscious or "shadow self." If the boat in a nightmare is sinking, this may symbolize "shadow work," or an excavation of the depths of the unconscious. The dreamer may be exploring or engaging an aspect of himself that is never revealed to others or to himself. If there is a lot of fear in the dream, this may indicate a discomfort with, or fear of, the unconscious thoughts and desires that have remained hidden for so long.

Skin Lesions

The skin is the human body's biggest organ. It grows, dies, regenerates itself, and is the first line of defense against the outside world. The most horrific diseases in history, such as leprosy and the bubonic plague, had symptoms that included grow-ing skin lesions, sores that open and ooze puss, and strange growths on sections of skin. To dream of a problem with your skin, such as open sores and lesions, may indicate feelings of sensitivity about perceived shortcomings and failures.

(See also *Leprosy*)

Skull

Skulls bode of danger and death, and a skull emblem on a flag is a gesture of dominance as well as a warning. Skulls are also associated with pirates (skull and crossbones), the Hell's Angels, and certain elite fighting units, indicating that they are capable of wielding deadly force.

(See also *Bones*)

Sleep Apnea

In Greek, *apnea* means "without breath." According to the National Institutes of Health, sleep apnea is a disorder that affects more than 12 million Americans. During sleep apnea episodes, the sleeper stops breathing for several seconds, forcing the brain to wake the sleeper so breathing can resume. Sleep apnea can be caused by a blocked airway (caused by the soft tissue collapsing in the rear of the throat), by the intermittent failure of the brain to tell the body to breathe, or by some combination of these two factors. This disorder makes for extremely poor sleep quality, which can lead to nightmares.

Sleep apnea most commonly affects overweight or obese men more than 40 years old, but it can affect people of all ages and sizes.

Sleep Paralysis

Most people have had the experience of feeling rooted to the spot in a dream or nightmare. Not being able to run away from some kind of danger or trying to run and only being able to move very slowly is a particularly common theme in dreams, probably because, on some level, we know that we truly are paralyzed when we dream. During the REM stage of sleep, when our most active dreams occur, a relay station at the top of the spinal column "disconnects" the motor cortex from most of the body (with the exception of the lungs and the eyes). This is a biological mechanism that prevents us from moving in our sleep, and is the reason why sleepwalking occurs only during non-REM sleep. This mechanism is also a factor of the sleep disorder referred to as sleep paralysis (which is distinct from normal REM sleep immobility), in which the sleeper finds himself completely paralyzed during the twilight state immediately before entering or after leaving sleep.

(See also *Old Hag Syndrome*)

Sleepwalking

Somnambulism, better known as sleepwalking, is one of the most fascinating and bizarre sleep phenomena. While in a deep, but non-R.E.M. sleep, the sleeper gets up and starts moving around. Some of these episodes can last as long as 30 minutes, sometimes taking the somnambulist as far away as the living room or beyond. Some sleepwalkers have been known to get into their cars and drive, and even, in extremely rare cases, commit murder. Sleepers typically make their way back to their bed, or they may wake up in a strange location with no idea how they got there. Contrary to popular belief, waking a sleepwalker will not provoke a heart attack or kill him—the best approach is to simply and quietly guide the sleepwalker back to bed.

Smoke

To be surrounded by choking smoke in a dream may indicate that the dreamer is suffering from confusion, anxiety, and a lack of clarity. Often a dreamer will be choked up and disoriented, suggesting a need to "clear things up."

Snake

Serpents are ancient symbols, often associated with evil, power, and even fertility. For Freud, serpent dreams were covert references to the male sex organ. Because they live in the ground, serpents may represent the healing, nurturing earth, or they may be emblems of the mysterious dangers of the underworld. Psychologically, they are the minions of the unconscious or representatives of the "shadow self." As a more general psychological symbol, snakes emerging out of the ground may indicate the emergence of unconscious (for example, repressed) material into the light of consciousness. Being bitten by a snake in a nightmare may simply be a phobic response, or it may indicate that the dreamer fears the harm that may come from the aspects of his psyche that are dark, undesirable, and/or uncontrollable.

Snoring

Snoring isn't necessarily a nightmare for the snorer, but it certainly is for the people who are obliged to sleep within earshot. Snoring is caused by air flowing through a partially obstructed opening in the back of the mouth and nose. The soft palate and the uvula (the small, fleshy object that hangs from the roof of the mouth like a punching bag) rest against each other, and the vibrations of the airflow cause the snoring sound. Some people tend to snore more often when they are extremely fatigued; for others it seems more indiscriminate. There are many treatments for snoring, but the treatments are really more for the snorer's partner and for the insomnia from which he or she has likely been suffering.

Solitude

Humans are social creatures, and the idea of being cut off from all human interaction is certainly a nightmare for some. A solitude nightmare is one in which the dreamer's emotions come to the fore more so than the imagery does. The setting is likely to be simple, such as an empty room or desolate landscape, but the silence and overwhelming sense of loneliness is the predominant feeling. This dream is usually quite literal, and suggests the dreamer is feeling isolated and/or abandoned in interpersonal relationships.

Somatic Phenomena

Somatic phenomena refer to the physical sensations the body experiences while dreaming. When our bodies experience the discomfort or annoyance of pressure or pain, or the discomfort from the uncomfortable position of our limbs while we sleep, this sensory input is often translated into our dreams.

The mind uses the dream to convey the uncomfortable state of our bodies, and because the dreaming mind does not present reality in the same way it does when we are awake, these messages often come to us in an exaggerated or symbolic way. Herbert Silberer, a German psychologist, recorded a dream he experienced while sick with a high fever and laryngitis—a condition that made it very painful for him to swallow. He reported drinking a bottle of water in his dream, only to find that another had taken its place as soon as he finished the one before it. This dream probably represented the saliva he had to swallow continuously, even though it was causing him pain. In a different study, blood-pressure cuffs were put around the ankles of subjects and slowly inflated while they slept. Each person reported a different variation on the theme of being tied down in their dreams, whether by snakes, ropes, or other similar items.

Spear

The spear is a hunting weapon, and its imagery in a dream usually relates to male sexual aggression, though not necessarily violent aggression. If a woman dreams of a spear or multiple spears, she may be feeling that a man (or men) in her life are after her sexually. If a male dreams of spears, it may indicate that he's feeling virile and "on the prowl."

Spider

Spiders are beneficial insects in that they trap other bugs. With the exceptions of

the black widow and a few other more rare poisonous types, most spiders don't harm humans. Regardless, many people are deathly afraid of the arachnids, and may suffer from full-blown arachnophobia. It's not uncommon for someone suffering from arachnophobia to have spider nightmares. For most people, however, spider imagery in a dream or nightmare may symbolize an intricate web that the dreamer has woven, or a web that has entrapped the dreamer. Alternatively, it may indicate feeling entangled in a sticky, clinging relationship.

STARGATE

STARGATE is one of the names given to the United States government's remote viewing (RV) project. By some accounts, the project was started by the Central Intelligence Agency (CIA) as early as 1951, and ran to as late as 1995 (some believe it is likely that the project still continues under some other, top-secret cover). STARGATE helped train and develop RV abilities in already gifted individuals. During the height of the Cold War with Russia, STARGATE was seen as the perfect form of espionage. The project was initially overseen by physicist H.E. Puthoff, Ph.D. Puthoff was amazed at the results his group was getting and was quoted as saying, "The results appear to provide unequivocal evidence of a human capacity to access events remote in space and time, by some cognitive process not yet understood." Such results may even point to the likelihood that precognitive dreams are a reality as well.

(See also *Remote Viewing*)

Stevenson, Robert Lewis

The author Robert Lewis Stevenson suffered from recurring nightmares throughout his whole life. Beginning in his early childhood and continuing throughout his adulthood, serious nightmares plagued him incessantly. He remained an uneasy, fitful sleeper until the end of his days.

The author claimed that his novel *The Strange Case of Dr. Jekyll and Mr. Hyde* (1886) found its origin and inspiration in an extremely vivid nightmare he experienced. Stevenson was hard-pressed for money, and for two days he brainstormed ideas for a book. He briefly considered the idea of a "double being" as the central character for a novel, but he discarded the idea. On the second night of brainstorming, he had a dream of Dr. Jekyll ingesting a powder and turning into Hyde before the astonished eyes of his pursuers. Stevenson claimed that this was only the first in a series of sequential dreams he experienced that explicated the story.

His dreams impacted his writing so definitively that he eventually wrote a book devoted to this theme, titled *Across the Plains* (L-D Allen Press, 1950). He made many references to the "nocturnal theater" taking place in his head, and attributed true authorship to the "little people" who ran it:

> The more I think of it, the more I am moved to press upon the world my question: Who are the Little People? They are near connections of the dreamer's beyond doubt.... They have plainly learned like him to build the scheme of a considerable story in progressive order; only I think they have more talent; and one thing is beyond doubt, they can tell him a story piece by piece, like a serial and keep him all the while in ignorance of where they aim. Who are they, then? And who is the dreamer?

Strangling

A dream about strangling someone or being strangled may indicate that you are denying, or being denied, a vital aspect of your expression and, thus, satisfaction in life.

(See also *Choking* and *Suffocation*)

Stress

Anxiety and fear provide the chief emotional context for many dreams—such as in dreams of falling, nakedness, and being chased—with fear dominating the dream landscape in nightmares. Anxiety-filled dreams can emerge as a result of inner conflicts, particularly the repressed conflicts that we attempt to hide from ourselves. Sigmund Freud and other therapists in the tradition of depth psychology have explored these dynamics at length, especially those conflicts rooted in childhood experiences.

However, the content of dream life is also shaped by external factors that operate independently of any inner, psychological conflicts. These factors can intrude upon our consciousness and thus give rise to unpleasant dreams and nightmares. Stress in our environments, whether it be stress arising from personal, social, vocational, or financial difficulties, may be the major cause of anxiety-filled dreams. The distinction between the inner and outer causes of dreams is fairly clear, but anxiety dreams can draw from both areas. For example, job stress may resonate with self-confidence issues from adolescence, or the present conflicts at home may remind the dreamer of certain childhood conflicts.

Some common dreams experienced while under undue stress include dreams of being chased, trapped, or attacked, or dreams of threatening animals or creatures.

Subconscious

The term *subconscious* is often used interchangeably with *the unconscious*. The unconscious or subconscious is the part of the psyche that is normally beyond the reach of consciousness. Psychoanalysis and certain other forms of psychotherapy claim to be able to access the unconscious through techniques such as dream interpretation. The term *subconscious* is also used instead of *preconscious*, which is Freud's term for the contents of the mind that, while not within the immediate spotlight of awareness, can be accessed simply by attending to them. For example, we are normally unaware of background noise or "white" noise, such as the hum of an air conditioner or the sound of the ocean, but it is easy to bring these sounds into the light of consciousness.

Suffocation

Gasping for breath in a tiny space that is running out of air, or feeling the lungs burn for oxygen as you are trapped underwater, is a horrifying experience. Suffocation in a dream demonstrates intense anxiety associated with being confined or smothered by a relationship or other situation. People who suffer from sleep apnea often report these feelings immediately before, and upon waking from, an episode.

Suicide

A dream about suicide may suggest that conditions in the dreamer's life are so frustrating or bleak that the dreamer is no longer willing or able to cope with them as he did in the past. The death indicates a drastic change is likely in the works.

Sunrise

Sunrise is the period from dark to light when the "veil" of mystery is lifted. This time symbolizes the transition from unknown to known, and indicates the dreamer is beginning to obtain clarity in what was once a muddy, confusing issue.

Sunset

As night begins to fall, shadows grow long and soon the color seems to run out of the landscape. The Irish call this time of day the *gloaming*. It's the time of transition from light to dark, from reality to unreality, from consciousness to unconsciousness, and can also serve as the backdrop for nightmares. The imagery denotes a time of change and confusion: things that were once clear have become cloudy and mysterious.

Swamp

Swamps are places of unknown dangers—the mud is ready to suck one under, snakes and other venomous creates lurk, and bugs swarm. This filthy and dangerous nightmare landscape may signify that the dreamer is currently walking through an enmeshing and potentially dangerous emotional landscape.

Sword

"He who lives by the sword, dies by the sword," the old adage says. Swords within a dream are symbols of power— especially male power and prowess. If one is wielding the sword, he is exerting power and dominance over others. If one dreams of being held at the sword's blade, he is feeling dominated and/or helpless in waking life. The sword may also represent a hostile male sexuality.

Symphonie Fantastique

In September of 1827, French composer Hector Berlioz watched Harriet Smithson play the role of Ophelia in a performance of Shakespeare's *Hamlet*. He was so struck with Smithson's beauty that he fell hopelessly in love with this unattainable actress. He channeled his feelings and passions into a composition entitled *Symphonie Fantastique*.

Berlioz obsesses over the actress, and Smithson becomes *Symphonie Fantastique*'s idée fixe (fixation/obsession). In the symphony's program, which Berlioz himself wrote, he explains the work's fourth movement, titled "March to the Scaffold." Berlioz wrote:

> Convinced that his love is unrequited, the artist takes an overdose of opium. It plunges him into a sleep accompanied by horrifying visions. He dreams that he has killed his beloved, has been condemned and led to the scaffold, and is witnessing his own

execution. The procession advances to a march that is now somber and savage, now brilliant and solemn. At its conclusion the idée fixe returns, like a final thought of the beloved cut, off by the fatal blow.

Symphonie Fantastique is an autobiographical work for Berlioz. Berlioz claimed to have dreamt up parts of the symphony from his own opium-infused nightmares: he saw the imagery of killing his beloved, and he heard the accompanying music. Berlioz used the symphony to not only channel his emotions, but to get the attention of Smithson as well. His efforts paid off, as the two were married October 3, 1833.

This symphony is a perfect example of dream art, in which the theme or aesthetics of a work are inspired or informed by a dream or nightmare.

Talmud

In the Babylonian Talmud, Berachot Folio 55a (29–35):

> 29 R. Hisda said: Any dream rather than one of a fast. 30 R. Hisda also said: A dream which is not interpreted is like a letter which is not read. 31 R. Hisda also said: Neither a good dream nor a bad dream is ever wholly fulfilled. R. Hisda also said: A bad dream is better than a good dream. 32 R. Hisda also said: The sadness caused by a bad dream is sufficient for it and the joy which a good dream gives is sufficient for it. 33 R. Joseph said: Even for me 34 the joy caused by a good dream nullifies it. R. Hisda also said: A bad dream is worse than scourging, since it says, God hath so made it that men should fear before Him, 35 and Rabbah b. Bar Hanah said in the name of R. Johanan: This refers to a bad dream.

The Talmud also states: "Although God turned away His face from Israel, yet He spoke in dreams to individuals." (Tr. Hag. 5b)

The Talmud and Jewish tradition in general are full of references to divine messages in the form of dreams. The Talmud describes a Ba'al HaChalom, the Master of the Dream, who is responsible for nightly dreams. The Ba'al HaChalom is consulted on matters of personal and legal disputes as well as bigger interpersonal issues.

(See also *Judaism*)

Tarot

As we know them today, tarot cards come in decks of 78 cards, each with very specific imagery, and some featuring archetypes. Some use the cards for divination, to glean some insight into the future, while others may use the cards for personal knowledge and development. Originally, tarot was developed sometime between 1440 and 1445 C.E. as a card game similar to

bridge for the noblemen in Northern Italy. The game evolved into an occult endeavor in the 18th century.

Today there are many hundreds of decks in circulation, but the most easily recognizable is the Rider-Waite. Named for Dr. Arthur Edward Waite, the occult scholar and member of the Order of the Golden Dawn, the deck was first published in 1910 by Rider & Company of London. Artist Pamela Colman Smith, who was also a member of the Golden Dawn, designed the deck under Waite's direction. The tarot deck, with its colorful, esoteric, and emblematic imagery on all of its 78 cards, was used to explore and teach the mysteries of the Golden Dawn.

Much of the imagery on the deck is dreamlike and archetypical. Two tarot cards from the Major Arcana, or the 22 cards not assigned to any of the four suits, that come to mind when discussing night and the dreamworld are the Star and the Moon. For tarot readers, the Star signifies abandonment and loss, and the Moon bodes of hidden enemies and dark terror that may be waiting around the corner.

Those who use tarot and are captivated by its imagery may find that the cards appear in their dreams. Those familiar with tarot have an understanding of what each card means in the context of a spread, and should use the same method of interpretation in a dream as one would in reading the actual cards. In a dream, a tarot reader's subconscious may use the tarot symbols because it is an imagery language that the dreamer will readily understand.

Tears

Tears come with sorrow, grief, and even joy. It is said that the chemical composition of tears of joy are qualitatively different than those stemming from sadness. Tears often represent cleansing and catharsis, indicating that a healing of some sort is taking place in the dreamer's life.

Teeth

Women experience dreams about teeth more frequently than men. Symbolically, teeth are often thought to represent the dreamer's sexuality. Loosing a tooth may represent the process of giving birth, in which a small object is removed from the body, resulting in pain and bleeding. (A related, widespread theme from folklore is that for every child a woman bears, she will loose a tooth.) Freud presented a more overtly sexual interpretation, suggesting that the pulling of a tooth is symbolic of male adolescent masturbation.

In some cultures, the loss of a tooth in a dream is sometimes interpreted as the unconscious desire of the dreamer for the death of a relative, with the loss of the central teeth representing the desired death of a parent, and the teeth further back in the mouth corresponding to more distant relatives. An ancient Egyptian interpretation, dating from around 2000 B.C.E., suggests that the loss of a tooth means that the dreamer will die as a direct result of the actions of his relatives. Other theories propose that dreams of tooth loss represent the desire for helplessness or dependency. They may also indicate a rejection of sex and sexual desire. Alternately, these dreams may signify a fear of aging, relating to the fact that we often loose our teeth as we age.

Research has been conducted comparing the personality traits of people with chronic teeth dreams to the traits of those who frequently experience flying dreams. While the "flyers" were calm, confident, and generally optimistic, those who dreamed about teeth were more anxious, prone to bouts of self-criticism, and more likely to feel helpless in situations with which they were unfamiliar. The reason for these personality differences is unknown and open to speculation.

Dreams about teeth indicate you may need to "get your teeth into" or "bite your way through" a situation. If you are being bitten, perhaps there is an aggressive struggle for control in a personal or business relationship. Losing your teeth may also indicate a perceived loss of power and control in life. In some of the more extreme cases of this nightmare, the dreamer finds himself trying to push the fallen, broken, or rotted teeth back into place. As in any nightmare, the more extreme the imagery, the more important the message is.

Falling Teeth

Darci Faiello is a 31-year-old marketing/sales professional living in Pittsburgh, Pennsylvania, with her husband. Since her early- to mid-20s, she has had nightmares about some of her teeth falling out.

The Nightmare:

> My worst nightmare is that my teeth are falling out. These dreams are very realistic—so realistic that for the entire day afterwards, I check my teeth, wiggling them around to see if they are ready to fall out. It is usually one of my front teeth or bicuspids, and it pops right out—no pain or blood. It just pops out. Then, in the dream, I spend a good amount of time trying to stick the thing back in. In one dream, I even used superglue!
>
> Several of my friends that I have talked to about this have had an occasional dream like this, but mine seems to occur on a monthly basis.

Darci claims that her teeth dreams often foretold of an unplanned event. "I just remember them happening, and then a drastic life change happening," she said. "I had one about a month before my position was eliminated from one company, and a few weeks before I landed a new job. The dream is so realistic that, when I do have it, it leaves quite an impression on me." She claims that it is her upper teeth that are most often affected in the dream.

The Analysis:

> It is very interesting to note that Darci had dreams about losing her teeth before she lost her job and just before landing a new one. The dream may indicate that at both times she was feeling a loss of control and confidence in her professional life. Perhaps she sensed troubles at work, and her dreams were working through some of those issues. Being out of work can also make one feel not very

confident professionally, so the second dream may be more related to those feelings as opposed to the foretelling of a positive event, such as landing a new job.

It's also interesting to note that she said the dream was occurring once per month at one point. In some folklore, dreams about losing teeth are related to childbirth. Perhaps childbearing is also on Darci's mind, and her dreams are a way of exploring those issues.

■　　■　　■

Telephone

The insistent ringing of a telephone demands our attention and usually requires us to stop whatever we're doing, even if it is only long enough to decide not to answer it. An ominous ringing in a dream may indicate a fear of a past life or situation coming to haunt you. To experience silence on the line in a dream may mean that you are feeling disconnected from a person in your life, whereas to hear the phone ring but not be able to find it signifies an even bigger disconnect.

Terrorism

On September 11, 2001, terrorism was thrust into America's public consciousness in a horrifying and immediate way. Those who lived through the attacks or lost people close to them have suffered the worst kind of trauma. Even those who didn't experience the attacks firsthand were traumatized, our lives changed suddenly and irrevocably by the horrifying scenes we witnessed on the news coverage. Many people have suffered, and continue to suffer, from recurring nightmares that replay the events of that day. Terrorism dreams express a very real sense of vulnerability, and, along with anger and fear, create the most dominant emotional context for any nightmare.

Tertullian

A third-century lawyer-turned-priest, Tertullian was the first important Christian philosopher and theologian to write in Latin rather than Greek. Eight chapters of his *A Treatise on the Soul* concerned sleep and dreaming. Tertullian's views on dreams were handed down as a legacy to Western Christendom, the effects of which are still felt today.

Tertullian believed in the sprit/body dichotomy first postulated by the ancient Greeks. He felt that the constant and persistent activity of the mind during dreaming, which occurrs while the body remains motionless, proves that the soul is an entity independent of the body, and thus immortal. Because of this he discounted the idea that the condition of the physical body, whether through diet or any other influence, could have an effect on dreams. Interestingly, he was critical of the idea that the soul could leave the body and travel unencumbered during sleep.

Tertullian classified dreams according to their sources, divine or otherwise. He maintained that God was responsible for many dreams, but allowed that demons were also the origin of certain kinds of dreams. Tertullian asserted that dreamers would not be held responsible for sins committed in their sleep during demonically influenced dreams, as the "acts" were not real but imaginary. He conceded climatic and even astrological influences on dreams, and cited the peculiar nature of the dreaming state itself as an influence as well.

Thorn

Like those found on Christ's "crown," thorns are usually associated with terrible burdens and suffering. Thorn imagery in a dream may signify that the dreamer is sacrificing parts of his own life for others, thereby becoming a martyr. This symbol could also mean that there is some "thorn in the side" of the dreamer—perhaps there is an unavoidable relationship or situation that is causing repeated distress.

Throat

Dreaming about a constriction or hoarseness of the throat means the dreamer is feeling stifled and cannot easily or fully express ideas or feelings. The dreamer has, in some way, lost his or her "voice" in a relationship or situation. This dream indicates a general perceived lack of agency or control in the dreamer's waking life.

(See also *Choking* and *Suffocation*)

Tibet

In Tibet, various deities and demons are thought to be responsible for dreams and nightmares. The various Buddhist *tantras*—texts dealing with rituals, meditations, and sexual practices—agree that auspicious omens that come true indicate the presence of a tutelary (guardian) deity in the dreamer's life, as well as success in the meditative process. Likewise, inauspicious dreams and nightmares indicate that the deity and future success are remote. However, Tibetan practitioners sometimes experience shamanic-type initiatory dreams in which they are dismembered and then reborn, and these dreams are not considered to be bad or negative.

In the Upanishadic tradition, Buddhist tantras assert that the four discrete states of consciousness are generated by energy passing up and down the central axis of the body. These four states are waking, dreaming, deep sleep, and "the state beyond the first three." The tantras often describe the production of an artificial dream state, often called "purifying or exerting the dream." The aim of these kinds of manipulations is to mix the states of dream, deep sleep, and waking, in the hopes of attaining the fourth and most desirable state.

Something similar to lucid dreaming is also discussed in a number of Tibetan Buddhist texts, and is the third of the six yogas introduced to Tibet in the 11th century. Tibetan lamas do not consider lucid dreaming itself to be a form of meditation, but rather a means of accessing the dream state in order to learn the doctrine of illusion or to practice meditation while in the dream. The ultimate goal of all meditation, in a dream state or otherwise, is to achieve *nirvana*, the transcendence of the awareness of individuality and the final liberation from reincarnation.

Tidal Wave

Tidal waves or tsunamis have been a part of our general consciousness, especially since the tsunami disaster of December 26, 2004, that killed more than 200,000 people in eight different countries. Although a full-blown tidal wave rapidly approaching the shoreline is a relatively rare sight, it can, however, be a very common theme in nightmares.

These kinds of natural disaster dreams (along with earthquakes, floods, storms, and the like) usually occur after the dreamer suffers from a traumatic experience, or when he is feeling extremely stressed. Survivors of fires, for instance, often report dreams of fire as well as dreams of being consumed by tidal waves. Water, especially deep or powerful bodies of water such as the ocean, usually symbolizes strong emotion and/or the forces of chaos, so nightmares about tidal waves can symbolize feelings of losing control or of being overwhelmed by strong emotion. Virtually all people, regardless of the traumatic experiences they may have suffered, share these kinds of feelings, which is why these dreams are so universal.

Tikopia

The Tikopia people live on the Polynesian island of the same name, located in the southeast corner of the Solomon Islands. These people invest great supernatural meaning in their dreams, and often cite supernatural influences on dreams.

Accurate dream interpretation is thought to illuminate the events of normal waking life. For the Tikopia, dream sharing with others is very common, and is usually done in a casual way at any time of the day. Not all dreams are regarded as significant, however, and for this reason many of them are not discussed at all.

The Tikopia explanation of dreams includes a more general theory of a mobile soul (similar to the astral body). It is thought that every person has an intangible spirit entity within his or her body that is capable of wandering abroad during sleep and transmitting its experiences to its "owner" upon return. The Tikopia explain dreams of visits to distant places with this theory of mobility of spirit. The spirit can also journey to the heavens and interact with dead souls.

According to the Tikopia, dreams are considered proof of the existence of the spirit realm, and they derive much of their information about supernatural beings from the dreams in which they appear. Many dream experiences are thought to be a result of the intrusion of purely supernatural spiritual beings that counterfeit familiar forms in order to deceive the dreamer. This kind of spirit is associated with nightmares of physical oppression. Violent nightmares with unpleasant emotional aftereffects are also very common among the Tikopia.

In general, dreams about fishing, birth, sickness, and death are regarded as the most significant, as these are aspects of human life particularly affected by chance, and the assurance provided through predictive dreams is usually welcomed. A dream's meaning and value is usually taken within the context of the immediate practical situation of the dreamer and his or her family. Dreams are generally shared and then discussed in the family unit so that its meaning and relevance can be determined.

Time Travel

Albert Einstein's theories showed that space is curved and time is relative, meaning that, theoretically, traveling through time is possible. The idea of time travel presents many paradoxes and conundrums (such as the possibility of one's very existence if one were to travel back in time to murder one's parents), and the great science fiction writers have manipulated this to great effect. Dream visions of being in the distant past or future may indicate that the dreamer is feeling awkward, isolated, and "out of step." The message of this dream is to reengage with those around you and reestablish your place in the world.

Tornado

Wind and water have long been traditional archetypal symbols of spirit ("which bloweth where it listeth") and emotion (which "runs deep," even when it's still). In certain religious narratives and myths, the voice of God often "speaks from out of a whirlwind." Undeveloped nations and traditional cultures (including our own ancestors, as far back as the Old Stone Age and beyond) have traditionally viewed the tornado as "the finger of God," which points with precision and un-paralleled power to the psycho-spiritual mysteries of guilt and divine justice. Like the imagined "hand of God," a real tornado is unpredictably powerful and de-structive, leaving one life relatively untouched while a life nearby is torn and shattered forever.

Each time we dream of tornadoes, these ancient, collective layers of symbolic association reveal themselves anew. Although only the dreamer can say for sure what his dream images mean, dream tornadoes can be compelling metaphors of the personal and collective social change that we sense is coming. As dreamers, our unconscious taps into the tornado image as a representation of our relation-ship to the deepest unasked and unanswered psycho-spiritual questions of life. A "dream tornado" is usually a harbinger of change or upheaval, in the psyche as well as the waking world.

For anyone who has ever seen a deadly funnel cloud come down from above to wreak havoc on the ground below, the power of the storm is both awesome and frightening. People experiencing undue amounts of stress tend to have natural-disaster dreams, such as floods, earthquakes, and tornadoes. As in all nightmares, tornado imagery may indicate that the dreamer is feeling commensurately help-less, powerless, vulnerable, and frightened in waking life.

(See also *Wizard of Oz, The*)

Transmogrification

Transmogrification is the process by which something transforms into something else. In the bizarre and irrational realm of nightmares, the occurrence is commonplace. An apple pie may turn into a coiled snake, or a tree within a dream may start walking and morph into a monster. The concept is an important aspect in the interpretation of the symbolism of a dream. In this, it is important to note what the object was and what it turned into in order to unpack the meaning of the dream.

Trapped

A feeling of being trapped in a nightmare may indicate a stifling personal relationship or job situation. Or the dreamer may in fact suffer from claustrophobia, and the fear is finding expression in a frightening dream. Pregnant women in their last trimester of pregnancy often have dreams of being trapped in small places—perhaps identifying with the growing fetus they are carrying.

(See also *Suffocation*)

Trees

Trees represent the self—the roots are the literal connection to family, friends, ancestors, and the world, and the branches are the many growth paths taken in life, including career choices, arts, hobbies, and other interests.

The Giant Tree Portal Nightmare

Melanie Durrell is a 47-year-old small business owner whose company services the technology needs of other companies. She lives in Overland Park, Kansas, and since 1990 she has experienced a series of nightmares that all begin the same way: standing in front of a large tree.

The Nightmare:

> *The nightmare always started the same: I would be getting ready to go into a tree. The tree was very large, very dark, and imposing. I would go to the tree, sometimes walking*

toward it, sometimes that dream-like flying or floating toward it, but most often there would be a door at the base of the tree, and sometimes I'd have to climb the tree to get inside. The tree was always extremely large and scary looking, reminding me of those old oak trees that grow in the southern United States.

Once I opened the door and was inside, I would be in a very large mansion with many large rooms, very high ceilings, and lots of detail in the house. There were elaborate mantels, plasterwork, large curving staircases, chandeliers, and beautiful furniture. In some versions of the dream, the inside of the tree would be a shopping mall with lots of people, escalators, and fountains. I never did get that—I hate shopping malls.

Within the house there would be secret passageways that visually became more like the tree instead of a house once I was inside of them. One of these passageways would be like a "wormhole," for lack of a better term, that would take me directly to the bottom steps of my Grandmother Lenore's attic.

This part of the dream is always comforting—I loved my grandma's attic—my sisters and I would play dress-up for hours up there. It's also where I used to hide if I was in trouble and she was looking for me. She never found me when I hid in the attic, and I avoided a few spankings as a kid by hiding up there.

There is a specific area of the dream house that I avoided out of fear. There was something unspeakable there, and I knew that something horrible would happen to me—being raped really stands out as the greatest fear. Sometimes the "thing" would stalk me through the house. Sometimes I would run all through the house trying to get away—from room to room to room—absolutely terrified. There would also be people in the house—mostly family who would not (or could not) help or protect me. It was like they couldn't see or hear me. The "thing" stalking me did not have shape or form. It was invisible.

Melanie hasn't had the nightmare in more than three years. She believes the reason she no longer has the dream is because she has conditioned herself to wake up as soon as she sees the giant tree in her dream in order to avoid the nightmare. She claims that, for several years, she was experiencing this nightmare three to four times a month. Melanie says, "I would wake up crying hysterically, tears running down my face, wet pillowcase, and shaking in fear, unable to go back to sleep and physically exhausted. My crying, moaning, and thrashing around would frequently wake other members of the house."

The Analysis:

Trees represent the self—the roots are the literal connection to family, friends, and the world, and the branches are the many growth paths taken in life, including career choices, arts, hobbies, and other interests. It is significant that Melanie always approaches the tree and then goes inside, meaning this dream is an inner journey. Because the dream is always frightening, the inner journey is to a dark place within herself.

The danger in Melanie's dream comes from the invisible stalker that she feels is out to do her harm. This "incubus" imagery signifies a potential assault on her physical environment or possibly her financial security from an unknown assailant (it could be a fear of job loss, the economy, or some big bills that may be piling up). Because she runs to her grandmother's attic within the dream—a location that was a safe haven for her in childhood—the message is that she has the tools needed to avoid the assault. Melanie claims she now controls the dream by avoiding the tree and waking up. What she fears is within and not without.

■   ■   ■

Trial

Being on trial in a nightmare reflects overt or latent guilt of some kind. It can also mean that the dreamer is being "tested" in real life. Dreaming of being on trial may indicate that the dreamer needs to be more self-accepting or less judgmental of others.

(See also *Judgment* and *Judge/Jury*)

Tunnel

Like a door or gate, tunnel imagery can represent transition, especially that of birth or death. The "light at the end of the tunnel" may represent relief from old conditions. A tunnel can also have the Freudian meaning of tunnel-as-vagina.

Uncanny, The

In 1919, Sigmund Freud penned an essay entitled *Das Unheimliche*, or *The Uncanny*. Freud examined literature and the underlying culture for events and concepts that frighten us or give us pause. "[T]he uncanny is that class of the frightening which leads back to what is known of old and long familiar," he wrote. He examined the ways the familiar becomes frightening. For example, a child's bedroom may be a pleasant place, but when night comes and the room is dark, the child may be frightened of his bedroom. Why? There's no rational reason, as it is still the same room. But because of darkness, the familiar is now unfamiliar. "[U]ncanny is frightening precisely because it is *not* known and familiar."

Uncanny was also the general term Freud used to describe all of the unexplainable yet persistent fears universal to humans. Examples include concepts of the afterlife and ghosts. "[T]he 'immortal' soul was the first 'double' of the body," Freud wrote. "This invention of doubling as a preservation against extinction has its counterpart in the language of dreams...." Freud believed the concept of the soul was created by the human ego's need for immortality and as insulation against the unknown. Death and what comes after is the greatest unknown of all, and the souls, ghosts, spirits, angels, and demons that populate that unknown are all extensions or projections of that fear.

The uncanny's relationship to dreams and nightmares is obvious. We often become fearful in dreams because we experience something familiar that also conveys an element of the unknown. Examples would include dreams of corpses or inanimate objects that come to life, or even dreams of people we know who are suddenly and frighteningly changed or mutated in their appearances. The central idea of the uncanny is "like, and yet unlike." It is not the fear of the unknown, but rather the fear that something *known* has suddenly become unknown, other—terrifying. In some dreams we may also

U

experience premonitions that come to pass, and the implications of this can be frightening. Freud may explain away these premonitions as simple "uncanny" coincidences, but the dreamer may be firmly convinced that some supernatural force was at work.

(See also *Freud, Sigmund*)

Underground

A dream of being underground in a dark and unpleasant place may indicate that the dreamer has unconscious thoughts and desires that are clamoring for attention. Going to great depths to retrieve them and bring them into the light of scrutiny (perhaps therapeutic scrutiny) shows a readiness to address and integrate this "shadowy" self as a legitimate part of the dreamer's consciousness.

(See also *Burial*)

Underworld

The notion of a world located beneath the surface of the earth, where the souls of the dead and other spirits reside, is a widespread theme in ancient and modern world religions and myth. In the psychotherapeutic tradition, the underworld is a rich symbol of the unconscious realm—the realm that we enter every night in our dreams. The idea of an underground abode of the dead probably finds its origin in the widespread custom of burying corpses in the ground (although it is difficult to tell which idea came first). For most ancient cultures, such as the Hebrews, Greeks, Romans, Egyptians, and Mesopotamians, the underworld was considered a less than pleasant place, but it was not the realm of eternal suffering and punishment of Christianity and related traditions. In some religions the underworld dimension can be reached through a tunnel or portal that leads underground, and many myths relate stories of heroes who enter the underworld to rescue a loved one, to gain the gift of immortality, or to accomplish some other heroic task. Likewise, some Christians believe that Christ traveled to hell, or *sheol*, and back in order to take the punishment for sin and redeem mankind.

The modern conception of the underworld is that it should be viewed psychologically, rather than literally, as a symbol for the unconscious. Jungian analysts in particular embrace this notion: even the term *depth psychology* seems to indicate a close, natural connection between the two ideas. So, for example, a myth that recounts the story of, say, a hero entering and reemerging triumphant from the underworld could easily be viewed as a symbol for the nightly journey through the world of sleep and dreams, and, hence, into the unconscious. Interestingly, many religious traditions describe this kind of heroic journey to the underworld realm of the dead as taking place in a dream state.

The personal unconscious, as opposed to the collective unconscious, is, in a sense, the repository or graveyard for the past—a past that continues to raise its head and "haunt" our waking life. The goal of the therapeutic process is to "resurrect" our once buried past and bring it into the harsh light of scrutiny. This process is not unlike an excavation or exhumation, in which the hidden becomes apparent, the unknown becomes known, and the unconscious becomes conscious. Like the heroes of the ancient stories and myths, clients of depth psychology are, in a sense, entering their own private and personal "underworld," hopefully becoming brave heroes in their own right.

Unpreparedness

Some dream symbols and themes are so common that almost everybody experiences them on at least one occasion in their lives. These themes include such familiar scenarios as falling and flying, public nakedness, and unpreparedness. Freud would argue that all such dreams are wish fulfillment, but the fact that people had flying dreams before the advent of aviation would indicate that these

dreams find their foundation in the collective unconscious of mankind. The reality is that such shared motifs probably arise from experiences and anxieties that are fundamental to all people.

The unpreparedness motif often expresses itself in examination dreams. For example, during finals, college students often have anxiety dreams in which they have not studied adequately. These dreams don't seem to be related to how much someone has studied or prepared—in fact, one can argue that the more conscientious the student, the more the fear of failure may be playing a part, and, hence, the greater the likelihood of unpreparedness dreams. The unpreparedness motif can also emerge as nightmares about public speaking. In these, the dreamer will usually be standing before a crowd on a stage or at a public forum and will be unable to remember his lines, or will realize that he hasn't prepared at all.

Although some unpreparedness dreams are an expression of real anxieties about test-taking or public speaking, these dreams may also represent more general fears and anxieties, such feelings of inadequacy, a fear of failure, or a fear of being "found out" in some way. The dreamer may feel that he will not "make the grade" or "pass the test" in some current life circumstance or endeavor, such as a job or relationship.

Urine

The bodily fluid that we all must expel when our bodies are finished processing liquids is a fact of life. Urine is also a dirty substance with which we generally avoid contact. Urine in dreams may represent discomfort or disgust with bodily functions, or it may signify a release of negative, toxic energy or emotions. To dream of urinating on others may mean that you are "marking your territory": someone or something is encroaching on your space in waking life and you are anxious about it. It may also show derision or contempt for the person or persons being urinated on.

(See also *Excrement/Feces*)

Vampire

"There are such beings as vampires, some of us have evidence that they exist. Even had we not the proof of our own unhappy experience, the teachings and the records of the past give proof enough for sane peoples," reads Dr. Seward's diary in Bram Stoker's *Dracula*. The original vampires of folklore were based on real people. Consumption (tuberculosis) victims were considered the walking dead—especially in the latter stages of the disease. A consumptive grows pale as he gets weaker from the illness, and the afflicted may wake up in the morning to find his bedclothes and sheets stained with blood coughed up during the night. As consumptives' flesh wastes away and their bones begin to show through their skin, they often resemble living corpses. The causes and mechanics of the disease were not well understood centuries ago, and, like so many other illness, it was laced with superstitious notions and old wives' tales. It was often thought that consumption was carried and spread through the work of evil. Traditionally, a vampire is a person who has been pronounced dead but who is able to prey on the living, causing others to become walking corpses as well.

In 1897, Bram Stoker took this walking corpse and made him powerful, sexual, and alluring. Hollywood embraced Stoker's vampire vision, and produced the *Dracula* that most think of when envisioning a vampire.

Psychic vampires are a related, modern-day phenomena. These are people in our lives who leave us feeling completely drained and exhausted after spending any length of time with them. These people usually are not conscious of what they are doing, but their way of venting, dishing gossip, and confessing all of their problems to us leaves us enervated and discouraged. Most of us have the misfortune of having at least one psychic vampire in our lives. Some researchers claim that the people who eventually become energy vampires were abused or neglected as children, and this type of "energy vampirism" becomes their only way to feel whole and accepted. Many, if not all, psychic vampires are probably not aware of the fact that they are

V

draining others, and are oftentimes bewildered and depressed when others ignore, become uneasy, and/or act strangely around them on a regular basis. This in turn can make the "deficiency" worse, because the vampire's behavior is a vicious, self-maintaining cycle. This individual is intensely craving contact with and assurance from other people, yet can never find anyone willing to endure the trying nature of being their friend/spouse/lover.

A vampire nightmare usually represents a relationship in your life that is draining you. Emotional strain can tax the mind and the body, and being sucked dry in a close relationship can make the body ill as well. Interestingly, people who live with abusive psychic vampires often exhibit the classic signs of anemia—pale complexion, lack of iron, listlessness, and fatigue—just as if they were actually being drained of blood on a daily basis. Just like vampires of folklore and Stoker's creation, vampires can be created, but they can also be destroyed. The only way to stop the vampire in your nightmare is to confront, and perhaps put a stop to, the relationship that is sapping your vitality.

Vedas

The Vedas (also referred to as Vedam) are part of the Hindu *Shruti*, or canon of Hindu scriptures. These religious scriptures form part of the core of the Brahminical and Vedic traditions within Hinduism, and are the inspirational, metaphysical, and mythological foundation for the later Vedanta, Yoga, Tantra, and even Bhakti forms of Hinduism. In Sanskrit, *veda* means "knowledge" or "truth," and has the same origin as the word *wisdom* in English. In chronological order, the four Vedas are the Rig Veda, Yajur Veda, Sama Veda, and Atharva Veda.

Among the original four Vedas, the Atharva Veda contains the most material concerning dreams. Prophetic dreams and their respective meanings are discussed; for example, riding on an elephant in a dream is considered auspicious, while riding on a donkey is inauspicious. Certain purification rites and rituals can counteract the effects of inauspicious dreams. Furthermore, the Atharva Veda asserts that the fulfillment of an omen dream will take place in accordance with when the omen occurred in the dream: if it occurs early in the night, the omen will be fulfilled later; whereas if it occurs later in the night, the omen is more likely to occur sooner.

Victim

Being a victim in a dream, or seeing another person being victimized, illustrates the unique unifying characteristic of nightmares—that is, a feeling of helplessness, vulnerability, and fear. Depending on personal history, dreams about

victimization, especially traumatic nightmares, can echo past traumatic experiences of trauma in which the dreamer was a victim. Alternately, the dreamer may simply be feeling more generalized feelings of anxiety in waking life, and these feelings translate into dreams in which the dreamer is victimized or rendered helpless.

Violence

Although violence is known to occur in the dreams of both men and women, it is more common in men between the ages of 12 and 35. Most theories suggest that committing a violent act in a dream, even if the dreamer is not usually a violent person, often suggests that he or she is dealing with unresolved issues of guilt, anger, and frustration. These negative emotions do not always result in violent dreams, and so it must be assumed that other factors contribute to their occurrence.

When reporting a violent dream, many subjects use descriptive phrases such as, "Just like in the movie I was watching," which seems to support the idea that that the media plays an important part in the imagery of our dreams. Movies and television programs tend to emphasize conflicts, and trivialize the virtues of compassion, empathy, co-creation, and love. The typical means of conflict resolution portrayed in the media is that of force and violence, and this idea may work its way into our unconscious, and, hence, our dreams.

Ultimately, the personal history of an individual is necessarily an integral part of the interpretation of all dreams, including violent dreams. Usually the seeds of violence and violent thoughts already exist before violent dreams occur. Personality type, socioeconomic circumstances, and parental role models affect every individual differently and must be taken into account when attempting to analyze the meaning of violent dreams.

To experience horrifying scenes of violence and destruction in a traumatic nightmare may simply be the replaying of an initial trauma or traumas. Such scenes in "ordinary" nightmares may indicate feelings of fear and a perceived loss of power and control in waking life. An upheaval may have taken place in the dreamer's work or personal circumstances, and the resulting feelings of fear and helplessness readily translate into scenes of aggression and brutality.

(See also *Anger* and *Aggression*)

Volcano

A terrifying dream about an erupting volcano represents a festering emotional issue that is building up within your psyche, and the explosive image is a warning to let off steam before a blowup.

Billy, Do You Want to Play?

Mark N. is a 35-year-old truck driver from Lancaster County, Pennsylvania. He is married with two boys. Billy is 14, and Robert is 11. Mark had a nightmare involving his children recently that shook him up for several weeks after.

The Nightmare:

My wife woke me up after she heard me whimpering, "No...no... no," in my sleep. I was so upset after I awoke because of what I had just seen in my dream. This is what I can remember: Robert, our 11-year-old, came into our bedroom and hit my wife over the head with a Maglite [a big, heavy flashlight] while she was lying in bed. He then left our room and went down the hall toward his brother Billy's room. I went downstairs to find something—though I don't remember what it was I was looking for—and in the kitchen, where the cabinets should have been, was a blank wall. Written on the wall in blood or chocolate (or worse), in real childlike handwriting was, "Billy, do you want to play?"

I couldn't move, and I kept screaming, "No!" over and over again while I read this on the kitchen wall. I wanted to go back upstairs, but I couldn't move from where I was standing. That's when my wife woke me up.

Mark said he assumed the handwriting on the wall to be that of Robert's. He also mentioned he couldn't wake himself up from the nightmare. According to Mark, Billy and Robert are at an interesting stage in their growing up. Billy is at a point where he doesn't want to hang out with his younger brother anymore because it isn't very "cool," which is something Robert isn't very happy about. Mark grew up as the middle child with an older and a younger sister.

The Analysis:

Violence in a dream indicates a loss of control and power. Considering Mark and his wife already have one teen and are just a short ways off from having two, the violence toward the mother indicates a breaking away of the child from his parents. Their little boy is growing up and doesn't need them like he used to.

The handwriting on the wall in the dream is likely rather specific regarding the other issue of the two boys not playing together like they had in the past because they're at slightly different maturity levels. The fear expressed in this dream may indicate a fear of the change happening within the family. Though this change is a normal progression of children growing up and needing their parents less, the change itself can be a scary time for parents.

■   ■   ■

Vomit

Vomiting or vomit in a dream often indicates a need to discard or reject something from one's life. It has been theorized that morning sickness is a way for a pregnant woman to reject the idea of being pregnant—her body expresses what her consciousness cannot admit. If you are vomiting in a dream, you may be feeling forced into a situation that you are not comfortable with, or you may have food issues or an eating disorder. Alternatively, feelings of nausea and sickness in a dream often mean that the dreamer is, in fact, sick, and often presages a real incident of stomach illness.

(See also *Nausea*)

Voodoo

Voodoo is a Caribbean belief system that has its origin in a combination of traditional African religion and Catholicism. The term is generally applied to the branches of a West African, ancestor-based Theist-Animist religious tradition. Its primary roots are among the Fon-Ewe peoples of West Africa, in the country now known as Benin, where Vodun is the national religion of more than 7 million people. The word *vodun* is the Fon-Ewe word for "spirit," "tutelary deity," or "demon."

Originally a slave religion, voodoo is especially associated with the island of Haiti, although identifiably "voodoo" forms of spiritual expression are also found in Jamaica, Brazil, Santo Domingo, Cuba, Puerto Rico, and even parts of the United States. Partially because of sensationalistic portrayals in the media, voodoo has come to have negative connotations.

Voodoo embraces a complex and extensive pantheon, referred to as *loas*. It acknowledges a supreme creator known as Bondye (from the French "Bon Dieu"), although he is too remote to be worshipped. Voodoo focuses instead on the immediate divinities or spirits (Iwa) and ancestors, who serve the loas in return for favors. The spirits are not seen as good or evil, but rather as demanding or less so. Each person has a kind of patron or "head" spirit, which may be revealed at a ceremony, in a reading, or in dreams.

As in most traditional cultures, adherents to voodoo believe that the soul literally leaves the body during sleep and experiences a different world in dreams. The human soul is thought to be composed of two opposites: the *gros bon ange*, or "big good angel," and *ti bon ange*, the "little good angel." The *ti bon ange* is one's individual soul or essence, and it is this "small soul" that journeys out of the body during dreams as well as during possession by a spirit. This traveling is viewed as potentially dangerous, because when the *ti bon ange* is away from the body, it is particularly vulnerable to attack by hostile forces—attacks that are then experienced as nightmares.

Vultures

Vultures are scavenger or carrion birds that circle above a fresh kill, waiting for their turn at leftover scraps of meat. The vulture feeds, parasite-like, off of the work of others who hunt and kill their prey. The image of vultures circling in a dream may indicate that someone in your life is feeding off of you and your hard work, and perhaps taking credit for your ideas or accomplishments.

War/Battle

Traumatic nightmares involving wars and battles are common in veterans who suffer from post-traumatic stress disorder. Nightmares of people who are "on the mend" from other kinds of trauma can involve battle scenes in which they are being pursued, trapped, or attacked. For most other people, a nightmare involving a field of battle may be a reenactment of an inner conflict, or it could

be symbolic of an interpersonal conflict that has been escalating.

(See also *Post-Traumatic Stress Disorder*)

Water

Symbolically, water has been a sign of everything from cleansing, purity, and forgiveness to anxiety, chaos (especially the ocean), and even God's wrath or judgment.

When a person dreams that he is emerging from a river, lake, ocean, or even a swimming pool, it may symbolize birth. This may be the birth of a child, or a metaphorical birth of an idea or project that the dreamer has been developing. Bathing in a dream can have a few different meanings depending on the state of the water in which one bathes: clean water may indicate good health, while dirty water may foretell sickness. A dream about water that floods the home is sometimes interpreted as a prophetic dream of the dreamer's own death.

Dreams about a large body of water are commonly thought to represent the dreamer's unconscious. While these dreams can be pleasant, they can also be very frightening nightmares—usually indicative of some kind of conflict within the unconscious. As always, one of the most important aspects

W

of personal dream analysis is observing the emotions evoked by the dream. In this case, if the dreamer is relaxed and calm in the water, it is doubtful that the unconscious is trying to send him messages of inner turmoil. However, if the dreamer is struggling, panicking, or even drowning, it may indicate that the dreamer needs to reflect on aspects of his life in which he feels helpless or out of control.

Werewolf

The werewolf legend has its origin in ancient Greek mythology. In this myth, Licao (from whose name we derive *lycanthrope* and *lycanthropy*), the king of Arcadia, learns that Zeus, the king of the gods, is in disguise and roaming without permission through his land. Because only a god would recognize the taste of human flesh, Licao kills his youngest son, Arcade, with the intent of serving his flesh at a banquet that Zeus attends. Zeus discovers the terrible deed and is thus found out, but he becomes so angry at the gratuitous murder of Licao's son that the king of the gods turns Licao into a wolf.

Wolves appear in the folklore narratives of many nations, spanning ancient Europe to modern-day America. The animal has come to represent the cunning, dark side of the human psyche. The familiar and bone-chilling nocturnal howl has become part of ancient stories as well as a common fixture in nightmares. In dreams, the half-human, half-wolf entity is interpreted as the representation of the power/fear dichotomy in sexual relationships. The werewolf represents both the quest for power and domination within the relationship, as well as the fear and rejection of that power. The werewolf is the inner "monster" within the dreamer or the dreamer's partner.

Interestingly, Webster's College Dictionary defines a *lycanthrope* as "a person affected with a delusion in which one imagines oneself to be a wolf" as well as "a werewolf."

Where the Wild Things Are

In 1964, author and artist Maurice Sendak created a children's classic with his picture book, *Where the Wild Things Are*. The story is about Max, a young boy in a wolf suit whose bedroom turns into a jungle when he is supposed to be getting ready for bed. Monsters (or "Wild Things") of every kind come forth intent on scaring Max, but the boy appropriates the nightmarish imagery by donning the wolf suit, and thus becomes king of the wild things. The story speaks to a child who can master his own monsters and realize that his warm bed at home isn't such a bad place.

Whip

A whip symbolizes authority and corporal punishment, which the dreamer can be imposing or receiving. In either scenario, the punishment represented is often abusive and disproportionate to the "crime"—an occasion for latent guilt and shame that might be playing out in the symbolism and larger dream narrative.

Whirlpool

A whirlpool is a mighty vortex in the water that pulls anything near it to the ocean bottom. To dream of being caught in a whirlpool's centrifugal current, with ever-increasing speed as one approaches the center, may represent being drawn into the infinite depths of emotion or passion, but in a rapid, violent, and uncontrollable way. The imagery may sig-

nify the fear of being sucked into an emotionally charged engagement or conflict that has a potential for destruction. As in most nightmares, the dominant emotional context for the dreamer is one of helplessness, vulnerability, and fear.

(See also *Water*)

Wind

A strong, uncontrollable wind in a dream indicates some kind of turmoil in the dreamer's emotions. As in most nightmares, the most significant emotional context in these dreams is often one of abject helplessness—the wind indicates that the dreamer is powerless over events that are beyond his or her control. Many people who have suffered various kinds of trauma (for example, a rape or terrible accident) tend to dream of threatening situations such as being caught in a wind, storm, giant wave, or tornado. In this case, the wind then becomes the symbol or metaphor that the dreamer's brain has chosen to represent the precipitating event or events.

(See also *Tornado* and *Tidal Wave*)

Witch

Colloquially, the term *witch* is applied almost exclusively to women, although, in pre-modern England, the term was applied to men as well. Modern self-identified witches and Wiccans continue to use the term *witch* for all who practice witch-craft. The modern conception of the the witches of history embraces elements of the familiar witch of folklore—the charmer, the cunning man or wise woman (crone), the diviner, and the astrologer.

Today, the term *witch* is most often used as a pejorative—just imagine the ugly, old hag or crone portrayed in the movies and books of popular culture—

and is sometimes appropriated in accusations against individuals who are suspected of causing harm via supernatural means. On occasion, such accusations have exploded into the mass paranoia of witch hunts. In the modern West, witchcraft accusations have often been accompanied by satanic ritual, abuse, and hysteria. Interestingly, such accusations may be found throughout history and across nearly all cultures.

For people from conventional religious backgrounds, witches can represent evil—specifically a feminized version of evil. Particularly for a male, witches in dreams can symbolize a malignant female (real or imagined), or, more generally, threats from his own mysteriously powerful unconscious that he and society have "gendered" as feminine. As in *The Wizard of Oz*, good witches *do* appear occasionally in popular representations—Glenda the "good witch" identifies herself as such, and being a witch in no way detracts from her beauty or benevolence. However, in most people's dreams, witches usually represent something dark, destructive, and uncontrollable.

Wizard of Oz, The

One of the film classics of our time, this 1939 film recounts a young girl's dream after she has been knocked unconscious during a terrible storm. This film is rich in symbolism, archetypes, and metaphor that are all fairly consistent with most commonly accepted theories of dreaming and dream interpretation. Dorothy's fears and anxieties, her petty grievances and real sorrows, are magnified and distorted in her dream via potent and exaggerated dream symbolism. In real life, she feels a restlessness and a need to see new places, yet in her dream she sets out

on a "quest perilous" to find her home. In real life, she fears and loathes the spinsterish and hag-like Mrs. Gulch. In her dream, Mrs. Gulch becomes the Wicked Witch, who is intent on destroying Dorothy and her chance for happiness. In real life, Dorothy feels disenfranchised and abandoned living with her hardworking but unsympathetic aunt and uncle (presumably her parents have left or are dead). In the dream, she adopts (or is adopted by) her three memorable consorts and thus finds a sense of place and belonging. The tornado in the beginning of the film

is real, yet, as in most nightmares, it too is a metaphor for Dorothy's inner turmoil and dissatisfaction.

The transition from black and white to Technicolor was used with great effect to indicate the transition from the flat, bland, waking world to Dorothy's infinitely more interesting, and frightening, dreamworld. Almost the entire movie is set in the dreamworld, and there is also a "dream within a dream" scene in the poppy field outside the Emerald City. (The association between poppies and dreams dates to antiquity; the Greek god of sleep, Morpheus, was said to live with his sons in a cave surrounded by poppy flowers.)

At times, Dorothy's dream takes on the truly bizarre and horrifying qualities of a nightmare. The evil Wicked Witch's relentless pursuit of Dorothy throughout the film—from the beginning of the movie, through the poppy field and the Emerald City, and finally to her own ultimate and memorable demise—is a dramatic example of the ubiquitous chase nightmare. The home of the witch, the Forbidden Forest, depicts the dark and eerie atmosphere that is frequently characteristic of nightmare dreamscapes. The hideous flying monkeys, who attack and kidnap Dorothy with gleeful cruelty and take her as a prisoner to the witch's tower, are a perfect example of the bizarre and irrational quality of much nightmare imagery. Dorothy's despair, her feelings of abandonment, her anxiety, her anger, and especially her feelings of helplessness perfectly encapsulate the negative emotions that are common fodder for nightmares.

Following the rescue by her friends and her eventual triumph over the dark forces of her imaginary dreamworld, Dorothy returns, like all nightmare sufferers eventually do, to waking reality, but not without a poignant sense of loss and anticlimax for the viewer.

Wound

Wounds in dreams are metaphorical representations of the impact of negative emotional experiences. These experiences are personal setbacks that are often painful, but ultimately are part of the growing experience. Alternately, the "healing of old wounds" can be positive—the connective tissue of old scars is often stronger and more resilient than the original material. In Christian iconography, the wounds of Christ are redemptive and represent hope and healing. Indeed the original root of the term *to bless* means "to wound," so wound imagery in dreams may not necessarily be a bad thing. As in any nightmare, pay attention to what is being wounded, the circumstances surrounding the injury, and especially the emotions that contextualize and are evoked by the event.

X-Files

The *X-Files* was a television show on the FOX network about a secret department within the Federal Bureau of Investigation (FBI) that tracks unexplained and paranormal phenomena. The show premiered in September of 1993 and ran until May of 2002. Not surprisingly, this show about the paranormal also made dreams (especially precognitive dreams) an integral part of the overarching narrative.

In the "Aubrey" episode, the lead character, FBI Special Agent Fox Mulder (played by David Duchovny) says the memorable line, "Dreams are answers to questions we haven't figured out how to ask." In the later "Paper Hearts" episode, Fox Mulder's partner, Dana Scully (played by Gillian Anderson) repeats the line back to him after Mulder tells her about a dream he's been having. "Paper Hearts" is thematically centered on Mulder's dream of a red light leading him to the bodies of little girls who were murder victims. The recurring nightmare helps Mulder find the bodies and, eventually, the killer. This show emphasized the popular connection between dreaming/nightmares and psychic phenomenon.

X

Yansi

Yansi belong to the central Bantu culture that spans central Africa, inhabiting the areas surrounding the lower Kwilu and Inzia Rivers in the Bandundu Province of the Republic of Zaire. Yansi society is characterized by a highly rigid and stratified system of kinship, marriage, and especially priesthood, which holds the vaunted spiritual power called *lebui*. There is a particular concern among the Yansi regarding boundaries and relations between the living and the dead, as well as with elders, medicine people, neighbors, and kinsmen.

Dreams play a fundamental role in the life of the Yansi, and are regarded with the same seriousness and weight as waking experiences. They are regarded as an extraordinary phenomenon, and evoke everything from admiration to fear. Dreams are frequently sought as a way of obtaining supernatural commentaries on current events. For instance, dreams are carefully examined when treatment begins for someone who is ill or before going on a hunt in order to assess the chances of success.

Dreaming is integral to the Yansi witchcraft-sorcery-medicine amalgam. Among Yansi clan-elders and medicine-owners (who are regarded as wise dream interpreters and accurate oracular dreamers in their own right), a distinction is made between the different categories and qualities of their dreams. The Yansi discriminate between recollected dreams that seem to dovetail with reality and those considered to be mere fantasy.

Dreams that later come to fruition are generally considered "true dreams." The instant of waking is generally thought to be the most auspicious time to interpret one of these dreams. The Yansi often fear the fetish- or medicine-owners who typically are the recipients of these dreams, because they are often the harbingers of misfortune and tragedy. However, these privileged few can also find solutions to difficult problems and foretell good fortune through their dreams. Ordinary people also experience these true dreams,

Y

in which they are informed about the state of their health and other problems. In contrast, the dreams of infants and mentally handicapped persons, as well as those dreams that could be classified as "fantastical" or unreal, are dismissed out of hand by the Yansi.

In Yansi society, dreams are not considered a source of information about the dreamer's inner life, but rather seem to provide a context of meaning for the actions and interactions of the individual and others. Most of all, dreams are the evidence of supernatural forces in relationship with human beings, and are an important means of acquiring knowledge about these forces.

Yoruba

The Yoruba are the largest ethnic group in Nigeria, and comprise approximately 26 percent of that country's total population. The majority of Yoruba people are

Christians, with the Church of Nigeria (Anglican), Catholic, Pentecostal, Methodist, and other indigenous churches having the largest memberships. Muslims comprise about a quarter of the Yoruba population, with the traditional Yoruba religion accounting for the rest. The Yoruba of southwestern Nigeria and Dahomey have a long history of Westernization, Christianity, and education, and, therefore, are considered (rightly or wrongly) to be the most "progressive" of the groups in this region.

Indiginous, or "pagan," Yoruba religious beliefs are complex, embracing a wide variety of dieties, myths, songs, histories, and other cultural constructs. The mythology of the Yoruba is sometimes claimed by its supporters to be one of the world's oldest widely practiced religions, and is cited as the source of several New World religions, such as Santería in Cuba and Candomblé (or Batuque) in Brazil. In Africa, traditional beliefs include such varied elements as a supreme being (Olorun), subordinate deities, ancestors, sacred kings, a variety of local spirits, and an elaborate system of divination that includes dreaming and dream interpretation.

According to the Yoruba, humans possess multiple souls, each representing a significant dimension of the human experience. Among these is the "life-breath" given by Olorun (Father-God) at birth, which is nourished by food and contains one's personal vitality and strength. If this life-breath leaves the body during sleep, witches may entrap it, which results in physical death.

The Yoruba interpret their own dreams and typically recount themes of social or spiritual estrangement, as well as the threat of isolation due to sickness, captivity, or long journeys. For the Yoruba, then, dreaming and dream interpretation are integrative in that they seem to provide a means to understand and "process" the stress that comes with significant, immediate, and enduring cultural change. As it does in any culture, the dream "contextualizes" the overriding emotion or emotions (in this case, anxiety), and provides a means for the dreamer and the culture at large to grapple with implications of such change. In this, the Yoruba appear to use their dreams to achieve both personal and social integration, and adapt them to the particular needs of profound religious change and the ensuing identity crisis.

Zezuru

The Zezuru are the Shona-speaking peoples in the Harare region of Zimbabwe. As in many cultures, this peoples' conception of the world is a dichotomy of the mystical, or supernatural, and what we could call the "rational," or empirical/verifiable. In Zezuru religious tradition, *Mwari*, or God, guides and orders the whole world, and the world is then divided into *Shona* and *non-Shona* phenomena. The *Shona* consists of the various clans that are linked to the spirits of heroes, which are subdivided into separate lineages allied to the ancestors. The *non-Shona* consists of the observable, physical world as well as the mystical conception of the *shave* spirits. Healers in this society generally maintain that they derive their special powers from their close association with a *shave* spirit.

In Zezuru society, it is believed that, at death, a man's soul or personality becomes a spirit that will play a fundamental role in the affairs of living men. The *makombwe*, or heroes, are believed to have lived on earth before the founding of Zezuru society, and have special powers of healing, prophecy, and rain-making. Likewise, the *vadzimu*, or ancestor spirits, are directly concerned with the day-to-day affairs of their descendants. The hero and ancestor spirits are a unifying force in Zezuru society in that they provide a code of mores and social conventions, whereas the *shave* spirits are responsible for the dissimilarities between people, such as individual talents and so forth.

Not surprisingly, the Zezuru believe that dreams provide a conduit between the spirit world and the living, and connect the present and the past in a very real and tangible way. It is thought that dreams also have a prophetic element, and as such can offer protection to the healers and the community at large by predicting major or cataclysmic events. The spirits are believed to initiate this contact and achieve their purposes through dreams, the dreams of the healers in particular. Through such dreams, the spirits can call, inform, guide, sanction, and even correct the healers, and thus reach

Z

the community at large and influence the actions of its members. The Zezuru also believe that the spirits of witches or lost souls can use dreams for nefarious ends: here they can cause harm, exact vengeance, or simply scare the dreamer in a nightmare.

The adults in Zezuru society also sometimes interpret children's dreams as direct messages from the spirits, though at times they are merely dismissed as meaningless. Sometimes children's dreams provoke anxiety in adults, which may result in punishment for the child. Usually families seek out a healer to interpret their children's dreams, which are always evaluated within the context of other events or "signs" in the community. The influence of the spirits is almost always cited in these cases.

Children seem to have a great deal of agency when it comes to enacting a culturally sanctioned response to their dreams. A child is usually made privy to the healer's interpretation, and he or she is free to accept or reject it as he or she sees fit. In addition, children can use dreams as a way to communicate with the healers (who are most often grandparents); indeed, a child's dreams may eventually become accepted as part of his initiation into his own role as healer.

Dreams do not play an ancillary role in this culture. Rather, they provide a forum for the sharing of privileged knowledge, and thus help to shape individual identity within the community while providing a means for socialization and integration.

Zombie

A zombie is one of the undead (or a reanimated corpse) in the Caribbean spiritual belief system of voodoo. The idea of the zombie has made its way into pop culture via zombie movies, fiction, and even video games.

In cultures that practice voodoo, zombies are supposedly created by witch doctors through supernatural means in order to serve as personal slaves. According to tradition, the witch doctor takes a sample of blood or hair from the deceased and uses the material in a ritual to reanimate the corpse. Herbs and other spells may also be used to create a concotion that has the same effect.

Historically, consumption (tuberculosis) epidemics in the 18th and 19th centuries furthered the notion that the sick were actually the walking dead or zombies, and with good reason: during the latter stages of this disease, the victim turns very pale and thin, and often coughs up blood. During sleep, a consumptive tends to cough more as the infection settles into the lungs, which causes the sufferer to wake up with splotches of blood on their mouths, bedclothes, and bed sheets. This, combined with the fact that consumption is highly contagious, created a kind of mass supernatural hysteria. As previously unaffected people came down with consumption, and as people observed blood around the mouths of others nearby, soon people inferred that these "walking dead" consumptives were feeding, zombie-like, off of the living, and turning others into the same horrifying state.

In the 1990s, and in the first several years of this century, zombie movies have experienced a renaissance. *Night of the Living Dead* (1990), *28 Days Later* (2002), *Dawn of the Dead* (1978 and the remake in 2004), and *Shaun of the Dead* (2004) are just some of the many zombie movies to hit the silver screen. In the movies, zombies are typically portrayed as mindless, shambling, decaying corpses with a hunger for human flesh. Often, the zombies will also have supernatural strength and constitution. Again, reminiscent of the vampire myth, one bite or even a scratch from a zombie and the victim joins the league of the undead. The most common method for stopping a zombie in the movies is to destroy the zombie's head.

With such gruesome imagery in both film and folklore, zombies have been known to stumble into our nightmares as well. A zombie nightmare may indicate that the issues or problems that have been sucking the life out of the dreamer are worsening and threatening to encroach upon, and extinguish, the dreamer's joy of living. In particular, zombie images in dreams may be a reflection of a mundane, plodding work environment. Perhaps the dreamer needs a creative outlet outside of the office as an escape from stultifying cubicle hell. If *you* are the zombie in the dream, perhaps you need to break through your apathy and take responsibility for creating more excitement and interest in your life.

Zulu

The Zulu are an Nguni people who have lived in southern Africa since the third century C.E. Dreams play a very important role in Zulu society. Clan, lineage,

and age establish the basic communal bonds of Zulu society. All individuals belong to a particular lineage, which consists of the descendants of a common founding ancestor. Within each lineage, various discrete subdivisions trace their ancestries back to a common grandfather. Clan consists of the numerous lineages linked together by a common founder, after whom the clan was initially named, and is the dominant shaping force in Zulu society.

Ancestors also play a fundamental role in Zulu society. Most Zulu dwellings—typically a roughly made hut—reserve a small area in the back that is devoted to the ancestors (who are believed to remain in the village after death as invisible dwellers). They are thought to visit the living either through dreams, in the form of a snake, or as a ghost. The appearance of a ghost is an extremely rare event and only occurs if the appropriate death rituals have not been scrupulously observed.

Zulu dreams principally function as a channel of communication with the ancestors. Ancestors must be respected and appeased for the protection they are thought to offer to members of their lineage. Through dreams, the ancestral spirits can express both approval and disapproval of the actions—past, present, and future—of their descendents. The tribal medical system draws on these dreams for prophesy and to inform diagnoses, especially in cases of what we would consider to be psychological disorders.

Many Zulu dreams are considered prophetic and, therefore, act as powerful guides and "scripts" for appropriate behavior. For example, a Zulu will suddenly treat a friend as an enemy in response to a dream in which his friend intended him harm. As in many Western theories of dream interpretation, the meaning or omen of a dream may either be in alignment with or opposition to its overt, or "manifest," content.

According to psychiatrist S.G. Lee, Zulu dreams can be segregated into only a very limited number of categories, as they seem to adopt a relatively narrow selection of central imageries or narratives. In this, the dreams of both men and women appear to be fairly constrained and heavily influenced by social pressures and sanctions. The dreams of women especially are not "free," in that they seem to be rigidly circumscribed by social mores, and they appear to correspond fairly predictably with their age, status, and role in the community. According to Lee, dream symbolism is rarely connected to the important events of private life; rather, it seems to be informed and limited by the concerns of the community at large. Interestingly, the Zulu's *own* interpretations of their dream symbols, as limited as they are, seem to coincide with our Western, psychoanalytical model.

Zuni

The Zuni (or Ashiwi) are a Native American tribe who live in the Pueblo of Zuni on the Zuni River, a tributary of the Little Colorado River in western New Mexico. The Zuni continue to practice their traditional shamanistic religion today, with its regular ceremonies and dances and independent mythology, as they have for the past 1,000 years.

The Zuni are loathe to speak the names of their dead. If a member of the tribe is visited by one of the dead in their dreams, it is considered a horrifying, nightmarish experience that requires an immediate "cure" in the form of the observance of specific religious rituals. In some cases, this includes being initiated into either the tribal organization known as the Kachina Society, which is an ancestral cult group, or into one of the 13 different medical societies.

The Zuni organize all natural and supernatural phenomenon and beings into two categories. The "raw," or "soft," beings include animals, insects, weather, plants, and the dead, all of which eat food that is raw or that has been sacrificed to them. Conversely, "cooked," or "daylight," beings subsist on cooked food and are protected by the Sun Father. This group includes living human beings exclusively. The living human is referred to as the *shi'nanne*, or "flesh," and the soul or

psyche as the *pinanne*, or "wind/air." The Zuni believe that the soul arrives at birth and departs the body at death, although it still maintains a close connection to the earth thereafter. Although the soul is inextricably linked to the heart, it can leave the body under certain circumstances, such as during trance, curing, singing, and especially dreaming. According to the Zuni, a part of the dreamer's self—typically the mind, emotions, or *pinanne* (breath)—wanders outside the body during a dream experience and is able to experience alternate locations or dimensions. The Zuni see themselves as passive recipients in this dreaming process.

The Zuni classify their dreams as either good or bad, as we do, depending on the emotions they evoke in the dreamer. They share their dreaming experiences among the members of their extended household as well as with friends, but not all dream experiences are reported right away, with some only reported years later. Accounts of old dreams consist of both the bad (nightmares) and the good dreams, whereas reports of recent dreams always concern nightmares. The Zuni always regard the appearance of a deceased person in a dream as a nightmare, and they believe that such a dream should be reported right away in order to diffuse its potential for harm. Thus, it is the recounting of a nightmare that weakens its potency and prevents it from becoming fully realized or completed.

Conversation With Dr. Ernest Hartmann

Ernest Hartmann, M.D., is professor of psychiatry at Tufts University School of Medicine and director of the Sleep Disorders Center at Newton-Wellesley Hospital in Boston. He is a former president of the International Association for the Study of Dreams, and was the first editor-in-chief of the journal *Dreaming*. He is the author of *Dreams and Nightmares* (Plenum Press, 1998; revised paperback version Perseus Press, 2001), which covers Dr. Hartmann's theory on the nature and function of dreams, and how to make use of them.

Q: What got you interested in dream study?

I've always loved my own dreams and I guess that got me interested. I always loved dreaming—there was a whole piece of me in dreams that didn't usually come out. I was interested in dreaming first, then I got into psychiatry and sleep research. I've had a whole career being very well known as a sleep researcher. I've written about 200 or 300 papers on sleep, the chemistry of sleep, the pharmacology of sleep, the basic mechanisms of sleep, and so on. But I was always interested in dreams first, and in the last 10 or 15 years I've gotten back into mostly studying dreams rather than sleep.

Q: Why do we need to sleep?

That's a very good question. At the moment there is no totally accepted answer. It's very well accepted that we need sleep, and that we need the two major parts of sleep, called non-REM [rapid eye movement] and REM sleep—they're both necessary—animals die without them. But exactly why we need them is not clear. We need them for some kind of restoration, and I would say that non-REM sleep is more for body restoration and REM sleep is more for brain and mind restoration—but that's a hugely oversimplified answer.

It turns out that rats who are completely deprived of REM sleep died of heat regulation problems, and they died from problems with homeostasis. So REM sleep might be responsible for regulating the body in all kinds of ways—not just the brain, though the brain is where the results show up most clearly in humans.

Q: Why do we dream?

Since we don't even know the functions of sleep, it's not likely that we would precisely know the functions of dreaming. So my simple answer is: I don't know. But I do have some ideas, some hypotheses [that] are carefully outlined in my book *Dreams and Nightmares*. My theory is that dreams make connections. We connect things more easily during dreaming than when we're awake. When we're awake, we keep things separate, and when we're dreaming we put them together. And dreams can be quite useful, for example, when something unusual or traumatic happens. The dreams seem to make connections and kind of weave this new material in so it's not as scary, and it doesn't stand out. The idea is if something else happens again, it won't be as disturbing or as frightening, because we already have that concept kind of integrated and woven in a little bit.

Q: What are nightmares?

Usually nightmares happen after a traumatic event—like you escape from a burning house, or you're attacked and raped—and you have nightmares for a while and then you gradually see the dreams kind of connecting this new trauma with images that remind you of old things that happened to you in childhood. So the dream is connecting up; it's weaving in this new traumatic material, and the nightmare becomes more ordinary. Gradually your dreams get back to normal—this is what happens with average people. People who develop PTSD [post-traumatic stress disorder] are the people where this process gets stuck, where the dreams aren't working the issue out, and they keep having the nightmare over and over again about the same thing.

Q: Why are nightmares more prevalent in children?

Children are just learning about the world, especially at ages 3, 4, 5, and 6. Even children in fairly ordinary circumstances have a lot that they don't quite understand. Their lives are being run by these large creatures known as parents—mostly they are reliable, but you never know because sometimes they start yelling at each other, sometimes they throw things, or they might hit you for no reason. Especially at ages 3, 4, and 5 when the child is learning how the world works, it can be a pretty scary world. Their dreams reflect that fear.

Q: What can we learn from our dreams, especially in the field of psychology?

A whole lot. We can use dreams in making scientific discoveries, artistic discoveries, we can use dreams to help decide what we're going to do with our lives. But the main thing is that we can get to know ourselves better. It's a whole big piece of our mental functioning. So why neglect it?

I'm a scientist. I want hard data, but this is a whole bit of our lives that we usually neglect. We spend at least two or three hours a night dreaming, and that's years of our lives. Something is going on and we might as well try and make use of it. And a lot of cultures do make use of it much more than we do.

Q: What is the purpose of the International Association for the Study of Dreams (IASD)?

It's a fascinating group. I've been a member for a number of years and I was president for a while. It's a group of people interested in dreams. It's partly a professional society—there are members doing research into dreams, it has clinicians, psychiatrists, psychologists, and social workers who are doing clinical work with dreams. We also have a lot of people who call themselves dream-workers—without having a specific academic degree. And we have artists, occasionally philosophers, and musicians who are interested in dreams from various points of view. It really is an international society that studies dreams from all points of view. The group prides itself in being eclectic and open; anyone can join. It's not a snobbish organization where you have to have a Ph.D. or an MBA, or anything like that.

Q: Do you think that [the perception of dream study] is changing in the Western world?

It's hard to say. A lot of people are more interested in dreams, but the trouble is it gets kind of relegated to the New Age-y kind of far-out sort of stuff. A lot of people are interested, but it hasn't become scientifically respectable. I'm very scientifically respectable. I'm a professor, I'm an M.D., I've written books and articles, I'm trying to make it more respectable.

Q: What other applications does dream study have?

There are a lot of applications in helping to run one's life. Dreams can also be used as a kind of measure of emotional arousal. I've done the first really systematic study of dreams before and after 9-11. I got 44 people who had been keeping dream diaries, who wrote down their dreams for years and years. This group sent me 20 dreams from their dream journals, the last 10 dreams they had before 9-11 and the first 10 afterward. We assigned the dreams random numbers and studied them all. It turns out once we broke the code that the dreams after 9-11 had more intense central imagery. The central image of the dream was more powerful after than before. This is surprising because we didn't see more towers or airplanes in these dreams, they weren't longer or more dreamlike, they were only barely more nightmare-like, but they were more intense. So the intensity of the central dream imagery is a kind of a measure of our emotional arousal or stress level.

There is also an interesting study going on with people who have cancer and people who are dying. This group sometimes seems to get a lot of benefit from dreamwork, from looking at their dreams. But I think that's part of the whole use of dreams: they help us understand ourselves.

Dreams make a connection we don't usually make.

For Further Information

The following is a list of organizations that are actively doing work in dream study, analysis, and other related subjects:

Association for Research and Enlightenment (A.R.E.)

> 215 67th Street
>
> Virginia Beach, VA 23451 USA
>
> Tel: 1 (800) 333-4499
>
> Web: *www.edgarcayce.org*

The Association for Research and Enlightenment was founded in 1931 by Edgar Cayce (1877–1945) with a mission to catalog and disseminate the many recorded readings of psychic Edgar Cayce.

Center for Consciousness Studies

> University of Arizona
>
> Department of Psychology
>
> Tucson, AZ 85721 USA
>
> Tel: 1 (520) 621-9317
>
> Web: *http://consciousness.arizona.edu*

The Center for Consciousness Studies was formed in 1998 at the University of Arizona with a mission to bring together the perspective of philosophy, cognitive sciences, neuroscience, social science, medical science, arts, and humanities for a complete understanding of human consciousness.

DreamMoods.com

Web: *www.dreammoods.com*

Email: contact@dreammoods.com

DreamMoods.com is an online resource offering a searchable dream dictionary, discussion forum, and other articles on interpretation and dream study.

Dream and Nightmare Laboratory

Hôpital du Sacré-Coeur de Montréal

Sleep Research Center

5400 boul. Gouin West

Montréal, Quebec

Canada H4J 1C5

Tel: 1 (514) 338-2222 ext. 2783

Web: *www.jtkresearch.com/DreamLab*

Established in 1991 in Montreal's Sacré-Coeur Hospital, the Dream and Nightmare Laboratory is dedicated to the study of dreaming and dream disturbances, and to the training of students and health professionals into the applications of dream science.

Dream Research and Experimental Approach to the Mechanisms of Sleep (DREAMS) Foundation

Box 513 Snowdon

Montréal, Quebec

Canada H3X 3T7

Tel: 1 (514) 990-2113

Web: *www.dreams.ca*

The DREAMS Foundation's objective is to inform the public as well as health and science professionals about the nature of dreams and how they relate to overall health and well-being.

Dreaming @ Swoon.com

Web: *www.swoon.com/dream*

Swoon.com is a popular personals, dating, astrology, and dream Website. Their tagline reads "Your everyday oracle." The Website includes a large dream interpretation guide where users can enter keywords based on their dreams and receive an interpretation.

The Farsight Institute

P.O. Box 49243

Atlanta, GA 30359 USA

Web: *www.farsight.org*

The Farsight Institute is a nonprofit organization founded in 1995 to conduct research into the process of remote viewing.

International Academy of Consciousness

45 Great Cumberland Place

3rd Floor

Marble Arch

London, England

United Kingdom W1H 7LH

Tel: +44 (0) 207-723-0544

Web: *www.iacworld.org*

The International Academy of Consciousness (IAC) is dedicated to the scientific study of consciousness, the human essence, and the soul. They have offices in Holland, Italy, Mexico, Portugal, Spain, Switzerland, the United Kingdom, and the United States, and run classes several times per month on how to do astral projection.

International Association for the Study of Dreams

1672 University Avenue

Berkeley, CA 94703 USA

Tel: 1 (209) 724-0889

Web: *www.asdreams.org*

The International Association for the Study of Dreams is a nonprofit organization comprised of doctors and researchers investigating the nature, function, and significance of dreams and dreaming.

The Quantitative Study of Dreams

> G. William Domhoff
>
> College Eight, UCSC
>
> Santa Cruz, CA 95064 USA
>
> Web: *www.dreamresearch.net*

A Website dedicated to providing dream meaning based on content analysis. The group also has a companion Website with thousands of dream reports (*www.dreambank.net*).

Select Bibliography

American Psychiatric Association. *Diagnostic and statistical manual of mental disorders*, 4th ed. Washington, D.C.: American Psychiatric Association, 1994.

Bliwise, D.L. "Historical change in the report of daytime fatigue," *Sleep* 19 (1996): 462–464.

Bloom, Harold, ed. *Modern Critical Views: Sigmund Freud*. New York: Chelsea House, 1985.

Campbell, Joseph, ed. *The Portable Jung*, translated by R.F.C. Hull. New York: Penguin Books, 1971.

Crisp, Tony. *Dream Dictionary: An A to Z Guide to Understanding Your Unconscious Mind*. New York: Gramercy Books, 2002.

Cunningham, Scott. *Dreaming the Divine: Techniques for Sacred Sleep*. St. Paul, Minn.: Llewellyn, 1999.

Freud, Sigmund. *The Interpretation of Dreams*, translated and edited by James Strachey. New York: Avon, 1965.

Guiley, Rosemary Ellen. *The Encyclopedia of Dreams: Symbols & Interpretations*. New York: Berkley, 1995.

Halloway, Gillian. *The Complete Dream Book*. Naperville, Ill.: Sourcebooks, 2001.

Hartmann, Ernest. *Dreams and Nightmares: The Origin and Meaning of Dreams*. Cambridge, Mass.: Perseus Publishing, 1998.

———. *The Nightmare*. New York: Basic Books, 1984.

Hopcke, Robert H. *A Guided Tour of the Collected Works of C.G. Jung.* Boston/ London: Shambala, 1989.

Krakow, B., M. Hollifield, L. Johnston, M.P. Koss, R. Schrader, T.D. Warner, et al. "Imagery rehearsal therapy for chronic nightmares in sexual assault survivors with posttraumatic stress disorder: A randomized controlled trial," *Journal of the American Medical Association* 286 (2001): 537–545.

Krakow, B., R. Schrader, D. Tandberg, M. Hollifield, M.P. Koss, C.L. Yau, et al. "Nightmare frequency in sexual assault survivors with PTSD," *Journal of Anxiety Disorders* 16 (2002): 175–190.

Lewis, James R. *The Dream Encyclopedia.* Detroit: Visible Ink Press, 1995.

Lukeman, Alex. *Nightmares: How to Make Sense of Your Darkest Dreams.* New York: M. Evans and Company, Inc., 2000.

Miller, Gustavas Hindman. *10,000 Dreams Interpreted: An Illustrated Guide to Unlocking the Secrets of Your Dreamlife.* New York: Barnes & Noble Books, 1996.

Summer Institute of Linguistics. *Notes on Anthropology and Intercultural Community Work* 18 (1995): 30–37.

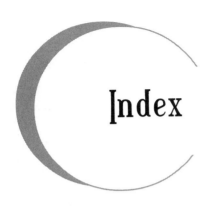

Index

About the Author

Jeff Belanger has been fascinated with exploring the unexplained aspects of our lives since childhood when he was first introduced to the subject of ghosts and the supernatural in the old New England town where he grew up. Since then, he has been studying the subjects that border on the fringe of the human experience.

Jeff has been a writer and journalist for various newspapers and magazines, and in 1999 he launched Ghostvillage.com as a repository for his writings on the unexplained. The site has since grown to become the largest paranormal community on the Web, attracting hundreds of thousands of visitors each year.

Over the years, Jeff has interviewed hundreds of people about their brushes with the profound. Dreams, and especially nightmares, have captivated him for years, as so little is understood about why they happen, but their effects on the dreamer are significant and often border on the supernatural. Jeff is also the author of *The World's Most Haunted Places: From the Secret Files of Ghostvillage.com* and *Communicating With the Dead: Reach Beyond the Grave*, and is the editor and compiler of *The Encyclopedia of Haunted Places: Ghostly Locales From Around the World*. Jeff is a regular guest on many regional and national radio programs, has lectured across the United States on the unexplained, and has been featured on television programs about the paranormal.

Kirsten Dalley is a writer and editor at an independent publisher.

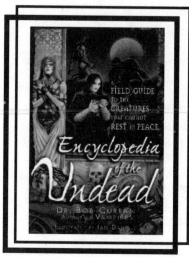
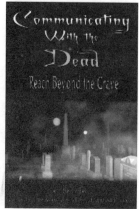
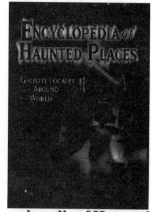